Covering the Border War

D0879011

Covering the Border War

How the News Media Creates Crime, Race, Nation, and the USA–Mexico Divide

Sang Hea Kil

LEXINGTON BOOKS
Lanham • Boulder • New York • London

Published by Lexington Books
An imprint of The Rowman & Littlefield Publishing Group, Inc.
4501 Forbes Boulevard, Suite 200, Lanham, Maryland 20706
www.rowman.com

6 Tinworth Street, London SE11 5AL, United Kingdom

British Library Cataloguing in Publication Information Available

Library of Congress Control Number: 2019950668

9781498561426 (cloth)
9781498561433 (electronic)
9781498561440 (paperr)

This book is dedicated to Han Sun Kil and Kale Carter.

Contents

Acknowledgments

This project began as a dissertation a long time ago, and there are many people that helped to make this into a book. I would like to thank my dissertation committee: Cecilia Menjívar (Chair), Thomas Nakayama, and the late Jane Hill for helping me tremendously in getting this project off the ground. Cecilia Menjívar continues to be amazing to me and consistently encouraged me to complete this book. I would also like to thank Zeynep Kilic, who has been in many different writing groups with me over the years and has seen many variations and drafts of my chapters. In addition, Patrisia Macías-Rojas, Soma Sen, Shireen Roshanravan, Claudio Vera Sanchez, Alessandro de Georgi, and many others, provided me substantive feedback on my most recent chapters, and Jordan Beltran Gonzales provided me helpful copy-editing skills. I also appreciate the insightful comments from the peer reviewers of this manuscript.

I would like to acknowledge prior publications and awards that relate to this book. My second chapter is based on my 2014 article titled "A Diseased Body Politic: Nativist Discourse and the Imagined Whiteness of the USA" published in *Cultural Studies* 28(2), 177–198, https://www.tandfonline.com/. Parts of my introduction and conclusion chapters draw from my 2019 article titled "Reporting from the Whites of their Eyes: How Whiteness as Neoliberalism Promotes Racism in the News Coverage of 'All Lives Matter'" that has been accepted for publication in *Communication Theory*, which is published by Oxford University Press on behalf of *International Communication Association (ICA)*. And part of my chapter 3 draws from my 2006 co-authored book chapter with Cecilia Menjívar titled "The 'War on the border': The Criminalization of Immigrants and Militarization of the US-Mexico border," in New York University Press' *Immigration and Crime: Race, Ethnicity, and Violence* (Eds. Martinez Jr., Ramiro, and Valenzuela Jr., Abel).

Finally, my chapter 6 won a top paper prize in 2019 at the *ICA* conference under the "Ethnicity and Race in Communication" division and I thank those reviewers for their comments.

In 2005, I was a Mellon fellow with the *Future of Minority Studies'* "Feminist Identities, Global Struggles" summer institute and participated in a kind of feminist bootcamp led by Chandra Talpade Mohanty and Beverly Guy Sheftall, along with a cohort of women junior faculty fellows at Cornell University. I thank the FMS 2005 group for providing me insightful feedback on my work when I shared my dissertation research proposal with the group, particularly Stacey Grooters who introduced me to literature on geographic scales.

My grassroots activism in Arizona greatly informed the analysis in this book. I would like to thank Jennifer Allen, former Executive Director of *Border Action Network*, where I served as a volunteer and board member, for her friendship and solidarity. I would also like to thank *Local to Global Justice,* a group I started with other graduate students, community members and Beth Swadener, a faculty member at Arizona State University, for collaborating with me and other students in starting a critical social movement on campus that continues to serve Arizona. I would also like to thank Ray Ybarra, who trained me as a legal observer under the *American Civil Liberties Union of Arizona* for the Minuteman Project (April–May 2005) convergence in the border region where I did several human rights observations in Cochise County, Arizona.

In addition, I want to appreciate the people on my campus at San Jose State University that supported me and helped motivate me in striving to make SJSU a better place for all and not some: Marilyn Easter, Maribel Martinez, Hyon Chu Yi-Baker, Sue Pak, and Jonathan Karpf. Also, Michelle Pujol, Latu Tapaatoutai, Gilbert Villareal Mendoza, and Nikki Borinaga inspired me with their dedication to social justice in fighting for transparency and fairness in the "justice" studies department and on our campus.

Moreover, the Holly Park Collective and in particular Izzy Alvaran gave me invaluable support to me and my writing process as well as Yaya and Umayu Ruiz. Furthermore, Julia Query, Sharon Sasaki, Sanya Richey, Lomi Kil, and Kyong Sung Kil also supported me in their unique ways and I am grateful. Eleanor Judis provided me help with grading in my classes when I needed it the most to carve out time for the revisions of my last chapters.

Finally, I would like to thank the late Free Speech Radio News, where I served as President of the Board of Directors until the end, for showing a model of how journalism can come from below and critically critique power holders with unique, local voices from a global spectrum.

My hope is that this book will help to stop the human-made, human rights crisis in the USA-Mexico border region by recognizing that all people inherently possess dignity and deserve rights, compassion, and love.

Any errors in this book are my own.

Introduction

Whiteness and the Nativist Imagination

President Trump wants to build a "great, great wall" that would attempt to seal the border between the United States and Mexico in order to stop immigrants he perceives as rapists and criminals from entering, working, and living in the United States. His presidential campaign promise resonated with many citizens who fear the permeability of the border and the intentions of the non-White immigrants who cross without official documents. His inability to fulfill his campaign promise to force Mexico to fund his wall led Trump to implement the longest government shutdown in U.S. American history that affected more than 800,000 federal workers—some were required to work without pay while others were furloughed or placed on temporary leave. The shutdown began after Trump requested an additional $5.7 billion in a new federal spending bill for his wall; this bill had needed to be passed on December 21, 2018, before the previous spending expired, but it failed to achieve an agreement with Democrats, thus the federal shutdown was declared the following day and lasted thirty-five days ("U.S. gov't shutdown," 2019). The federal government reopened January 25, 2019, as negotiations ensued to prevent another shutdown, which led to the passing of the congressional bill that provides $1.375 billion for Trump's border wall that he signed February 15, 2019.

On that same day, President Trump declared a national emergency and stated, "So we're going to be signing today, and registering, [a] national emergency and it's a great thing to do. Because we have an invasion of drugs, invasion of gangs, invasion of people and it's unacceptable" (Paschal, 2019, para. 22). He clarified that "we are declaring it for virtual invasion purposes—drugs, traffickers, and gangs" (Paschal, 2019, para.32). The national emergency declaration could provide Trump another $3.6 billion diverted from military construction projects, $2.5 billion from diverted from counternarcotics programs, and $600 million diverted from asset forfeitures, that combine with the $1.375 spending package on the border barriers to give Trump about $8 billion for his "great wall" (Baker, 2009). However, as Trump explained, "we will have a national emergency, and we will then be sued" (Paschal, 2019, para. 30), acknowledging the legal challenges of declaring a national emergency over a "virtual invasion" of the southern border simply because, as Trump put it, "I could do the wall over a longer period of time. I didn't need to do this, but I'd rather do it much faster . . . I just want to get it done faster, that's all" (Benin, 2019, para. 3). His zealous focus on the border wall escalates the "war on the border" policy that has existed in the region for decades and has directly contributed to the deaths of thousands of migrants who risk their lives for better economic opportunities by crossing this increasingly militarized, territorial boundary.

Donald Trump's demand for a greater border wall is a culmination of the racist nativism that began this most recent wave with California's Proposition 187. California's Proposition 187 (1994), the "Save our State" initiative sought to bar undocumented immigrants from health and educational services. In addition, Arizona's SB 1070 (2010), the "Support Our Law Enforcement and Safe Neighborhoods Act," would have allowed the use of racial profiling by law enforcement against immigrants. While both policies have been neutralized due to legal challenges, the symbolic message of these policies in addition to the continued militarization of the border have created an extremely anti-immigrant discourse that the media, politicians, or general public seldom deem racist. This wave of nativism attempts to formalize a *petit apartheid* (Georges-Abeyie, 2001) system by driving immigrants further underground making them more exploitable. Nativism is an intense opposition to immigrants because of their perceived foreignness or anti-US American values and relates to a defensive feeling of nationalism (Higham, 1955). While the mainstream media cover Trump's inflammatory rhetoric as racial at times, the general trend of today's media coverage minimizes structural and everyday racism. The Obama Administration seemed to signal this "postracial" reality, but really just signaled a "postracial racism" (Haney-López, 2010), reflected in the White backlash against a Black president (Hughey, 2014). This White backlash also reflects Trump's ascendency to the office of the president.

I provide two illustrations from the border region, to show how this recent wave of nativist discourse can greatly harm immigrants by naturalizing racism through imagery and metaphors that seem merely descriptive but hide a deeply racist and hierarchal imagination. First, a discrete event occurred in 1997 in Chandler, Arizona, located just outside the state capital of Phoenix. The city of Chandler, in an effort to economically revitalize their downtown area through "Operation Restoration," partnered their police officers with

Immigration and Naturalization Services (INS) agents in order to clear the area of undocumented residents. In the end, though, this immigration partnership violated the civil rights of many legal citizens and residents who were racially targeted and harassed. While the news media seemed to be sympathetic to the legal residents and undocumented immigrants who were profiled by their race and class as "illegal aliens," and the news seemed to be very critical of the poor standards used to racially profile people in Chandler, like clothing that did not appear to be middle-class, people's use of Spanish language, and dark skin color, the news still used headlines like "raid," "roundup," and "sweep." So over and over again, the news implied that immigrants were "criminals," "animals," and "dirt" respectively. This reflects how news discourse could communicate racist ideologies about immigration matters without having to utter a single racial slur, especially within this postracial, political milieu. What was the connection to racial ideologies among the images of immigrants as criminals, animals, and dirt?

The problem arose when City of Chandler's effort to clear the downtown area only seemed to target poor and working-class people of color and left alone those perceived to be middle-class or White (Romero, 2006). The raid focused on where they lived (apartment complexes and trailer parks), how they traveled (by sidewalk or type of car), where they worked (construction sites) and shopped for necessities (grocery stores and gas stations). Thus, the raid policed citizenship, human movement, and urban space by remaking a culturally Mexican-American location into a White space (Romero, 2006). In fact, scholars note that the raid bears great similarity to the repatriation campaign during the Great Depression when the U.S. American government forcibly removed about one million people (both U.S. American citizens and undocumented immigrants) deemed "Mexican" from the Southwest region to Mexico (Johnson, 2005). In addition, other scholars have noted that Arizona's SB1070 that allows the use of racial profiling on immigrants assumed to be without documents is a formalized version of the Chandler event in the sense that poor racial and economic class criteria are used to determine someone's citizenship or legal residency (Castro, 2011; Magaña, 2013; Provine & Sanchez, 2011).

By law enforcement standards, the five-day raid was successful because it detained 432 people. However, it was an unauthorized operation since the city of Chandler did not get permission for the joint operation from the State Attorney General's Office as required by policy. And by civil rights standards, the raid had violated people's rights; two multi-million dollar lawsuits were filed by legal residents who had been illegally detained by law enforcement. Later, two separate investigations of this event narrated immigration as a problem in the city in two very different ways (Romero, 2006). When the City of Chandler's internal investigation focused on immigrants as laborers, criminals, and "aliens" as justifications for the raid, it summarily erased the traditions and heritage of Mexican culture from the local history. In contrast, the Attorney General's investigation acknowledged squarely that the downtown revitalization project prompted the city to conduct the raid, and as a consequence, citizens' civil rights were violated in the process (Romero, 2006). This Chandler event reflects how Whiteness continues to overdetermine perceptions of U.S. American citizenship and legal residency.

The second illustration reflects an ongoing border policy (see chapter 2). In 2005, the U.S. Department of Homeland Security Border Safety Initiative reported a record-high death toll along the U.S.-Mexico border at 492 (U.S. Border Patrol SW border deaths by fiscal year). Human rights organizations put the death toll at 516 for that year, much higher than the officially stated number. Each year, hundreds of people die attempting to cross a border that is increasingly militarized. Militarization in this sense refers to strategies and tactics that relate to "low-intensity conflict" (Dunn, 1996).

Low-intensity conflict originally characterized the U.S. American military and security force's counterinsurgency techniques used against revolutionaries in the Global South, especially in Central America during the 1980s (Dunn, 1996). It is a broad term that encompasses guerilla warfare, avoidance of a sustaining or escalating involvement of U.S. American troops with minimal causalities of personnel, and preemptive measures that prevent outright conflicts. Basically, low-intensity conflict provides social control over a certain civilian population through a form of militarization where military forces take on police functions and vice versa. Low-intensity conflict has increased domestically "in our own backyard" in the drug war and border control efforts with militarized training, equipment, mentality, and approach (Dunn, 1996).

While militarized border practices grew over the Carter, Reagan, and Bush, Sr.'s presidential administrations, militarized border practices took a dramatic turn under the Clinton administration when the INS launched an offensive border strategy called "prevention through deterrence." This strategy began with "Operation Hold the Line" (in El Paso, Texas in 1993) and continued with "Operation Gatekeeper" (in San Diego, California in 1994), "Operation Safeguard" (in Nogales, Arizona in 1994), and "Operation Rio Grande" (in the Brownsville corridor that extends from the Lower Rio Grande Valley to Laredo, Texas in 1997). Walls, stadium-style lighting, surveillance equipment, increased criminalization, and improved border patrol staffing characterize this strategy (Andreas, 2000). The goal was to move the migration path away from safer, urban areas—namely San Diego and El Paso—into remote, unsafe regions of the Arizona desert, to deter people from crossing into the United States and to make apprehension easier in the remote areas. Consequently, the premeditation of using the harsh desert as a migration deterrent resulted in far more deaths and human tragedies. However, this "gatekeeper state" politically crafts the border as "out of control," which demands more policing capacities that focus the problem not on border statecraft but on individual border crossers, which dismisses the state's responsibility in fostering undocumented immigration (Nevins, 2002). Indeed, this border enforcement strategy has "backfired" in the sense it does not control the border, but only encourages undocumented border crossers to stay in the United States and settle with their families in all fifty states, eliminating the long-standing practice of circular migration by men border crossers to three states (Massey, Durand, & Pren, 2016).

Since there is no comprehensive official count of the deaths associated with border migration overall (Eschbach, Hagan, Rodriguez, Hernández-León, & Bailey, 1999), the "total number of deaths in the past 20 years is estimated between 5000 and 8000, but there is no accurate account of the people who have lost their lives trying to cross the border" (Nienass & Délano, 2016, p. 288) due to animal predation on bodies, the scattering of skeletal remains by the elements, a lack of comprehensive DNA databases, and the deaths that remain uncounted on the Mexican side of the border as a direct result of these militarization policies. In addition to the rise of border-crossing deaths, "the use of mass hearings to prosecute apprehended migrants, and abuses of migrants in immigration detention" reflect a layered and complex human rights crisis in this border region (Androff & Tavassoli, 2012, p. 1; Macías-Rojas, 2016). And yet the immigration and border discourse in the news media somehow does not reach an alarmist level about the historical, economic, political, and legal factors that create a policy-driven human rights crisis. Rather, the alarmist frameworks are more consistently used to highlight immigrants as criminals, with the added suggestion that they are animals, dirt, and other social and symbolic disorders.

Both of these examples, the Chandler incident and the record-breaking border deaths, show how the criminalization of immigrants makes racism seem like common sense while denying any racism. The Chandler example shows how racialized discourse about immigration has become naturalized and hidden in everyday news about crime by reducing immigrants to criminals, animals, and dirt despite the critical coverage of the operation itself. The record-high death toll in the border region shows how criminalizing policies that use metaphors of "war" as frameworks have excessively deadly effects.

This study makes sense of how deeply racist conceptualizations can be communicated without overtly racist rhetoric through the deployment of spatially suggestive and embodied imagery. This is an interdisciplinary endeavor that makes the most of a wide range of research in race theory, social geography, anthropology, feminist theory, Chicana(o)/border studies, justice studies, cultural studies, and media studies. Additionally, the border region becomes the geographic line between an "Us and Them" binary that becomes an ideological foil for meanings of race, crime, and nation in relation to immigration. The defense of this border region becomes a productive place for researching how the media constructs Whiteness through innuendo, symbolism, and imagery. This study reveals the subtle equation of *USA* = *White Body* and *Immigrants* = *Disease* by using critical discourse analysis methods to examine the border states' newspaper coverage (*Los Angeles Times, Arizona Republic, Albuquerque Journal,* and *Houston Chronicle*) during a peak epoch of border militarization (1993–2006). The next section overviews the most recent wave of nativist discourse by highlighting two alarming events in the border states that correspond to period under study: California's 1994 Proposition 187 and the 2005 Minutemen spectacle in Arizona. The discourse generated from this nativist wave contributes to a "racist dirt fixations" theoretical model that I expand upon in the next chapter. I then review the literature on the continuing significance of Whiteness and situate my work within the Whiteness studies literature. Finally, I describe my methodology for the study and provide an overview of the remaining chapters.

CONTEMPORARY NATIVIST DISCOURSE

California's 1994 voter-approved ballot initiative called Proposition 187, or the "Save our State" or "S.O.S" initiative, is a watershed moment in the nation's post-civil rights racial history (Jacobson, 2008). Its racialized intent to exclude immigrants from vital and basic services like health and education services heralded a new nativist wave that continues today against mostly Brown people of color. After the measure passed, lawsuits followed and a court injunction was placed, where a subsequent court decision found Prop 187 unconstitutional (Jacobson, 2008). However, Prop 187's true and lasting intent was to send a symbolic political message from the Californian voters to the federal government and undocumented immigrants about their anger over the perception that immigrants are a fiscal burden to the state (Calavita, 1996). Prop 187 was an angry SOS message that California was a sinking boat due to immigration. It is no coincidence that Prop 187 passed one year after "Operation Hold the Line" in El Paso, which marked an upward tick in the militarization of the border. "Literally and metaphorically, the 'border' was one of the primary grounds on which Proposition 187 was fought," where the news covered proponents of the proposition "as favoring a border that maintains the economic and ideological unity of the nation, in part through the process of greater and greater measures of enforcement" (Ono & Sloop, 2002, p. 51).

While each nativist wave in U.S. American history had different targets ranging from Catholics and Chinese immigrants to political radicals and immigrant strikebreakers (Calavita, 1996; Higham, 1955), Leo Chavez (2001) argues that the recent discursive patterns used to describe Mexican immigrants are "overwhelmingly alarmist" (p. 215), which breaks from the historical pattern of immigration discourse that uses both positive and alarmist imagery. The rhetoric and discourse of Prop 187 fundamentally altered the understanding of the nation to its southern border that shifts in meanings and functions (Ono & Sloop, 2002). Now, "suspect bodies carry the border on them. These bodies, even when present at physical locations quite distant from the geopolitical border, are susceptible targets" (Flores, 2003, p. 381, citing Chang & Aoki, 1998). Thus, border vigilante activity has moved from the border into the interior of the nation where they target immigrant employment, public buildings and officials, and educational institutions (Kil, Menjívar, & Doty, 2009).

Ono and Sloop (2002) analyze dominant civic discourse in the national media coverage of Prop 187 and find that the news discourse portrays immigrants as the "new enemies" in three ways: economic drain, criminals, and disease. These Prop 187 themes of enemy, economy, crime, and disease overlap and are not mutually exclusive in the discursive conceptualizations.

Mehan (1997) also makes the case that these immigrants have become our new, post–Cold War enemy in an "Us vs. Them" war frame. Official political frameworks like the "War on Drugs" and "War on the Border" only help to see immigrants as symbolic national enemies that encourage racialized enforcement policies (Kil & Menjívar, 2006). Chavez (2003) contends that central to the war metaphor are that "immigrants are a threat to national security, sovereignty, and control of territory" (p.423). He further argues that Proposition 187 targets reproduction while ignoring production, meaning that Prop 187 attempts to sever social services which target the reproduction of the immigrant families while ignoring production by leaving alone immigrant workers and employers given that Prop 187 did not propose to reduce incentives for hiring undocumented labor or propose to increase employer sanction enforcement (Chavez, 2003). Moreover, Santa Ana (2002) found that contemporary discourse imagines Latinos as "invaders" and "outsiders," as well as "burdens," "parasites," "diseases," "animals," and "weeds." Ono and Sloop (2002) note that regardless of whether the news discourse was in favor of or opposed to Prop 187, both sides of the discursive debate deployed a "collective rhetoric . . . that uses suspicion of the other as a strategy for the preservation of self" (p. 41).

The economic downturn fueled nativism that was the salient factor that motivated voters to support Proposition 187 (Alvarez & Butterfield, 2000). Santa Ana, Moran, and Sanchez (1998) also note the fiscal focus of Prop 187 in the news media that emphasized the theme of "immigrants as commodity." These arguments attempt to be proimmigrant but nevertheless rely upon perceiving immigrants essentially as a labor resource or a thing rather than focusing on the damage to the rights and dignity of humans as a result of the proposition's implementation. Similarly, Ono and Sloop (2002) found that news discourse both for and against Prop 187 assume that "immigrants are human capital" (p. 31). Additionally, Hasian and Delgado (1998) analyze economic arguments of Prop 187 as a way to communicate racism and xenophobia in non-racial, economic terms that scapegoat the immigrant as a source of the problem. Moreover, Suárez-Orozco (1996) uses a psychocultural perspective to analyze the economic worries and social anxieties experienced by Californians during the 1990s, from the economic recession, to earthquakes, and to urban race riots, all of which helped to craft the immigrant "Other" image. The trope of immigrants as the "Other" contains anxieties that otherwise could not be easily controlled. The result is the fantasy of immigrants as "parasites draining the economy or as criminals taking our limited and diminishing resources" that affect the public discourse with anxiety, envy (in relation to racial group competition) and paranoia (Suárez-Orozco, 1996, p. 157).

The accusation of immigrant criminality stems from the perception that new immigrants arrive with a lawless intent. Ono and Sloop (2002) note that the discourse for and against Prop 187 assume immigrants' criminal proclivities because of the crime committed in their undocumented border-crossing and the immorality of cutting in front of others in line to immigrate. The public imagines the criminality of immigrants either through a victim lens or water imagery. For example, Cacho (2000) describes an ideology of White injury in the race-neutral language of Prop. 187 that depicts the people of California as "victims" who suffer personal and economic injury caused by immigrants. In addition, she argues that this White injury ideology conceals the economic reliance on immigrant labor, denies its racism, and foists an additional economic crisis onto immigrant workers and their children by legally, culturally, and socially disenfranchising them (Cacho, 2000). Hasian and Delgado (1998) note that the rhetoric of victimage in Prop 187 invited Californians to see immigration as a tax burden and obscures the racism that immigrants experience after they cross the border. Peter Brimelow's (1996) *Alien Nation: Common Sense About America's Immigration Disaster* popularizes this notion of White victimhood. Scholars also note the use of water imagery to suggest immigrant criminality during the Proposition 187's debate. The media uses water imagery to describe immigration as a large and uncontrollable phenomenon (Chavez, 2001) much like a crime wave, which overlooks an individual immigrant's humanity by focusing on the deadly fantasy of floods or *"inundating surges of brown faces"* (Santa Ana et al., 1998, p. 153, emphasis in original).

Ono and Sloop (2002) show that Prop 187 debates displayed a concern over the "health of the social body," where border crossers are seen as carriers of disease (p. 34). Santa Ana (2002) writes that the "Nation as body" has a long history as a political metaphor and it allows the nation to possess characteristics of a body because of the shared quality of bounded, finite spaces; except that the biological body encourages meanings of the nation in distinctly corporal and emotional ways. In addition, Gabriel (1998) argues that the construction of immigrants as "pollutants" leads to paranoias around the physical body as well as the imagined body of the nation where metaphors freely exchange between these two scales to the benefit of both. Cisneros (2008) also notes that the media represented "immigrants as pollutants," which serves a unifying, nationalistic function that normalizes U.S. American identity as "pure."

Despite Prop 187's failure to become state policy, the measure helped to contribute to the racialized climate that ended affirmation action and bilingual education in California, inspiring other states to enact similar versions of these nativist policies (Jacobson, 2008). And as Clinton's "prevention through deterrence" strategy moved the migration path into the harsh Sonoran desert, racist vigilante groups followed this new migration path from California and Texas and converged in Arizona in 2005 (Kil & Menjívar, 2006).

Doty (2009) analyzes these border vigilantes who call themselves the Minutemen (or other variation of that name) for their anti-immigrant media message and argues their overarching theme is that a crisis threatens U.S. American security. For these border vigilantes, undocumented border crossers threaten the cultural integrity, national identity, and physical security of the United States. She writes these border vigilantes see the USA as

"under siege." Laws are being flaunted, and thus the respect for laws is diminishing, as is the government's willingness to uphold them. "We" are under siege from "them." "We" are victims of the crisis; "they" are perpetrators. A deeply complex situation involving two historically intertwined countries and peoples is reduced to a black and white, illegal- and -legal phenomenon in which certain individuals and groups become the "enemy" and a "state of emergency is declared. (p. 80)

Doty (2009) notes a related theme in the border vigilantes' beliefs is that the state is eroding citizen's property rights, or at least leaving property unprotected like the ranches on the border (see chapters 2 and 4), which they believe requires a declaration of a state of emergency (see chapter 6).

In addition, the vigilantes see immigrants as criminal trespassers on the U.S. American property, where vigilantes portray themselves like a neighborhood watch group (Doty, 2009; Kil & Menjívar, 2006). Cacho (2012) argues that this type of argument that accuses immigrants of infringing on property

rights appeal to the White expectations of entitlement and reflect the "con-
flicting property interest of whiteness [that] underlie immigration debates"
(p. 26). Moreover, DeChaine (2009) argues that these vigilantes promote a
discursive "fence logic" by focusing the problem more on the physical border
rather than the immigrant, in what he refers to as a "project of alienation,"
where alienation reduces anxieties regarding national disunity by shoring up
what is inside the border and marking what is outside. He furthers argues that
the vigilantes' rhetorical alienation in its official discourse is not overtly racist but rather blames the condition of the border on the federal government.
In contrast, Oliviero (2011) notes that the Minutemen use White supremacist tropes that construct immigrants as invaders and diseases of the body
politic that invoke the rape of the nation which "genders national insecurity"
(p. 691). She argues that the Minutemen's citizenship logics depend on
"unmarked tropes of masculinity, whiteness, and heteronormativity, despite
their gestures of multiculturalism" (Oliviero, 2011, p. 702).

Donald Trump's racist nativism toward undocumented, Brown border
crossers draws from these border vigilantes and the rhetoric of Prop 187
where Trump seems to repackage these nativist talking points as his own to
demand a greater wall, more military, and a declaration of a national emergency based on racial myths of rampant immigrant crime. However, studies
show that the positive association between immigrants and crime is largely
false, and in fact, immigrants are more likely to be the victims rather than
perpetrators of crime (Martinez & Valenzuela, 2006).

Suffice it to say, the new nativist rhetoric is alarmist but somehow not
considered racist by the public and the news media that actively deploy these
negative images. On the surface, the rhetoric seems to have little pattern or
cohesiveness in the imagery generated, outside of its negativity, because
immigrants cannot be both weeds and waves or invaders and diseases all at
once. It seems like a *blitzkrieg* of alarmist ideas with little rhyme or reason.
However, it is my contention that below the surface of these nativist constructions is an emerging structure about the nation in relation to geographic scale
that privileges space and place in particular ways that relate to Whiteness
and notions of "purity," which contributes to deeply racist constructions of
immigrants' intentions and place vis-à-vis the nation.

I advance a "racist dirt fixation" theoretical framework that I elaborate in
the next chapter to better understand and make sense of the disparate nativist imagery of this recent wave. This "racist dirt fixations" framework draws
upon Cornel West's (1998) genealogies of racism that derive from religious,
scientific, and sexual ordered systems and Mary Douglas' (1966) symbolic
"dirt," which ontologically represents disorder and "danger" for the physical
body and breaches each of West's ordered systems in a racialized way that
represents a violation of "purity." Religious, scientific, and sexual ordered

systems and the "dirt" that violates these systems work with the scale of the physical body that nests within and projects outward toward larger geographic, bounded scales, like a house, region, and the nation. Each scale possesses embodied, symbolic "dirt" hidden within the narratives of the scale's imagined border between inside/outside, order/disorder, purity/pollution and health/disease. In addition, various intersections of race, class, gender, sexuality, and disability in the news discourse simultaneously construct as well as hide these racialized fixations. "Racist dirt fixations" explain how the physical body contributes to the immigration debate, and particularly how the worries over the USA-Mexico border influences the White body politic that produces racial genealogies, justifications, and nightmares about border crossings at each level of geographic scale.

THE CONTINUING SIGNIFICANCE OF WHITENESS IN AN AGE OF RACE NEUTRALITY

Whiteness Studies emerged out of several academic, literary, and activist influences and can be thought of in three waves: (a) the historic and intellectual work of Blacks who fought Whiteness mostly before the civil rights era, (b) late-twentieth century contributions to the continuing power of Whiteness, and (c) the global growth of Critical White Studies with empirical studies (Gallagher & Twine, 2017; Garner, 2017; Twine & Gallagher, 2008). These three waves examine "how power and oppression are articulated, redefined and reasserted through various political discourses and cultural practices that privilege Whiteness even when the prerogatives of the dominant group are contested" (Twine & Gallagher, 2008, p. 7). These waves also reflect a commitment to make visible the institutionalization of White supremacy and its attempts to recuperate its dominance in changing racial, political and economic contexts.

The first wave of Whiteness studies focuses on the historic, Black intellectual work of scholars, activists, journalist, and artists who critiqued White supremacy. Many cite the work of W.E.B Du Bois'(1936) book titled *Black Reconstruction in America 1860-1880* as a pivotal staring point of Whiteness studies (Gallagher & Twine, 2017; Garner, 2017; Roediger, 1991; Twine & Gallagher, 2008). W.E.B Du Bois (1868–1963) was founder of the National Association of the Advancement of Colored People (NAACP) as well as a scholar and activist who observed that low-wage White workers were paid a "public and psychological wage" for their Whiteness which prevented any class solidarity with recently freed slaves (Roegider, 1994, p. 12; citing Du Bois, 1936). Du Bois also was the first to observe that Whiteness and institutional racism were mostly invisible to Whites because Whiteness operates as a normative center and he predicted that this "colorline" problem of White supremacy would only go global in scope in the coming centuries (Twine & Gallagher, 2008, citing Du Bois, 1903).

In addition to Du Bois, Black writers, activists, and scholars examined Whiteness, its supremacy and its impact on Black lives. James Baldwin (1924–1987), Zora Neale Hurston (1891–1960), Langston Hughes (1902–1967), Ralph Ellison (1914–1994), Ida B. Wells-Barnette (1862–1931), among many other Black intellectuals and artists contributed to understanding the power of Whiteness because they have been the "nation's keenest students of white consciousness and white behavior" (Roediger, 2010, p. 4). Moreover, the Black literature on racial passing contributes to the cultural production of Whiteness as "pure" (ostensibly without "one drop" of Black blood), by forcing a denial of kinship with any Blacks in order to pass as White (Mullen, 1994). Many in this first wave would also witness the first wave of White backlash marked by George Wallace: "Segregation now, segregation tomorrow, segregation forever" speech in 1963 and that would continue into the 1970s with claims of the White worker as the victim of people of color's demands for rights to justice and equality (Hughey, 2014, p. 722).

Outside the United States, Frantz Fanon (1925–1961), a Black French Martinique psychiatrist, contributes to early Whiteness studies with his psychosocial analysis of how possessing Black skin under imperial oppression and subjugation forces the Black colonial subject to internalize White superiority by wearing self-loathing "White masks" (Nayak, 2007, citing Fanon, 1986). Additionally, Fanon analyzed the imperial "White gaze," a technique of discipline that controls the Black colonial subject's actions but also thoughts (Nayak, 2007, citing Fanon, 1993). Fanon (1961) was notably the first philosopher to advocate for a psychological decolonization of the colonized mind from the culture of White supremacy in his book *The Wretched of the Earth.* Indeed, Fanon was a revolutionary who urged the colonized people of Africa to strike back against injustice and the brutality of White colonial exploitation and occupation. Later, White scholars of Whiteness studies would reemphasize his decolonization point (Ignatiev, 1995; Roediger, 1994).

The second wave of Whiteness studies began in late 1980s/early 1990s and initially arose out of the humanities tradition from both Great Britain and the United States and corresponds with a second wave of White backlash that marked the rise of Reaganism and Thatcherism during the 1980s and continued into the 1990s (Hughey, 2014). In the late-1980s, British film scholar Richard Dyer (1988) analyzed the representation of Whiteness in popular film and noted that "white power secures its dominance by seeming not to be anything in particular" but upon closer inspection, Whiteness can become emptiness, lack, or even death (p. 1). He would later expand his argument in his book titled *White* that analyzed Whiteness in popular Western media where

Whiteness stands for the ordinary as well as all humanity and draws its various abstractions from both Christianity and colonialism (Dyer, 1997). Across the Atlantic Ocean and in the same year of Dyer's first publication on Whiteness, Peggy McIntosh's (1989) essay on White privilege as an "invisible knapsack" from a gender studies perspective offered a practical way to make visible the privileging system of Whiteness that had seemed naturalized. A few years later, bell hooks (1992) argued that Blacks, from slavery onward, have studied Whiteness as a "special," partially recorded knowledge in order to cope and survive White supremacy. She draws from the Black writers of the first wave of Whiteness studies to explain how they typically imagined Whiteness as type of terror in their stories that had practical implications on Black safety and survival. A year later, Toni Morrison (1992) argued in her book *Playing in the Dark* that notions of individualism, freedom, masculinity, and innocence among classic works by White authors like Melville, Hemingway, and Poe rely on the reflexive construction of Blackness as inherently unfree. She argued that this was a literary means for these authors to project a "dark" terror and desire without having to acknowledge these racialized feelings as their own. Morrison shifts the "critical gaze from the racial object to the racial subject; from the described and imagined to the describers and imaginers; from the serving to the served" (p. 90). Thus, the abstraction of Whiteness in films, the invisible knapsack of White privilege, the terror of Whiteness represented by Black writers, and the White construction of Blackness as a literary foil for White liberal values helped to inspire academia from a variety of fields to investigate Whiteness once again with increasing participation by White scholars with each additional wave.

Hence, White men historians contributed to this second wave by focusing on how whiteness impacted European immigrants in their racial formation in the United States. Roediger (1991) led the way with his book *Wages of Whiteness* that examined how race, class, and sometimes gender contributed to the identity formation of the White worker, where embracing Whiteness was a response to the fear of dependency on wage labor (or fear of White slavery) that related to the capitalist work discipline of the New Republic. Ignatiev's (1995) book, *How the Irish became White*, traces how the Irish immigrants, fleeing a famine and brutal caste system in their homeland, were initially treated poorly upon arrival to the United States and often racially associated with Blacks. Eventually, the Irish embraced White supremacy as a choice and strategy to gain material advantages in society. Ignatiev (2019) is particularly controversial for encouraging White people to be a traitor to and abolish Whiteness (http://racetraitor.org/abolishthepoint.html), which is also advocated by Roediger (1994). Allen (1994) and Jacobson (1998) additionally contribute to the story of how new European immigrants' racial formation relates to social control and labor practices that contributed to the

invention of Whiteness. These Whiteness scholars help theorize class identity, historicize race, and center the nation in the formation of race (Hattam,
2001). These studies demonstrate how historical materialism, racial formation, politics, and White supremacy made Whiteness and offer hope and/or
mandate for its abolishment.

Frankenberg's (1993) *White Women Race Matters* contributed to this
second wave by examining how race and gender affect White women where
their Whiteness is a location to structural privilege, a standpoint or way of
knowing, as well as set of practices. Nakayama and Krizek (1995) from a
communication studies perspective map the discursive space or territory of
Whiteness and offer six rhetorical strategies through which Whiteness dominates: Whiteness is closely tied to raw power or the "majority," Whiteness is
negatively and invisibly defined by what is not (not Black, not Brown, etc.)
and can stand for the universal/all humanity, Whiteness is naturalized through
scientific classification that empties Whiteness of its sociohistorical power
and hides its true functions, Whiteness conflates with nationality where "the
vision of whiteness is bounded by national borders and recenters whiteness"
(p. 300), Whites (particularly White men) refuse to label their Whiteness,
and some Whites symbolically claim European ethnicity in a manner that
is similar to accessorizing a wardrobe (Nakayama & Krizek, 1995, citing
Waters, 1990). In addition, Nakayama and Martin (1998) coedited *Whiteness:
The Communication of Social Identity*, and this collection analyzes Whiteness from a sociohistorical, postcolonial, and poststructural framework as
well as in United States and international contexts. On a comparative level,
Gabriel's (1998) *White Wash* looks at race and the media in the U.K. and U.S.
American experience, given that both countries are grounded in imperialism
and interwoven racial histories, and traces the numerous ways Whiteness
stays invisible yet powerful while making the case that the Far Right (or
White backlash culture) discourse like the "white victim" trope influences the
popular media in portraying and policing racialized bodies as criminals and
threats. *The Making and Unmaking of Whiteness* (Rasmussen, Klinenberg,
Nexica, & Wray, 1997) is an edited anthology that emerged from a 1997
academic conference at Berkeley California and was an effort to understand
the role of Whiteness in the racist nativism of California, which included
that passage of Proposition 209 (1996) that ended affirmative action in state
agencies. Arizona would also follow California in 2010 by ending affirmative
action through a state voter proposition. Rasmussen et al. (1997) assessed the
divergent state of Whiteness studies with five working conceptions: Whiteness is invisible/unmarked, Whiteness is empty (as in lacking culture) and
appropriates (other cultures to fill the void), it is structural privilege, it is
violence/terror, it is institutionalized colonialism, and Whiteness studies is
an antiracist practice.

Critical Race Theory, which emerged from Critical Legal Studies, analyzes how the law maintains White supremacy historically, institutionally, and intersectionally and contributes to Critical White Studies (Delgado & Stefancic, 1997). For example, Cheryl Harris's (1992) groundbreaking work on Whiteness as property analyzes the historical and legal co-evolution of White supremacy and property rights through the institution of enslaving Blacks and the seizure of Native American lands. Chattel slavery helped to merge Whiteness and property so that "Whiteness was the characteristic, the attribute, the property of free human beings" (p. 1721). The cultural and economic practices of White settler colonial land use facilitated the deprivation of Native American land by defining legal possession through White uses of land only, thereby negating Native American claims to possessing the land first. "Whiteness and property share a common premise—a conceptual nucleus—of a right to exclude. This conceptual nucleus has proven to be a powerful center around which whiteness as property has taken shape" (p. 1714). Harris analyzed her Black grandmother's ability to pass as White for work as a form of Whiteness as property in an illumining example of Critical Race Theory's emphasize on storytelling and personal narrative in legal analysis. In addition, Haney-Lopez's (1996) *White by Law* critically examines the early racial prerequisite legal cases (1878–1952) in immigration law that helped to determine citizenship for the few immigrants deemed White by the courts, demonstrating that Whiteness was legally constructed and informed by racist judicial thinking, which dramatically and forever altered the current racial make-up of the United States.

Additional contributions to the second wave of Whiteness come from a sociological perspective. Lipsitz (1998) describes how neoliberal social policies and racial animus creates a "possessive investment in whiteness" that impact housing, education, wealth accumulation, and employment by advantaging Whiteness. "Whiteness has a cash value . . . a social fact, an identity created and continued with all-too-real consequences for the distribution of wealth, prestige, and opportunity" (vii). In addition to its cash value, Lipsitz agrees with Harris (1992) that Whiteness is like property "but it is also a means of accumulating property and keeping it from others" (viii). Thus, Lipsitz echoes Harris' exclusion principle where "whiteness has been characterized, not by an inherent unifying characteristic, but by the exclusion of others deemed to be 'not white'" (p. 1736). Doane and Bonilla-Silva's (2003) edited book, *White Out*, attempts to direct Whiteness toward more theoretical complexity, empirical studies, and dynamic understandings of Whiteness and how it reifies its supremacy in changing social, economic, and political structures, which leads us to the third wave of Whiteness studies.

Twine and Gallagher (2008) make the case for an emerging third wave of Whiteness studies that is more localized and empirical and offer three salient features to this current wave. First, they argue that the third wave employs innovative methodologies. In particular, they highlight the use of race conscious biographies to examine how Whites produce and practice Whiteness in their lives (Twine & Gallagher, 2008; citing Twine, 2004 and Kinney, 2005), though Doane and Bonilla-Silva (2003) are critical of Whiteness studies that focus on the construction of White identities as a fruitless academic inquiry.

Second, they argue that the third wave examines how White cultural and discursive practices and strategies attempt to regain and recover Whiteness and its supremacy in the "post-apartheid, post-industrial, post-imperial, post-Civil-Rights" age (Twine & Gallagher, 2008, p. 13). One example is the mainstreaming of White supremacist discourse since the global economic collapse of 2008 that contributed to a renewed White backlash that delivered the Presidency for Donald Trump and a British exit from the European Union (Garner, 2017). This study provides another example of how the "war on the border" paradigm with its border militarization policies is a strategy of Whiteness to regain its supremacy in seemingly nonracial ways that colludes with neoliberal economic transformations in making immigrants materially surplus and discursively disposable.

Thus, Whiteness as neoliberalism is another illustration of this third wave of Whiteness that expands Harris' Whiteness as property concept to the global-transformations of late capitalism (see chapter 7). Hohle (2015) argues that neoliberalism initially emerged as a Southern White strategy among Jim Crow segregationists and the business class to counter the gains of the civil rights movement and reassert White advantage over Blacks which paved the way for U.S. American neoliberalism characterized by austerity, privatization, deregulation, and tax cuts for the rich. Neoliberalism "is not about free markets" (p. 141). Moreover, Giroux (2003) argues that "under neoliberalism all levels of government have been hollowed out and largely reduced either to their policing functions or to maintaining the privileges of the rich and the interests of corporate power both of which are largely White" (p. 197). Goldberg (2009) argues that racial neoliberalism is a response to the "impending impotence of whiteness" (p. 337) that seeks to privatize property by privatizing race to better protect those racial exclusions in the private sphere that is beyond state intervention. Mohanty (2013) clarifies that "while neoliberal states facilitate mobility and cosmopolitanism (travel across borders) for some economically privileged communities, it is at the expense of the criminalization and incarceration (the holding in place) of impoverished communities" (p. 970).

Given that the neoliberal transformation of culture, politics, and economy reinvents Whiteness with a nonracial discourse that obscures its rise in corporate bodies, mergers, and extreme concentrated wealth, the institution of policing becomes an interesting and emerging inquiry into the third wave of Whiteness. Much like slaves were policed as property in the past, police target poorer, darker bodies and their communities for their failure to thrive in this rigged market that manages them as surplus populations though austerity policies (like ending welfare with workfare) and criminalization practices (exemplified by the prison industrial complex). As early as 1904, W.E.B. Du Bois called slave patrols "a system of rural police," yet today's introductory criminal justice/policing textbooks largely dismiss the relevance of patrolling slaves as property to modern policing (Turner, Giacopassi, & Vandiver, 2006, citing Du Bois, 1904). Singh (2014) agrees that policing began with the U.S. American history of settler colonialism and suggests it continued with the management of the racial domination throughout the centuries, and that police power regulates "an unequal ordering of property relations, that is, *the whiteness of police*" (p. 1092, emphasis in original). Singh continued, "Whiteness carries a tremendous price . . . [and] such valuation is made concrete and realizable through the work of policing" both in the daily surveillance that maintains the racially valued and devalued spaces and the "exemplary spectacles by which forms of overt police violence tutor publics in the value of whiteness" (p. 1097). Burton (2015) also sees a link between the history of Southern slave patrols and the modern practice of "order-maintenance policing" (aka, broken windows policing) and argues that police "protect and serve whiteness." I would add that Whiteness as neoliberalism consolidates Whiteness as property to create exclusivity in wealth, space, and territory that the Whiteness of police then protects and serves. For example, Kahn, Goff, Lee, and Motamed (2016) applied regression analysis to police use of force and the mug shots of suspects in official case files and found that police use less force the more a suspect looks stereotypically White, which provides an additional protective privilege for Whites encountering the criminal justice system. Given this context, it should then come as no surprise that the "blue lives matter" flags—a Black/White USA flag with a center "thin blue line" that represent police backlash to the "Black Lives Matter" social movement that has protested police brutality and violence against Blacks—appeared beside Confederate flags and White Power symbols at the violent, neo-Nazi demonstration in Charlottesville, Virginia in August 2017 (Rossman, 2017). In addition, President Trump's former Attorney General Jeff Sessions gave a speech to the National Sheriffs Association and said, "The office of sheriff is a critical part of the *Anglo*-American heritage of law enforcement. We must never erode this historic office" (Sit, 2018, para. 2, emphasis added). In regard to policing the border, Hernández (2010) argues that historically controlling immigration at the southern border meant "expanding the boundaries of whiteness while hardening the distinctions between whites and non-whites" (p. 42). Hernández charts how the Black/White racial binary shaped the "Border Patrol's Mexicanization of the legal/illegal divide" (p. 11), where

xxviii   Introduction

immigration control and the ever-expanding prison system perpetuate a caste of undocumented immigrants.

Third, Whiteness studies scholars of this third wave are shifting away from the European immigrant experience in the United States toward racialized immigrants and their negotiations with Whiteness (Twine & Gallagher, 2008; citing Basler, 2008). For example, Basler (2008) analyzes interviews that uncover Mexican American voting patterns on Prop 187 and the 2004 presidential race to demonstrate that their voting significantly relates to their racial identity and nationalism, as more support for Republican candidates demonstrate a claim to "a white identity to place them in the 'imagined community' of 'real Americans' like California nativists and President W. Bush-unquestioned and uncompromised white Americans" (p. 159). In addition, Foley (2008) argues that while Mexican Americans are White by law, they have historically been treated as the racial other, resulting in Faustian bargains with Whiteness that divide Mexican Americans by race and class.

Additionally, Whiteness studies are now global in outlook especially in regions that were former European colonies (Garner, 2017), where crossing borders also means crossing racial lines of the nation imagined and guarded as White. For example, Bebout's (2016) *Whiteness on the Border* examines how Whiteness and U.S. Americanness are co-constituted against Mexicanness, which allows the access to advantages and resources for Whites but renders Mexicans, Mexican Americans, and Mexico as anti-citizens/anti-United States. Further north at the USA-Canada border, "officially perceived Whiteness" provides "significant material and ontological rewards" against racial profiling in a post-9/11security regime with little acknowledgement of this power dynamic by White Canadian border residents (Helleiner, 2012, p. 128). In fact, the war on terror helps to impose a Canadian national identity through border policing practices that reflect White nationalism and foster a passport culture that contributes to a global apartheid where rich states keep the poor out so that certain nationalities are criminalized as "existential and juridical 'foreigners'" (Sharma, 2006, p. 124). Additionally, Sarah Ahmed (2007) argues that Whiteness should be seen as a phenomenology, where some bodies are oriented in a certain direction, space, with certain abilities, that allows White "bodies to move with comfort through space, and to inhabit the world as if it were home" (p. 159; also see chapter 4). While bodies of color experience "a phenomenology of 'being stopped'" (Ahmed, 2007, p. 161) and move in a different way than White bodies with mobility, where borders can produce "stranger danger" toward bodies of color

> politics of mobility, of who gets to move with ease across the lines that divide
> spaces, can be re-described as the politics of who gets to be at home, who gets

to inhabit spaces, as spaces that are inhabitable for some bodies and not others, insofar as they extend to the surface of some bodies and not others. (p. 162)

Thus, Whiteness is a "form of positive residence: as if it were a property of persons, cultures, places" (p. 154).

This study is unique to the scholarship on Whiteness because it regionally analyzes newspaper discourse from the Border States most impacted by border militarization policies in order to find the discursive constructions of order/disorder, law/crime, and White/Brown. Whiteness studies helps to situate this border region within a continuum of colonialism and neoliberalism, where multiple histories of European colonization, various layers of neoliberal trade agreements, and post-9/11 border security concerns contribute to the criminalization of the Brown border crossers. *War on the Border* engages the deadly relationship between news discourse and militarized border practices and calls attention to the important reality that race neutral new(s) racism can help to ignore a human-made, human rights crisis. The study moves past the White-Black binary that characterizes the first two waves of Whiteness studies to show how Brownness is emerging as a significant, racially defining "Other" for the nation.

The core argument of this study is three fold: (a) an ontological understanding of the physical body in relation to symbolic "dirt" of religious, scientific and sexual ordered systems affects the ways in which the "purity" of national body is imagined as threatened by undocumented Brown border crossers; (b) the news media determines how the public defensively sees immigrants by targeting them as agents of crime and associating them with dangers and disorders that threaten the body politic at various geographic scales; and (c) the analysis of the media's framing of immigrants and the border as a crime issue reflexively reveals the hidden ideological construction of Whiteness as nation that intersects with inequalities of class, race, gender, disability and other categories of difference.

CRITICAL DISCOURSE ANALYSIS AS METHODOLOGY

Critical Discourse Analysis (CDA) guides the news media analysis of this study. CDA is a repertoire of methodological approaches with theoretical similarities that focus on social problems (Wodak & Meyer, 2001). van Dijk (1993), a founder of CDA, argues that CDA focuses on abuse of power and encourages the critical discourse analyst to take an "explicit sociopolitical stance" (p. 252) that also resonates with Whiteness studies' activist aims for transformative racial justice. In particular, he argues that CDA focuses on social power (privileged access to resources) and dominance (controlling and managing the minds of others through social representation) and how discourse reproduces this power and dominance in a hegemonic, institutionalized manner that serves power elites. Consequently, CDA is dynamic tool in uncovering how Whiteness is communicated through the news media in covert ways.

CDA enables a systematic assessment of veiled communication strategies that help in the production of social dominance (van Dijk, 1993). Based on the "racist dirt fixation" theoretical model of this study, there are three levels of discursive obfuscation of Whiteness in the border news discourse that CDA helps to uncover. First, the body as an image schemata provides a structure for organizing comprehension (Johnson, 2013). In the case of the body politic, where the body is an image schemata for the nation, the metaphor contains embodied complexity, a hierarchy of parts, states of health or illness, the latter of which requires diagnosis and treatment in order to prevent death or serious injury (Musolff, 2010). It helps form the "Us vs. Them" attitude toward those that are perceived as undocumented border crossers who "violate" boundaries. Second, racist genealogies that derive from religious, scientific, and sexual ordered systems (West, 1998) and the symbolic "dirt" that violates these ordered systems (Douglas, 1966) work on an intertextual level as genres to help communicate what is "pure." CDA promotes intertextual analysis in order to examine text "from the perspective of discourse practice, aiming to unravel the genres and discourses which are articulated together" (Fairclough, 1995, p. 70). Third, geographic scales like the body, house, region, and nation help to hide racist thinking in nonracial ways. For example, the scale of the ship that represents California and Prop 187's "SOS" signal for help hides a fuller narrative that California is a White victim/ship to the sinking disaster that is Brown immigration.

CDA also uncovers ideological motivations not readily seen in text and talk (Fairclough & Wodak, 1997). Following Morrison's (1992) literary methodology in examining Whiteness that shifts the "critical gaze from the racial object to the racial subject; from the described and imagined to the describers and imaginers; from the serving to the served" (p. 90), CDA not only analyzes what exists in the text but also pays sensitive attention to what is absent or the "implicit meaning" that is taken as a given or a presupposition (Fairclough, 1995, p. 106). In addition, CDA allows for an intersectional analysis (Lazar, 2017) that includes race, class, gender, sexuality, disability, and citizenship to help flush out the discursive, imagined dimensions of Brownness and Whiteness. This study examines how the border news coverage represents Brownness in order to access the implicit meaning of Whiteness as a presupposition to expose what hooks (1995) calls the "the vernacular discourse of neo-colonial white supremacy" (p. 5).

For CDA, "the media are not a neutral, common-sensed, or rational mediator of social events, but essentially help reproduce preformulated ideologies" (van Dijk, 2013, p.11). Thus, it is not the intention of this study to analyze individual journalists or newspapers as racist but to treat racism as structural, systemic and institutionalized which also characterizes the neoliberal transformations in the news media industry in advancing Whiteness (see chapter 7).

Since the power of Whiteness is rhetorically silent (Crenshaw, 1997) then it becomes important to decolonize the discursive dimension of Whiteness (Nakayama & Krizak, 2009) with an anti-racist commitment. In order to expose the power of Whiteness, the scholar-activist goal for this study is to then discover the deep structures of language, mythology, fantasy, terror, and desire at play in the news discourse about crime and the USA-Mexico border. Scholar activism means that as a researcher I am not neutral to the political situation of this study's setting. During my time in Arizona as a graduate student, I was a political activist and participated and led grassroots mobilizations to foster social justice and counter hate and racism. I served as a volunteer and board member of Border Action Network from June 2002 to May 2006. Border Action Network (BAN) is a grassroots, membership-based, nonprofit organization in Tucson, Douglas, and Nogales, Arizona. BAN works to protect the human rights, civil rights and the environment of the bi-national border communities against the militarization of the USA-Mexico border (Kil, Allen, & Hammer, 2011). Additionally, I was trained as a legal observer by the American Civil Liberties Union of Arizona for the Minuteman Project (April 2005–May 2005) and did several human rights observations in Cochise County, Arizona (Ybarra, 2005). Lastly, I am one of the original student founders of Local to Global Justice in Arizona established in 2002, which is currently a statewide teach-in and forum held annually at Arizona State University that merged academia with activism and was the key organizing platform for anti-war, direct action protest in the state (Farago, Swadener, Richter, Eversman, & Roca-Servat, 2018).

Using newspaper databases such as Lexus Nexus, NewsBank, Proquest, as well as some archival research, this analysis drew on leading newspapers in each border state: *Los Angeles Times, Arizona Republic, Albuquerque Journal,* and *Houston Chronicle.* These four Border States are the most impacted by militarized immigration policies and their newspapers reflect this in their coverage. Furthermore, these outlets cover immigration issues more frequently and negatively than states in the interior (Branton & Dunaway, 2009). Newspaper articles from these four outlets reflect a thirteen-year period of heightened border enforcement, beginning with "Operation Hold the Line" in El Paso (September 19, 1993) and ending with the passing of the Secure Fence Act (October 26, 2006), which further attempts to "seal" the border with an additional 700 miles of militarized fencing (White House, 2006). This thirteen-year period is significant because of the intense focus on the "War on the Border" as a policy and paradigm for immigration enforcement. This "border-centered strategy of immigration control" (Cornelius, 2004) began to shift thereafter and subsequent media and governmental attention turned toward the interior of the nation with stepped up ICE raids and an increase in racial profiling as reflected in bills like SB1070 and attempts at copycat legislations in other states (e.g., Utah, Alabama, Georgia, South Carolina, and Indiana).

Each news article in the data contains the three words "border," "immigration," and "Mexico." I narrowed the search to include articles flagged as "news" by the databases that include features and articles, as opposed to editorials, reviews, commentaries, letters to the editor, obituaries, and so forth. I additionally culled articles for a crime frame either in the headline or first few paragraphs, which reduced the number of stories that focused on the political contests, the border economy, or the cultural happenings in the region. Finally, I eliminated duplicates and further eliminated editorials and commentary that were misfiled as "news" by the database search engines, leaving only harder news items. A limitation to this study is a reliance on the search databases to accurately gather all news stories within the search parameters applied to the data.

The total number of news articles for the study is N=3,393: *Los Angeles Times* n= 630, *Arizona Republic* n=848, *Albuquerque Journal* n=457, and *Houston Chronicle* n=1458. Journal Publishing Company owns the *Albuquerque Journal* and is the only outlet that is not a conglomerate or multinational company (Bloomberg, 2018). In 2000, Tribune Media Company bought *The Los Angeles Times* from Times-Mirror Company (Shaw & Hofmeister, 2000). Gannett purchased *The Arizona Republic* in 2000 from Central Newspapers (CNN Money, 2000). The Hearst Corporation has owned *The Houston Chronicle* since 1987 (Hearst, 2018).

Nvivo is a qualitative software program that tracked and counted word references that related to each of these bodily scales—the body, house, region, and nation—as well as discourse that insinuates "dirt" or disorder. Coding initially started as a bottom-up approach where I read and coded each article by the strategy illustrated in Table 0.1. NVivo later added a word frequency function which allowed the determination of the 1,000 most-frequents words in the data. Of those words, each was organized according to the coding strategy (Table 0.1) in a top-down approach. The word "frequency" functions produced words like "and," "not," "Arizona," and "Houston," which were not analyzed given the ubiquity of the words in the data, and instead only analyzed words with references in the data below 4,500 as the limit to this study based on computational capacity. Concepts that relate to "racist dirt fixations" and the bodily scales include stemmed versions of a word and

Table 0.1 Coding Strategy

Tier 1: Theory	Racist Dirt Fixations			
Tier 2: 4 Scales	Body	House	Region	Nation
Tier 3: Themes	Embodied discourse	Home or Shelter	Location of conflict or disaster	Medicalized discourse

sometimes synonyms as well. For example, the concept "cross" (see chapter 3) encompasses stemmed versions like crossed, crossing, crosses, and so forth. Additionally, the concept "fence" also includes stemmed versions of that word as well as the stemmed versions of its synonyms "wall" and "barrier" that are used interchangeably with "fence" (see chapter 4) in the data. Occasionally, Nvivo did not fully include stemmed versions of a word search, thus an aggregate of individual stem word searches simulated this function. This occasional inconsistency of stem word searches within Nvivo's search functions is another limitation of this study.

Overall, I analyzed leading concepts in order of frequency of references in the data (with some minor exceptions noted in the analysis), then selected a news example of the concept that best represented their (a) relevance to "racist dirt fixations" and (b) ability to demonstrate the scale under analysis. In addition, examples from news articles were left intact as much as space permitted (in most cases this includes the headline and lead paragraphs) to show the fuller picture of the news narrative. For purposes of efficiency, I analyzed some concepts in pairs.

ORGANIZATION OF THIS BOOK

Chapter 1 lays out the theoretical framework for the analysis of everyday news discourse for Whiteness and nativism. West's (1988) concept of White racist logics and Douglas' (1966) concept of purity and danger help build the "racist dirt fixations" approach. These racist dirt fixations elide and hide in modern news discourse because the embodied nature of these fixations allows them to jump several geographic scales. Beginning with the physical body and moving to other scales like the house, region, and nation, nativist discourse can convey racism by using these four scales to imagine the dangerous borders between inside/outside, order/disorder, and nation/immigration. The result is a portrait of a White body politic in danger that is embodied in four general scales used in nativist discourse to discursively construct the nation as both bounded and vulnerable.

Chapter 2 describes the setting of the study that includes the political, social, and economic forces that factor into our contemporary state of militarized nativism at the border. I begin with an analysis of President Trump's promise to "Build that Wall" and then discuss the social construction of border crossers as racialized enemies. Next, I provide a brief history of the militarization of the border by analyzing the Clinton, Bush, and Obama administrations' contributions to the situation. Additionally, I offer meanings of the border, nativist ideology that motivate border militarization, and the impact of this militarization on local people and communities. I assert that the bipartisan Border Militarization policies are a form of Necropolitics (Mbembe, 2003) that brutalizes the public and incites racial hatred toward immigrants (Kil & Menjívar, 2006; Kil et al., 2009). I further contend that the border region is a Necropolitical Deathscape that affects immigrants' lives well beyond the discrete border region, making them more vulnerable and exploitable.

In turn, chapter 3 describes how the news media imagines and scales the nation as a "vulnerable body" while providing intersectional analysis on the discursive imagery in the border coverage. An analysis of racist dirt fixations reveals a fear of disability that intersect with racist, classist, gendered, and sexualized ideas about the immigration disorder and its impact on the health of body politic and its association with Whiteness. Three dominant themes compose this "vulnerable body" scale: "body aches," "body functions," and "body parts." "Body aches" is the most dominant theme and illustration of news narratives to show how immigrants are painted as a danger to the well-being of the nation. Four concepts lead this theme—"Cross," "Death," "Help," and "Problem." "Body Functions"—which characterize the functions and capacities of the body, offer striking imagery about how the nation "suffers" immigrants with leading concepts of "Secure," "Services," and "Jobs" that each criminalize immigrants as agents of harm and abusers of state resources. The final theme of "body parts" includes references to physical organs or appendages with "Face," "Hand," "Arm," "Foot," and "Heart." These concepts show that body politic can speak to a fear of disability or disfigurement with the "changing face" of the nation. "Hand" and "Arm" reflect border enforcement efforts, while immigrants who must cross the border by "Foot" are poor and associated with the lowest-valued part of the body politic. "Heart" shows a medicalized understanding of the body politic that is more modern and imagines immigrants as a type of blood clot or virus/bacteria that travels to the "heart" of the United States.

Chapter 4 offers an empirical analysis of the second of four nested scales: house. The news industry ascribes scripts and imagery to immigrants that renders them as less-than-human abstractions in the narratives by portraying them as criminals, enemies, and wild animals in contrast to the nation's concrete humanization as a house in need of defense. At the scale of the house, the border is like a "Revolving Door" or gate to the nation. Immigrants are primarily seen as two threats, either as a criminal home invader or as frightening wild animals that reflect scripts of a White, middle-class, hetero-patriarchal family under threat by security breaches to the national house.

Chapter 5 analyzes the next larger scale of the region, which is dominated by two themes. The "Battlefield" theme characterizes the narrative of the bor-der region, where immigrants are an invading army and any immigrant deaths in the border region are collateral damage, a by-product of this imagined "war." The region scale is also dominated by the "Flood" theme that associ-ates immigration with menacing waters that could drown the nation, either by natural forces or by means of a biblical flood.

Chapter 6 elaborates on the nation scale with a specific focus on the con-temporary, medical discourse informed by a popularized, scientific under-standing of disease that reflects concerns about the White body politic and "dirt." The news media's construction of this "diseased politic" communi-cates Whiteness and nativism about the border through discursive "border symptoms" and "technological remedies." I provide a brief overview of the studies on the modern discourse of health and illness to establish the ways that this medicalized discourse contributes to embodied racializations. In addition, I also discuss the rhetorical intersection of the medical, military, and law enforcement field within a medicalized discourse in communicating rac-ist, nativist ideologies. Four themes are detailed: "growing number," "busy time," "congested space," and "technological operations." The first three themes represent a pattern in the discourse of "border symptoms" of the body politic. In response to these "symptoms," the state invests in medicalized and militarized science and deploys "technological operations" in order to treat and control the border.

The concluding chapter summarizes the key findings about Whiteness and the nation in news discourse about the border. News media tenets like objectivity and neutrality contribute to the new(s) racism. Neoliberal transfor-mations that vertically restructure corporate media, concentrate ownership, and advance Whiteness over the past thirty years illuminates the journalistic failings in covering the border as a human rights crisis. I conclude with some recommendations for resisting this everyday new(s) racism.

REFERENCES

Ahmed, S. (2007). A phenomenology of whiteness. *Feminist Theory, 8*(2), 149–168.
Allen, T. W. (1994). *The Invention of the White Race: The Origin of Racial Oppres-sion in Anglo-America* (Vol. 2). London: Verso.
Alvarez, M., & Butterfield, T. (2000). The resurgence of nativism in California? The case of Proposition 187 and illegal immigration. *Social Science Quarterly, 81*(1), 167–179.

Andreas, P. (2000). *Border Games: Policing the U.S.-Mexico Divide*. Ithaca, NY: Cornell University Press.

Androff, D., & Tavassoli, K. (2012). Deaths in the desert: The human rights crisis on the U.S.-Mexico border. *Social Work, 57*(2), 165–173. DOI:10.1093/sw/sws034.

Baker, P. (2009). Trump declares a national emergency, and provokes a constitutional clash. *The New York Times*, February 15. Retrieved from https://www.nytimes.com/2019/02/15/us/politics/national-emergency-trump.html.

Basler, C. (2008). White dreams and red votes: Mexican Americans and the lure of inclusion in the Republican Party. *Ethnic & Racial Studies, 31*(1), 123–166. https://doi-org.libaccess.sjlibrary.org/10.1080/01419870701538950.

Bebout, L. (2016). *Whiteness on the Border: Mapping the U.S. Racial Imagination in Brown and White*. New York: New York University Press.

Benin, S. (2019). A quote Trump may come to regret: "I didn't need to do this." *MSNBC*, February 15. Retrieved from http://www.msnbc.com/rachel-maddow-show/quote-trump-may-come-regret-i-didnt-need-do.

Bloomberg. (2018). Company overview of journal publishing co. *Bloomberg*. Retrieved from https://www.bloomberg.com/research/stocks/private/snapshot.asp?privcapId=1605394.

Branton, R. P., & Dunaway, J. (2009). Spatial proximity to the U.S.-Mexico border and newspaper coverage of immigration issues. *Political Research Quarterly, 62*(2), 289–302.

Brimelow, P. (1996). *Alien Nation: Common Sense about America's Immigration Disaster*. New York, NY: HarperCollins.

Burton, O. (2015). To protect and serve whiteness. *North American Dialogue: Newsletter of the Society for the Anthropology of North America, 18*(2), 38–50.

Cacho, L. M. (2000). "The people of California are suffering": The ideology of White injury in discourses of immigration. *Cultural Values, 4*(4), 389–418.

Cacho, L. M. (2012). *Social Death: Racialized Rightlessness and the Criminalization of the Unprotected*. New York: New York University Press.

Calavita, K. (1996). The new politics of immigration: "Balanced-budget conservatism" and the symbolism of Proposition 187. *Social Problems, 43*(3), 284–305.

Castro, R. F. (2011). Xenomorph: Indians, Latina/os, and the alien morphology of Arizona Senate Bill 1070. *Harvard Civil Rights–Civil Liberties Law Review, 46*, 1–12.

Chavez, L. R. (2001). *Covering Immigration: Popular Images and the Politics of the Nation*. Berkeley: University of California Press.

Chaves, L. R. (2003). Immigration reform and nativism: The nationalist response to the transnational challenge. In M. C. Gutmann, F. V. Matos Rodriguez, L. Stephen, & P. Zavella (Eds.), *Perspectives on Las Américas: A Reader in Culture, History, and Representation* (pp. 418–429). Malden: Blackwell Publishers.

Cisneros, D. (2008). Contaminated communities: The metaphor of 'immigrant as pollutant' in media representation of immigration. *Rhetoric and Public Affairs, 11*, 569–602.

CNN Money. (2000). Gannett to buy publisher. *CNN Money*, June 28. Retrieved from https://money.cnn.com/2000/06/28/deals/gannett/.

Cornelius, W. (2004). Evaluating enhanced US border enforcement. *Migration Information*. Retrieved from http://www.migrationinformation.org/feature/display.cfm ?ID=223.

Crenshaw, C. (1997). Resisting Whiteness' rhetorical silence. *Western Journal of Communication*, 61, 253–278. DOI:10.1080/10570319709374577.

DeChaine, D. R. (2009). Bordering the civic imaginary: Alienization, fence logic, and the Minuteman Civil Defense Corps. *Quarterly Journal of Speech*, 95(1), 43–65.

Delgado, R., & Stefancic, J. (Eds.). (1997). *Critical White studies: Looking Behind the Mirror*. Philadelphia, PA: Temple University Press.

Doane, A. W., & Bonilla-Silva, E. (Eds.). (2003). *White Out: The Continuing Significance of Racism*. New York, NY: Psychology Press.

Doty, R. L. (2016). *The Law into their own Hands: Immigration and the Politics of Exceptionalism*. Tucson: University of Arizona Press.

Douglas, M. (1966). *Purity and Danger: An Analysis of Concepts of Pollution and Taboo*. London: Routledge & Kegan Paul.

Dunn, T. (1996). *The Militarization of the U.S.-Mexico Border, 1978–1992: Low-intensity Conflict Doctrine Comes Home*. Austin, TX: CMAS Books.

Dyer, R. (1988). White. *Screen*, 29(4), 44–65. DOI:10.1093/screen/29.4.44.

Dyer, R. (1997). *White: Essays on Race and Culture*. London: Routledge.

Eschbach, K., Hagan, J. M., Rodriguez, N. P., Hernández-León, R., & Bailey, S. (1999). Death at the border. *International Migration Review*, 33(2), 430–454.

Fairclough, N. (1995). *Media Discourse*. London: Edward Arnold.

Fairclough, N., & Wodak, R. (1997). Critical discourse analysis. In T. van Dijk (Ed.), *Discourse as Social Interaction*, (pp. 258–284). London: Sage.

Fanon, F. (1961/1963). *The Wretched of the Earth* (2nd ed.; Constance Farrington, Trans.). New York, NY: Grove Press.

Farago, F., Swadener, B. B., Richter, J., Eversman, K. A., & Roca-Servat, D. (2018). Local to global justice: Roles of student activism in higher education, leadership development, and community engagement. *Alberta Journal of Educational Research*, 64(2), 154–172.

Flores, L. A. (2003). Constructing rhetorical borders: Peons, illegal aliens, and competing narratives of immigration, *Critical Studies in Media Communication*, 20(4), 362–387. DOI: 10.1080/0739318032000142025.

Foley, N. (2008). Becoming hispanic: Mexican Americans and whiteness. In P. S. Rothenberg (Ed.), *White Privilege: Essential Readings on the Other Side of Racism*, (3rd ed., pp. 55–66). New York, NY: Worth Publishers.

Frankenberg, R. (1993). *White Women, Race Matters: The Social Construction of Whiteness*. Minneapolis: University of Minnesota Press.

Gabriel, J. (1998). *Whitewash: Racialized Politics and the Media*. New York, NY: Routledge.

Gallagher, C., & Twine, F. W. (2017). From wave to tsunami: The growth of third wave Whiteness. *Ethnic and Racial Studies*, 40(9), 1598–1603.

Garner, S. (2017). Surfing the third wave of Whiteness studies: Reflections on Twine and Gallagher. *Ethnic and Racial Studies*, 40(9), 1582–1597.

Georges-Abeyie, D. (2001). Petit apartheid in criminal justice: The more things change, the more things remain the same. In D. Milovanovic & K. Russell (Eds.), *Petit Apartheid in the U.S. Criminal Justice System: The Dark Figure of Racism* (pp. 9–14). Durham, NC: Carolina Academic Press.

Giroux, H. A. (2003). Spectacles of race and pedagogies of denial: Anti-Black racist pedagogy under the reign of neoliberalism. *Communication Education, 52*(3–4), 191–211. Retrieved from DOI: 10.1080/0363452032000156190.

Goldberg, D. T. (2009). *The Threat of Race: Reflections on Racial Neoliberalism.* Malden, MA: Wiley Blackwell.

Haney-López I. F. (1996). *White by Law: The Legal Construction of Race.* New York, NY: New York University Press.

Haney-López, I. F. (2010). Post-racial racism: Racial stratification and mass incarceration in the age of Obama. *California Law Review, 98*(3), 1023–1074.

Harris, C. I. (1992). Whiteness as property. *Harvard Law Review, 106,* 1707–1791. Retrieved from DOI:10.2307/1341787.

Hasian, M., Jr., & Delgado, F. (1998). The trials and tribulations of racialized critical rhetorical theory: Understanding the rhetorical ambiguities of Proposition 187. *Communication Theory, 8*(3), 245–270.

Hattam, V. C. (2001). Whiteness: Theorizing race, eliding ethnicity. *International Labor and Working-Class History, 60,* 61–68.

Hearst. (2018). Houston Chronicle. *Hearst.* Retrieved from https://www.hearst.com/newspapers/houston-chronicle.

Helleiner, J. (2012). Whiteness and narratives of a racialized Canada/U.S. border at Niagara. *Canadian Journal of Sociology, 37*(2), 109–135.

Hernández, K. L. (2010). *Migra!: A History of the U.S. Border Patrol.* Berkeley: University of California Press.

Higham, J. (1955). *Strangers in the Land: Patterns of American Nativism, 1860–1925.* New Brunswick, NJ: Rutgers University Press.

Hohle, R. (2015). *Race and the origins of American neoliberalism.* New York, NY: Routledge. Retrieved from DOI:10.4324/9781315735962.

hooks, b. (1992). Representing Whiteness in the Black imagination. In L. Grossberg, C. Nelson, & P. A. Treichler (Eds.), *Cultural Studies* (pp. 338–346). London: Routledge.

hooks, b. (1995). *Killing Rage: Ending Racism.* New York, NY: Henry Holt & Company.

Hughey, M. W. (2014). White backlash in the "post-racial" United States. *Ethnic and Racial Studies, 37*(5), 721–730.

Ignatiev, N. (1995). *How the Irish became White.* New York, NY: Routledge.

Ignatiev, N. (2019). *The Point Is Not to Interpret Whiteness but to Abolish It.* Retrieved from http://racetraitor.org/abolishthepoint.html.

Jacobson, M. F. (1998). *Whiteness of a Different Color: European Immigrants and the Alchemy of Race.* Cambridge, MA: Harvard University Press.

Jacobson, R. D. (2008). *The New Nativism: Proposition 187 and the Debate over Immigration.* Minneapolis: University of Minnesota Press.

Johnson, K. R. (2005). The fifteenth annual Dyson Distinguished Lecture: The forgotten "Repatriation" of persons of Mexican ancestry and lessons for the "War on Terror." *Pace Law Review, 26,* 15–49.

Johnson, M. (2013). *The Body in the Mind: The Bodily Basis of Meaning, Imagination, and Reason*. Chicago, IL: University of Chicago Press.

Kahn, K. B., Goff, P. A., Lee, J. K., & Motamed, D. (2016). Protecting Whiteness: White phenotypic racial stereotypicality reduces police use of force. *Social Psychological and Personality Science, 7*(5), 403–411.

Kil, S. H., Allen, J., & Hammer, Z. (2011). Border Action Network and human rights: Community-based resistance against the militarization of the U.S.-Mexico Border. In W. T. Armaline, D. S. Glasberg, & B. Purkayastha (Eds.), *Human Rights in Our Own Backyard: Injustice and Resistance in the United States* (pp. 146–154). Philadelphia: University of Pennsylvania Press.

Kil, S. H., & Menjívar, C. (2006). The "War on the border": The criminalization of immigrants and militarization of the USA-Mexico border. In R. Martinez, Jr. & A. Valenzuela, Jr. (Eds.), *Immigration and Crime: Race, Ethnicity, and Violence* (pp. 164–188). New York: New York University Press.

Kil, S. H., Menjívar, C., & Doty, R. L. (2009). Securing borders: Patriotism, vigilantism and the brutalization of the U.S. American public. In W. F. McDonald (Ed.), *Immigration, Crime and Justice: Sociology of Crime, Law and Deviance* (Vol. 13, pp. 297–312). Bingley, UK: Emerald/JAI Press. DOI:10.1108/S1521-6136(2009)0000013019.

Lazar, M. M. (2017). Feminist critical discourse analysis. In J. Flowerdew & J. E. Richardson (Eds.), *The Routledge Handbook of Critical Discourse Studies* (pp. 372–387). London: Routledge.

Lipsitz, G. (1998). *The Possessive Investment in Whiteness: How White People Profit from Identity Politics*. Philadelphia, PA: Temple University Press.

Magaña, L. (2013). Arizona's immigration policies and SB 1070. In L. Magaña & E. Lee (Eds.), *Latino Politics and Arizona's Immigration Law SB 1070* (pp. 19–26). New York, NY: Springer.

Macías-Rojas, P. (2016). *From Deportation to Prison: The Politics of Immigration Enforcement in Post-civil rights America*. New York: New York University Press.

Martinez, R., Jr., & Valenzuela, A., Jr. (Eds.). (2006). *Immigration and Crime: Ethnicity, Race, and Violence*. New York: New York University Press.

Massey, D. S., Durand, J., & Pren, K. A. (2016). Why border enforcement backfired. *American Journal of Sociology, 121*(5), 1557–1600.

Mehan, H. (1997). The discourse of the illegal immigration debate: A case study in the politics of representation. *Discourse & Society, 8*(2), 249–270.

Mbembe, J. (2003). Necropolitics. *Public Culture, 15*(1), 11–40.

Mohanty, C. T. (2013). Transnational feminist crossings: On neoliberalism and radical critique. *Signs: Journal of Women in Culture and Society, 38*(4), 967–991. DOI:10.1086/669576.

Morrison, T. (1992). *Playing in the Dark: Whiteness and the Literary Imagination*. Cambridge, MA: Harvard University Press.

Mullen, H. (1994). Optic white: Blackness and the production of Whiteness. *Diacritics, 24*(2/3), 71–89.

Musolff, A. (2010). Political metaphor and bodies politic. In U. Okulska & P. Cap (Eds.). *Perspectives in Politics and Discourse* (Vol. 36; pp. 23–41). Amsterdam: John Benjamins Publishing.

Nayak, A. (2007). Critical whiteness studies. *Sociology Compass, 1*(2), 737–755.

Nakayama, T. K., & Krizek, R. L. (1995). Whiteness: A strategic rhetoric. *Quarterly Journal of Speech, 81*(3), 291–309.

Nakayama, T. K., & Martin, J. N. (Eds.). (1999). *Whiteness: The Communication of Social Identity*. Thousand Oaks, CA: Sage.

Nevins, J. (2002). *Operation Gatekeeper: The War on "Illegals" and the Remaking of the US–Mexico Boundary*. New York, NY: Routledge.

Nienass, B., & Délano, A. (2016). Deaths, visibility, and the politics of dissensus at the US-Mexico Border. In A. Oberprantacher & A. Siclodi (Eds.), *Subjectivation in Political Theory and Contemporary Practices* (pp. 287–304). London: Palgrave Macmillan.

Oliviero, K. E. (2011). Sensational nation and the Minutemen: Gendered citizenship and moral vulnerabilities. *Signs: Journal of Women in Culture and Society, 36*(3), 679–706.

Ono, K. A., & Sloop, J. M. (2002). *Shifting Borders: Rhetoric, Immigration, and California's Proposition 187*. Philadelphia, PA: Temple University Press.

Paschal, O. (2019). *The Atlantic*, February 15. Retrieved from https://www.theatlantic.com/politics/archive/2019/02/trumps-declaration-national-emergency-full-text/582928/.

McIntosh, P. (1989). *White Privilege: Unpacking the Invisible Knapsack*. Wellesley, MA: National SEED Project on Inclusive Curriculum.

Provine, D. M., & Sanchez, G. (2011). Suspecting immigrants: Exploring links between racialised anxieties and expanded police powers in Arizona. *Policing and Society, 21*(4), 468–479.

Rasmussen, B. B., Klinenberg, E., Nexica, I. J., & Wray, M. (Eds.). (2001). *The Making and Unmaking of Whiteness*. Durham, NC: Duke University Press.

Roediger, D. R. (1991). *The Wages of Whiteness: Race and the Making of the American Working Class*. London: Verso.

Roediger, D. R. (1994). *Towards the Abolition of Whiteness: Essays on Race, Politics, and Working Class History*. New York, NY: Verso.

Roediger, D. R. (2010). *Black on White: Black Writers on What It means to be White*. New York, NY: Random House.

Romero, M. (2006). Racial profiling and immigration law enforcement: Rounding up of usual suspects in the Latino community. *Critical Sociology, 32*(2/3), 447–473. DOI:10.1163/156916306777835376.

Rossman, S. (2017, August 18). "Thin blue line": What does an American flag with a blue line mean? *USA Today*. Retrieved from https://www.usatoday.com/story/news/nation-now/2017/08/18/thin-blue-line-what-does-american-flag-wit-flag-maker-condemns-use-white-supremacists-charlottesvill/580694001/.

Santa Ana, O. (2002). *Brown Tide Rising: Metaphors of Latinos in Contemporary American Public Discourse*. Austin, TX: University of Texas Press.

Santa Ana, O., Moran, J., & Sanchez, C. (1998). Awash under a brown tide: Immigration metaphors in California public and print media discourse. *Aztlán: A Journal of Chicano Studies, 23*(2), 137–176.

Sharma, N. (2006). White nationalism, illegality and imperialism: Border controls as ideology. In K. Rygiel (Ed.), *En-Gendering the War on Terror: War Stories and Camouflaged Politics* (pp. 121–143). New York, NY: Routledge.

Shaw, D., & Hofmeister, S. (2000). Times Mirror agrees to merger with Tribune Co. *Los Angeles Times*, March 13. Retrieved from http://articles.latimes.com/2000/mar/13/news/mn-9216.

Singh, N. P. (2014). The Whiteness of police. *American Quarterly*, *66*(4), 1091–1099. Retrieved from DOI:10.1353/aq.2014.0060.

Sit, R. (2018). Jeff Sessions faces fresh racism charge after praising "Anglo-American heritage of law enforcement." *Newsweek*, February 12. Retrieved from https://www.newsweek.com/jeff-sessions-racism-anglo-american-sheriff-803624.

Suárez-Orozco, M. (1996). California dreaming: Proposition 187 and the cultural psychology of racial and ethnic exclusion. *Anthropology and Education Quarterly*, *27*(2), 151–167.

Turner, K., Giacopassi, D., & Vandiver, M. (2006). Ignoring the past: Coverage of slavery and slave patrols in criminal justice texts. *Journal of Criminal Justice Education*, *17*(1), 181–195. Retrieved from DOI:10.1080/10511250500335627.

Twine, F., & Gallagher, C. (2008). The future of whiteness: A map of the "third wave." *Ethnic & Racial Studies*, *31*(1), 4–24. DOI:10.1080/01419870701538836.

US gov't shutdown: How long? Who is affected? Why did it begin? (2019). https://www.aljazeera.com/news/2019/01/gov-shutdown-long-affected-190107150120233.html.

van Dijk, T. A. (1993). Principles of critical discourse analysis. *Discourse & Society*, *4*(2), 249–283.

van Dijk, T. A. (2013). *News as Discourse*. New York, NY: Routledge.

West, C. (1988). Marxist theory and the specificity of Afro-American oppression. In C. Nelson & L. Grossberg (Eds.), *Marxism and the Interpretation of Culture* (pp. 17–29). Urbana: University of Illinois Press.

White House. (2006). Fact Sheet: The Secure Fence Act of 2006. Retrieved from http://georgewbush-whitehouse.archives.gov/news/releases/2006/10/20061026-1.html.

Wodak, R., & Meyer, M. (Eds.). (2001). *Methods of Critical Discourse Analysis*. London: Sage. DOI:10.4135/9780857028020.

Ybarra, R. (2005). *Rights on the Line: Vigilantes at the Border* [film]. American Friends Service Committee, Witness, and American Civil Liberties Union of Texas.

Chapter 1

Dirt, Scales, and the White Body Politic

In this interdisciplinary chapter, I theorize how racism functions in recent nativist discourse. The incorporation of cultural studies, social geography, race theory, anthropology, feminist theory, and immigration studies contribute to a theoretical framework that attempts to better make sense of how racist conceptualizations can be communicated without overtly racist rhetoric through the deployment of spatially suggestive and embodied imagery. In the last chapter, I introduced the variety of seemingly disconnected ways that recent nativist discourse is commonly expressed in contemporary discourse. This chapter reveals a pattern that connects the hodgepodge of negative imageries commonly used against immigrants in order to create a deeper understanding of how nativist discourse stealthily communicates New Race Neutral Racism (NRNR).

I build my theoretical analysis in two parts: First, I begin with an overview of how "racist dirt fixations" work in a new race neutral racist manner with the geographic scales to make sense of the wide range of dissimilar images in nativist discourse. I start with the work of Cornel West (1988) on White racist logics and apply it to the work of Mary Douglas (1966) on dirt fixations in order to develop a "racist dirt fixations" framework. This framework draws on West's genealogies and justifications for racism that are historically suggestive and derive from religious, scientific, and sexual ordered systems and Douglas' "dirt," which ontologically represents disorder and breaches each logic's system in a racialized way. These fixations function with the geographic scale of the physical body that "nest" within larger scales—like a house, region, and the nation—with each scale possessing embodied qualities. Then I explain how embodied, nested, and scaled nativist discourse creates a naturalized portrait of a White national body in danger from the criminal immigrant who represents dirt, disgust, abjection, and disorder in a

1

variety of symbolic ways depending on the scale. These four scales undergird nativist discourse and possess powerful material, metaphoric, and ideological meanings that have been underanalyzed in the current scholarship on nativist discourse, race theory, and Whiteness studies. Each of these bodily scales, the body, house, region, and nation, insinuates "dirt" or disorder by employing intersectional associations with race, class, gender, sexuality, and disability in order to communicate a threat by geographic contagion. This novel theoretical framework explains how immigration and particularly the worries over the USA-Mexico border factor into the production of nested scales and produces racial tensions, anxieties, and nightmares about borders and crossings at each level of representation.

RACIST DIRT FIXATIONS AND NESTED SCALES

Within this new nativist discourse, two additional concepts help make greater sense of how nativism produces Whiteness in veiled ways: (a) White racist logics in relation to "dirt" fixations, and (b) nested scales. I build upon West's (1988) postulations about White racist logics and apply the work of Douglas (1996) on dirt fixations by ordered systems to make more sense of how racist logics function within nativist discourse. For simplicity, I refer to my nexus of West's and Douglas' concepts as "racist dirt fixations." These "racist dirt fixations" are a form of NRNR and allow older forms of racist logics to be repackaged in a new race neutral way. The nested scales of the four bodies provide details on how these "racist dirt fixations" move and "jump scales" (Smith, 1992) to create powerful, persuasive discourses that link the body to the nation, nation to the house, house to a region to help make sense of the seemingly random imagery used by nativist discourse. The discursive jumps among nested scales and allows racism to avoid overt racial terminology, which then seemingly makes racist intentions invisible. I engage both these concepts to theorize how discursive racism covertly functions in public discourse about immigration.

Cornel West (1988) explains that there are three modes of European domination based on White supremacy. These logics are discursive and derive from a genealogical condition:

Judeo-Christian racist logic [that] emanates from the biblical account of Ham looking upon and failing to cover his father Noah's nakedness and thereby receiving divine punishment in the form of blackening his progeny . . . . The scientific racist logic rests upon a modern philosophical discourse . . . that promote and encourage the activities of observing, comparing, measuring, and ordering physical characteristics of human bodies . . . . The psychosexual racist logic arises from the phallic obsessions, Oedipal projections, and anal-sadistic orientations in European culture that see non-"white" people as sexual, frivolous, passive, and dirty. Generally, the psychosexual racist logic is concerned with acts of bodily violation and impurities and sees the potential of non-"whites" as dangerous transgressors of these actual and metaphorical bodily boundaries. (pp. 22–23)

These three discursive logics provide a way to rearticulate the justifications of historical racism into contemporary discourse and practice. But instead of using direct and clear rationalizations, these logics now work inferentially.

In order to expose a commonality among the three White racist logics West puts forth, I elaborate on West's racist logics by applying the work of Mary Douglas (1966), who analyzes social pollutions and taboos. Douglas argues that violations of ordered systems create "dirt" and if West's White racist logics are ordered systems, then symbols of dirt contribute to the racialization of the "Other" as a breach of each logic's order. Douglas describes "dirt" as

matter out of place. This is a very suggestive approach. It implies two conditions: a set of ordered relations and a contravention of that order. Dirt then, is never a unique, isolated event. Where there is dirt there is a system. Dirt is a by-product of a systematic ordering and classification of matter, in so far as ordering involves rejecting inappropriate elements. This idea of dirt takes us straight into the field of symbolism and promises a link-up with more obviously symbolic systems of purity. (p. 48)

For Douglas, "dirt is essentially disorder" (p. 2). Dirt, however, is less a hygienic concept and more an ontological one. Direct and racist accusations that a group of people is dirty, either morally, physically, or sexually, is generally no longer acceptable in public discourse because of its more obvious link to historical racism. But insinuations that a group of people are ontologically dirty in that they violate ordered systems allows historical racism to reappear in more suggestive and imaginative forms.

Given Douglas's analysis on dirt, West's three logics can then be perceived to be "pure" or eternal systems threatened by danger. For example, non-Whites violate religious rules and systems as reflected by the story of Ham and his progeny who are cursed, supposedly with darkened skin, for violating Noah's dignity. Non-whites violate scientific precepts when they demand political privileges equal to that of Whites when sciences continually support inferiority and deficiency among people of color. And the impure, non-white body (usually imagined as male) threatens the controlled and ordered sexual purity of the White body (imagined as female) in a psychological projection of a racialized sexual fantasy that implies the brutality of rape. Each of these logics reflects a symbolized fear of "matter out of place" that threatens physical and social order. Thus, I argue that racial logics are essentially a fixation on disorder. Religion, science, and sexual purity are then "ordered relations" or systems that fear and reject dirt. Additionally, the dirt, disorder, or "matter out of place" for each system helps to reify dichotomies within each of the three logics. For example, the biblical logic demarcates the sacred/profane or the graced/damned. Scientific logic defines order/disorder or normal/pathological. And the sexual logic of purity rejects dirt, pollution, and bodily violations. Eliminating the ontological dirt for each racialized ordered system is a constitutive effort toward an ordered "purity."

Today, these "racist dirt fixations" function under the cloak of NRNR, which allows for the reproduction of deeply racist ideas to flourish in new forms without much challenge. Bonilla-Silva's (2010) *Racism without Racists* offers four central frames of a new "colorblind racism" (for the purpose of this study, the less ableist term "race neutral racism" will be used instead) deployed by Whites in racial discourse to deny systemic racism: abstract liberalism, naturalization, cultural racism, and minimization of racism. Abstract liberalism stems from the political philosophy of liberalism that emphasize individualism and meritocracy to deny racism at the group level. Naturalization makes racism seem like simple common sense, or biologically driven, or just the way things just are. Cultural racism blames people of color for their marginalization by denigrating their culture. Minimization of racism communicates a postracial reality and blames minorities for being over sensitive to race matters (Bonilla-Silva, 2010). NRNR perpetuates racism as it denies the recognition of racial inequalities and explains these inequalities in nonracial ways. For example, whereas Jim Crow pointed to the biological inferiority of Blacks to justify apartheid and racial segregation, the NRNR protects White dominance by viewing minorities' current status as a product of economic markets or cultural limitations and differences, thereby avoiding racial terminology and mystifying the actual process of racial exclusion (Bonilla Silva, 2010). For a nativist example, Fox's journalist Lou Dobbs (formerly of CNN) and border vigilante groups like the Minutemen Project express views that immigrants are here to conquer the nation but regularly deny having any racist motivations. NRNR has euphemized discussions about race to the point that Whites can easily dismiss non-White concerns as a type of "racial paranoia" (Jackson, 2010). Thus, "racist dirt fixations" are a form of NRNR that subtly rearticulate qualities of old school racism in a manner that is covert and avoids overt racist terminology. A key mechanism that helps "racist dirt fixations" to remain invisible is the discursive use geographic scale.

The scale is very simple but highly complex idea about levels of representation. Scale is as simple as representing a mile on a map and as complex as talking about the nation as a "diseased body politic" that suffers immigrants. Discursive racism colludes with the social construction of scale because scale utilizes metaphors and images that enable it to inhabit cartographic, material, spatial, literary, and ideological dimensions at once. Smith (1992) writes that the power of metaphor greatly enhances "our understanding of material space, physical space, territory, just as our spatial practices and conceptions of material space are fecund raw material for metaphor" (p. 62).

In the past three decades, human geographers have shown an interest in how the production of scale relates to the production of space. Generally, human geographers have taken a constructionist perspective with a focus on capitalistic production, social reproduction, and at times social consumption in attempting to understand the ways of sociospatial re-structuring through scale (Marston, 2000). Brady (2002) explains:

> "[s]caling" is the name given to the process by which space is divided, orga-nized, categorized . . . . By demarcating spaces, by establishing limits and thus contents, and by fixing spaces within a framework of spatial relations, or "nested hierarchies," scale narrates and thereby helps to organize and produce space. (pp. 173–174)

Marston (2000) adds that scale is not merely a product of geographic rela-tions. Like space, place, or environment, scale factors "in the construction and dynamics of geographical totalities" (Marston, 2000, p. 220, as cited in Howitt, 1998). Thus, scaled places are "the embodiment of social relations of empowerment and disempowerment and the arena through and in which they operate" (Marston, 2000, p. 221, as cited in Swyngedouw, 1997).

Conceptualizations of geographic scale tend to begin with the physical body and then link to larger scales (Brady, 2002; Smith, 1992). For example, Smith discusses how a political art piece in the form of a "homeless vehicle," which functions like a scaled-down house built on the platform of a shopping cart, can express the contestation for spatial access to the urban landscape by converting "spaces of exclusion [like homelessness] into the known, the made, and constructed [like the homeless vehicle] . . . redefining the scale of everyday life for homeless people" (p. 60). Scale in this sense becomes important at the level of the physical body. And the scale of the body is socially constructed with social differences such as gender, race, age, ability, and class inscribed onto that body. In his examination of the homeless vehicle as a geographic production of scale, he also explores other scales that start with the body, then extends to the home, and continues in larger scales such as the community, urban, region, nation, and global in a nested but not nec-essarily hierarchical fashion. Smith's purpose is to provide a framework for thinking and theorizing about spatial difference through scale that "defines boundaries and bounds the identities around which control is exerted and contested" (p. 66). Smith adds that scale both contains social activity and is also the site where social activity takes place. Thus, geographic scale possesses the significant ability to control social processes and define boundaries of identities.

First, "Racist dirt fixations" work on the scale of the body. Beginning with the religious racist logic, the ontological "dirt" for the Christian system that bears greatly on systems of racism is the invention of the savage whose body was socially constructed with dark skin and a libidinous nature. Religion is an old purveyor of racialized and sexualized logics (Smedley, 1993; West, 1988). Science like religion also makes race an object of systematic investigation with a focus on physical differences. Science communicates a qualitative difference between the "normal" and "pathological" (Canguilhem, 1989), distinct from the "graced or damned" model of the Christian tradition, where "dirt" is pathology or abnormality. Much scientific knowledge has been dedicated to justifying the physical and mental inferiority of non-Whites (Graves, 2001). Unfortunately, this type of scientific inquiry is still popular today as reflected in the *New York Times* bestseller by Herrnstein and Murray's (1994) titled the *Bell Curve: Intelligence and Class Structure in American Life*, which states that intelligence dictates social standing rather than race, class, or social inequality and that IQ is genetic, which supports the notion that IQ is racially correlated. The psychosexual logic codes the scale of the physical body in interesting ways in relation to dirt, such as fixating on threats to an imagined purity of the White body. This "pure/impure" logic also crosscuts with other bodily binaries such as human/animal and mind/body (Haraway, 1989). And these binaries contribute to the social construction of Whiteness that emphasizes purity, humanity, and the mind. "[W]hite is a color code for bodies ascribed the attribute of the mind, and thus symbolic power, not to mention other forms of power, in social practices like 'intelligence' tests. The body is coded darker, denser, less warm and light" (Haraway, 1989, p. 153). Hence, the popularity of the *Bell Curve* again reinforces the association of Whiteness with the mind and non-Whiteness with the body. Indeed, the White body is almost a "pure spirit" (Dyer, 1997, p. 39). These three racist dirt logics can reverberate to other, larger geographic scales like the nation. It allows the body politic to suffer from the profane, the deviant, or the impure in ways inspired by the physical body. And there is a "continual exchange of meanings between the two kinds of bodily experiences so that each reinforces the categories of the other" (Douglas, 1970, p. 93).

WHITE BODY (POLITIC) AND DANGER

Geographic scale helps "racist dirt fixations" remain covert and hidden and it does so in three ways. First, because a sense of scale begins with the body and "jumps" toward other, larger scales, the scale can inspire borders in various embodied ways, point to what threatens those borders, and link them all back to the personal and political in a manner that is material and ideological. Second, scale helps to discursively hide the historical rearticulation of White racist logics in a contemporary, race neutral manner through a metaphoric and geographic process that obscures direct racism through the comparative use of neutral, nonracialized scales. Third, because scale seems like fixed space that is divided, ordered, categorized, and bounded, controlling social processes and defining boundaries of identities within a scale becomes an active process of excluding dirt. Thus, geographic scale helps "racist dirt fixations" produce and reproduce Whiteness as the nation and immigrants as the disorder through the literary imagination of scales.

As mentioned earlier, scaling typically begins with the physical body. And the physical body possesses a basic and constant desire to maintain boundaries between the self and the other (or nonself). Douglas (1966) argues that "boundaries can represent any boundaries which are threatened or precarious. The body is a complex structure. The functions of its different parts and their relation afford a source of symbols for other complex structures" (Douglas, 1966, p. 116). Bodily fluids such as feces, urine, spit, blood, and other discharges become "dirt" and a dangerous pollutant to the system. Bodily excretions are anomalous because they were once a part of the self before they transformed into nonself upon exiting the body. What the body expels is symbolized in societal ways as powerful and perilous. "Danger lies in transitional states, simply because transition is neither one state nor the next, it is indefinable" (Douglas, 1966, p. 97).

Typical reactions to danger come in emotional forms like disgust. Generally, animal, food, and bodily waste can illicit disgust. Disgust accentuates that boundary between animal and human. Rozin and Fallon (1987) note that when people feel disgust it tends to be related to animals, parts of animals, animal products, or objects that have touched these animal items or resemble them. Disgust is also a food-related emotion. Disgust objects tend to be repulsive because of the link to an animal origin, the idea of taking that object into the body as food, and the irrational belief that people take on the properties of the disgust object through contact or ingestion. Bodily wastes of animals, even human animals, are disgusting because they are essentially expelled animal products. The one exception would be tears, which is understood to be a human ability that accentuates the difference between human and animal since animals do not shed tears emotionally (Rozin & Fallon 1987, as cited in Ortner, 1973).

Another form of emotional reaction to danger is abjection. Kristeva (1982) builds upon Douglas's anthropological notion of dirt and danger with her feminist, post-Lacanian analysis of abjection. Kristeva asserts that

[i]t is thus not lack of cleanliness or health that causes abjection but what disturbs identity, system, order. What does not respect borders, positions, rules. The in-between, the ambiguous, the composite. The traitor, the liar, the criminal with a good conscience, the shameless rapist, the killer who claims he is a savior. . . . Any crime, because it draws attention to the fragility of the law, is abject, . . . immoral, sinister, scheming, and shady: a terror that dissembles . . . . (p. 4)

Kristeva agrees with Douglas's argument that danger comes from system violations, but Kristeva's focus is on abjection. Like Douglas, Kristiva agrees that borders represent dangerous ambiguity. However, Kristeva advances Douglas' argument beyond beliefs about pollution, taboo, dirt, and danger into a more complex moral realm where crime is abject, for example, because it causes terror by dissembling the identity of the moral order. Kristeva grounds her argument in the psychology of the individual self and accounts for the psychic mechanisms of disgust that stem from the experience of borderlessness between the self and other/nonself. Abjection can range from food loathing to corpse avoidance, but the basic underlying principle is that abjection challenges and disturbs bodily integrity by emphasizing the reality of death and decay through bodily fluids and functions. Like Douglas, she also claims that the abject can also have a double meaning and existence because it can affect the self as well as society in helping to create rituals and symbols of exclusion at both levels of representation. For example, she agrees with Douglas that pollution rituals reflect abjection and disgust toward women's bodies that correspond to sexual taboos intended to divide men from women and insure the dominance of the former over the latter. However, unlike Douglas, Kristiva (1982) emphasizes the psychological need of the abject by society because the process of abjection functions much like a "security blanket" (pp. 136–137). Abjection safely removes humans and humanity from the territory of nature by marking out an area of human culture removed from the threat of nature and animals, which are "imagined as representatives of sex and murder" (Kristeva, 1982, p. 13).

What is common among the work of West, Douglas, and Kristeva is the divide between culture and nature. For West, his racist logics stem from valuing Western religion, science, and White bodies, which are institutions and symbols of culture, over the heathen savage, the degenerate, or Black bodies, respectively, which are associated with nature. For Douglas, the body as a symbol of society divides what is ordered and dangerous. Bodily fluids and processes represent nature and control over the body associates with culture. This resonates with Ortner's (1972) classic feminist argument that culture is associated with men and nature with women because a woman's body and its functions keep her symbolically closer to nature (e.g., pregnancy, lactation, and menstruation) in contrast to a male physiology whose functions permit him more freedom to contribute to culture. Kristeva extends Ortner and Douglas' arguments. For Kristeva, animalness, which is psycho-socially represented in pregnant or menstruating women, is abject and challenges the border between self/society, human/animal, and culture/nature. For example, nativists fear that immigrant women's bodies contribute to an "invasion" through sexual reproduction (Chavez, 2008). So no matter if it is racist logics, dirt, or abjection, the underlying principle that relates all three methodologies together is that systems (culture, Whiteness, men) find danger in disorder (nature, racial other, and women's bodily functions and fluids). The continued marginalization of immigrants based on their race or noncitizen status reflects this tradition that associates the other with nature, dirt, and disorder.

Additionally, emotional reactions to boundary violations that lead to disgust and abjection also lead to fantasies of geographic contagion based on racialized fears that the other is taking over. In relation to disgust, Rozin, Millman, and Nemeroff (1986) study the operation of the laws of sympathetic magic in disgust (citing Frazer, 1890, and Mauss. 1902). The first law deals with contagion and proposes that once an object or thing has had contact with another object that properties or traces can transfer and linger long after the initial contact. This allows for magical action to be applied, for example, to a fingernail or hair clipping that can affect the original source or person to whom the clipping belonged. The second law deals with similarity and holds that things that look alike share essential properties; in other words, a resemblance equals the source. For example, people who like chocolate tend to avoid eating it if it is shaped like dog feces. Rozin et al.'s study is important because it demonstrates that patterns of thinking normally ascribed to developing or traditional societies also occur in thinking patterns of modern Western societies.

I believe that a type of sympathetic magic in relation to moral disgust occurs in relation to nativist concerns about immigrant takeovers. There is an anxiety about immigration in relation to geographic contagion in that immigrants are seen as invaders. This relates to the first law of sympathetic magic. Since immigrants reside and work in the nation, magical thinking permits contagion to spread through this contact with the discursive image of a national assault by immigrants. This train of thought is best illustrated by Samuel Huntington's (2004) book, *Who are We? The Challenge to America's National Identity*, where he sees immigration from Mexico contributing to a demographic *reconquista* of the Southwest region as well as generally undermining the national "Anglo-Protestant" identity. Nativist rhetoric also conveys geographic contagion by extending the invasion image to immigrant women. Chavez (2001) points out that women are featured in news media as an "insidious invasion, one that includes the capacity of the invaders to reproduce themselves" (p. 233). Immigrant women suggest the formation of families and communities that lead to racial conquest (see chapter 4). Many conservative political figures like Pat Buchanan (2002) promote the idea that immigrant women give birth to more children than native White women. His book title reveals much of his line of thought: *The Death of the West: How Dying Populations and Immigrant Invasions Imperil Our Country and Civilization*. Finally, the French racial riots of 2005 sparked alarmist worries in the United States about the contagion of racial unrest affecting Mexican immigrants in a similar manner (Koff, 2009). While no riots manifested, in 2006, the immigrant rights movement marched nationally in the largest protest ever seen across many cities in almost every region of the United States. In 2007, immigrant students and activist participated in the largest school walkout to protest the criminalization policies that affect them.

Moreover, racial dynamics are changing as the White-Black racial binary transforms into a more complicated racial reality. Bonilla Silva (2010) contends that the United States is moving toward a triracial structure of White, honorary White, and collective Black categories similar to countries in Latin America. This racial transformation relates to the second law of sympathetic magic in that magical thinking allows racialized groups to share essential racial properties with the source. This works in two ways: those with darker skin whether they are Black, Brown, or Pilipino are in the "collective Black" category and those non-Whites with lighter skin who uphold White values occupy the "honorary White" category. Thus, resemblance equals the source for the former and resemblance equals an "honorary" status to the source for the latter. Note that resemblance to a White source does not make those who occupy this honorary White category necessarily White. This serves two functions: first, model minorities' occupation of an "honorary White" category helps to deny White racism (fourth dimension of NRNR) and second, the "honorary White" category disciplines the "collective Black" population by undermining the latter's claims of a racially unjust society.

This reality is best illustrated by Francis Fukuyama (1995), a former student of Samuel Huntington, who argues that Asians possess model, cultural, and civic values and that poor, inner-city Blacks create their own marginalize circumstances. In addition, Carbado and Gulati (2004) claim that as model minorities gain economic success and become more agreeable for Whites, then there is little incentive to share this economic success with minorities at the bottom of the racial hierarchy through either racial reforms or "door-opening" opportunities. In fact, there is a strong urge for some minorities to race to the top to occupy an honorary White status and "lift the ladder up behind them when they get there" (p. 1646). So while race is a sociohistorical process that is context specific in its formations (Omi & Winant, 1986), the emotional reaction to the racial other, even as group composition changes, expresses magical and suspicious thinking about racial powers from the margins. Consequently, the racialized fear of geographic contagion collaborates with a win/lose narrative that characterizes nativism. In short, if you lose, you are taken over by racial pollution or infection that threatens the imagined Whiteness of the nation.

Fear about geographic contagion and its threat to the Whiteness of nation takes dramatic symbolic and material form with the militarization of the USA-Mexico border. Haney-Lopez (1996) argues that early immigration laws helped to shape the current racial demographic of the United States by permitting certain groups their citizenship based on their successful claims to Whiteness. It is also arguable that current militarization policies do much the same in attempting to shape the current racial demography through the material defense of borders and the symbolic protection of Whiteness. How racism is co-constituted with nationalism (Miles, 1987) takes on deadly dimensions in the border region. The following chapter details the current militarized border policies and the resulting human rights crisis reflected in the border deaths and racial profiling in that region.

The crime of violating the nation's borders is met with moral disgust and abjection and the nativist discourse about immigrant crime is a new race neutral racist way of talking about race. Thus, nativist discourse is not directly and honestly racist. The covert, invisible, nonracial articulations of NRNR that occur in nativist discourse allow Whiteness to reproduce itself without much challenge. If NRNR is the method of nativist discourse, then Whiteness is the result. And the discourse about crime allows "racist dirt fixations" to resurface within nativist discourse. The symbolic and metaphoric fixations on dirt by the three modes of religion, science, and sexual fixations influence the four discursive scales: body, house, region, and nation. These logics work to create constructions of the profane, deviant, and danger in relation to immigration. It is an exercise in imaginative geography (Said, 1978) that helps to socially construct the nation as sacred, normal, pure, and White. Moreover, religious, scientific, and sexual logics work at each level of representation to communicate racialized danger in specific ways. Scale becomes the vehicle in which older forms of racist logic make reasonable sense in a newer, more race neutral form. Scale permits deeply racist logics to become referential and metaphoric instead of direct and blatant.

I contend that new nativist discourse socially constructs the nation as a White body (Santa Ana, 2002) through four scales (See Figure 1.1). Each scale has its own internal rationale that provides coherency. Each scale also has its own internal differences; for example, the parts of a house differ greatly from parts of a body. These scales share borders and overlap in meanings. For instance, the meaning of a fence surrounding a house can overlap in meaning with the border walls of a nation. And each scale can convey

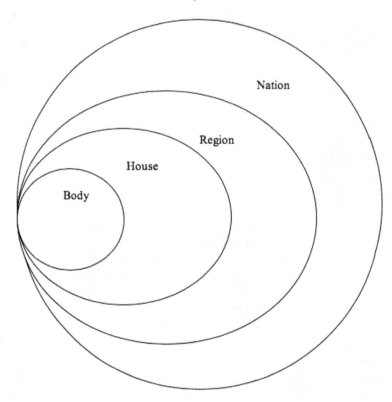

Figure 1.1   Four Scales.

religions, scientific, and sexual racist logics through images, symbols, metaphors, intimations, metonyms, and other rhetorical devices, which all help to
deny nativist racism.

   Body. This "Nation as Body" metaphor is typically treated as an outdated
metaphor with roots in classical political thinking (Plato uses it in *The Republic* and Aristotle in *Politics*) and peaks in medieval and early modern times
where the King's body was often seen as representing his kingdom (Rasmussen & Brown, 2005). However, Santa Ana's (2002) analysis of metaphors
of Brownness in public discourse features "immigrants as disease" to the
"Nation as Body" as the most dominant metaphoric image for the nation (p.
255). Frequently, public discourse socially constructed immigrants as a "burden" on the nation (p. 256). Historically, medical discourse has been used
to marginalize immigrants and associate them—their living spaces, habits,
culture, and genetics—with disease causation rather than seeing immigrants
as victims of social inequality that contributes to disease (Kraut, 1994). Racist
dirt fixation at this scale plays upon uneasiness around disability. The crime
frame also evokes an economic burden and warfare frame, which then works

with the "Immigrant as Disease" frame because illnesses take away from the body, whether it is health, blood, or vigor.

Inda's (2000) research on the rhetoric of Proposition 187 reveals the hidden nativist logic that constructed immigrants as an illness, particularly the image of the parasite, to describe immigrants' role in relation to its "host." Suárez-Orozco (1996) also noted the use of parasitic images in describing immigrants' use of social services. While Inda (2000) notes there was some resurgent discourse that turned the tables on this host-parasite relationship by describing the nation as a parasite taking advantage of marginalized immigrants and their labor, the continued strength of nativist discourse is clearly winning over any resurgent discourse, allowing any conception of a "Nation as Parasite" configuration to fade in comparison. "In public discourse, to put it bluntly, Latinos are never the arms or heart of the United States [of America]; they are the burdens or diseases of the body politic" (Santa Ana, 2002, p. 10).

House. Santa Ana's (2002) second dominant metaphor for the nation is "Nation as House" in his analysis of metaphors of Brownness in public discourse (p. 260). Immigrants are seen as criminal home invaders, weeds, foreigners, enemies, and dangerous waters to the national house (p. 260). Nativist discourses use the scale of the house to create the psycho-sexual racist nightmare of a "Home Invasion" where the immigrant is the intruder. This is further reinforced by the creation of the DHS, where "home" figures as a vulnerable abode. The use of the concept of "homeland" by the DHS echoes a familial and genealogical strain in the national imagination, where solidarity is based in common blood and shared territory. The home is an idealized, private space that provides safety and shelter from the forces of nature exemplifying the binary between culture and nature. Because of its idealization, "home" can convey a variety of meanings that speak to its importance for the family as a paradigm of the intersection of race, class, gender, sexuality, and age (Collins, 1998). House and home convey both unity and hierarchy. The home is a gendered place where women are still associated with feminine, interior spaces in contrast to men who are associated with public life outside the home.

In addition, patriarchal norms dictate that men defend their home and family from natural forces and social dangers. The home is also a racialized space with an absence of otherness, and consequently this represents White racial purity (Garner, 2007), the context in which White men defend White women's sexual purity against racialized intruders by closing and reinforcing gates or doorways into the home. Similarly, the nation's border is commonly imagined as a "gate" and border enforcement is "gatekeeping," as reflected in the iconic militarization efforts along the Tijuana-San Diego border called "Operation Gatekeeper." The border is imagined as a thin, fragile, and permeable line between pure and impure, harmony and hostilities, shelter and wilderness, calm weather and cataclysm. Thus, both home and nation are imagined as "sacred" that helped to reify the purity of White women and the White bloodline that resides in the home as well as the purity of the nation's Whiteness which is the genealogical strain that occupies the homeland. A racialized male intruder sexually threatens this imagined scale. The suggestion of rape, of "bestiality storming the citadel of civilization" and its potential of miscegenation, threatens the racial and gendered purity (Dyer, 1997, p. 26) of the nation in this particular construction.

Furthermore, this image is also class-based, as the intention of the intruder is to rob and steal something treasured and valued as sacred. The foreign, dark, and guilty invader threatens with a type of bodily invasion the innocence of Whiteness and the nation. On the other hand, national territory and space then become a type of property "whose perpetuation is secured by the state" (Alonso, 1994, p. 383). It is in this sense that the house is a home and the family within it are not only raced and gendered but also issues of economic class and the constructions of the nation as White also figure into the idealization of home and family. Racial otherness is imagined as outside the "Nation as House" where immigrants are seen as dangerous, wild animals. The reasoning of equating immigrants with animals includes a birth-placed, biological hierarchy that naturalizes greater power and privileges to some people over the rest, allowing superior beings to rule over inferior ones that echo the biblical edict found in Genesis (Santa Ana, 2002, p. 88).

Region. While this study builds on Santa Ana's (2002) work on dominant images about immigration and the nation, it departs from his work by offering the scale of the region to help make sense of the variety of nativist images used against Brown border crossers. Thus, fears about war and dangerous waters occupy a regional scale in this study and are not bound to "Nation as House" as in Santa Ana's study. First, the border region is a "battlefield." This complements Harris' (1993) argument that Whiteness and property are deeply interrelated concepts since historically Whiteness has been a prerequisite to own property via the expropriation of Indian land and the reduction of Black people to enslaved property. Harris argues that even today, Whiteness has become a legally enforceable form of property that privileges all Whites. Thus, if Whiteness is a prerequisite to enforceable property rights, and the nation is a type of property, then the state secures the Whiteness of the nation with militarized border enforcement. Where the nation by virtue is feminized as innocent and pure, the state by virtue is masculinized as "rough and ready," muscularly well-armed in protecting the nation from degradation and harm (Kil, 2011).

Second, the White racist logic of religion features predominantly at the scale of region contributing to the construction of "immigration as biblical flood." Chavez (2001) notes that the "water-flood imagery" in immigration news communicates a large and uncontrollable magnitude in regard to immigration. Again, the culture/nature dichotomy is used in this racist "dirt" fixation. Here, the nation is imagined as an inhabited geographic area (culture) that suffers immigration as forces of nature like cataclysmic flood. This image in particular evokes biblical anxieties of natural destruction by divine punishment. Santa Ana (2002) describes the ontology of "immigration as dangerous waters" in four ways: (a) immigration corresponds to kinetic water; (b) the United States is a landmass subject to flooding; (c) more immigration equals increased threat to the nation; and (d) the nation's vulnerability to flooding equates with change (p. 75). Fears of "dangerous waters" indicate an implied takeover by immigrants of "Anglo-American cultural dominance" (Santa Ana, 2002, p. 78) as penalty for the failure to protect Whiteness.

Nation. The scale of the nation further articulates the "diseased body politic" with more contemporary, scientific understandings of the body, illness, and technological treatments at a cellular scale within the imagined body politic. New race neutral racist and nativist discourse deploys a subtle, medicalized framework that capitalizes on the intersection of law enforcement, warfare, and medicine in making its racist justifications for "operations" in the border region. It moves beyond medieval notions of "Nation as Body" and makes suggestive use of the modern understandings of an immune system, where the immune system is like militarized border enforcement and undocumented immigration is like a cancer that is growing, quick, and hard to detect. Emily Martin (1994) researches the intersection of scientific discourse, social construction of the body, and economic systems and transformations. Martin (1992) argues that the body of late capitalism contains two contradictory and co-existing body formations: "a body organized as a global system with no internal boundaries and characterized by rapid flexible response, and a body organized around nationhood, warfare, gender, race, and class" (p. 129). The late capitalism body is also informed by more advanced knowledge of the immune system, which possess hallmarks of "technological innovation, specificity, and rapid, flexible change" (p. 123) that also describe global capitalism and its dramatic restructuring of the economic system motivated by profitmaking. A similar phenomenon takes place at the border where knowledge about cancer and the immune system help to influence public discourse about immigration and the nation.

For example, General Barry McCaffrey, President Clinton's drug czar (1996–2001), began his tenure backing away from military concepts like the "war on drugs" and instead treating drug abuse issues like a type of social cancer (Wren, 1996), he thus advocates antidrug efforts that focus on treatment and education over a focus on stopping drug traffic at the USA-Mexico border (staff, *LA Times*, 1996). Susan Sontag (1978) critiqued the intersection of cancer and warfare imagery and argues that to "describe a phenomenon as a cancer is an incitement to violence. The use of cancer in political discourse encourages fatalism and justifies 'severe' measures—as well as strongly reinforcing the widespread notion that the disease is necessarily fatal" (p. 84). Today, new knowledge about HIV and the immune system offers systems of "purity and danger," where the job of the immune system is to maintain the boundary between self and other, where the other is "foreign and hostile" (Martin, 1992, p. 126). These medicalized distortions effectively criminalize these immigrant border crossers as surplus populations, which make them more vulnerable to economic exploitation because of their "dirty" status as violators of the boundary between self and other, in which the imagined militaristic, immune system of the body politic needs to maintain the boundary between self and the "foreign and hostile" border crossers. The nation scale represents the intersection of medicalized discourse, the racial construction of the body politic, and postmodern economic transformations.

In conclusion, the need to uncover the "postracial" power of nativist discourse is greater than ever as political platforms (Trump presidency) and social movements (Minutemen), and legislations (SB1070) increasingly take a bigoted position toward immigrants while claiming innocence when accused of racism. "Racist dirt fixations" offer symbolic ways in which new racism draws on old racist ideologies and mystifies the process through binary dichotomies and symbolisms. Geographic scale helps "racist dirt fixations" elide and hide in public discourse through its seeming neutral, nested scales that actually inspire borders and threats in personal and embodied ways, which give meaning to social processes and defining boundaries of identities through an active process of excluding dirt or "matter out of place." This framework of "racist dirt fixations" and the nested scales offers a novel theoretical argument that (a) expands our knowledge of race and its metaphoric and geographic dimensions; (b) shows how old racism can still express itself in new racism albeit in more stealthy, race neutral ways; and (c) reveals that discourse about crime on a national scale goes beyond mere reporting and public debate and points to the imagined racial identity of the nation.

From the physical body that experiences disgust and abjection projected symbolically onto the nation in a sexualize nightmare about crime, to the nation where the militarization of the border protects the imagined line between pure and impure, harmony and hostility, calm weather and cataclysm, nativist discourse maximizes the use of "racist dirt fixations" and the nested scales in a veiled way to impose Whiteness on the nation. However, by limiting scale to the nation, nativist discourse intentionally ignores the global scale. This makes invisible the global development of economic migration and the responsibilities that the United States possesses in stimulating that development. In turn, the irony is that as the Global North increasingly turns to and practices a "gated globe" paradigm, where immigration is highly restricted and regulated (Cunningham, 2004), this nativist discourse ignores this larger political and economic process that directly bears on immigration and the nation, and further bamboozles this situation by describing immigrants—who do the vital but least desired work—as a disease on the body politic.

The next chapter explores the current militarized state of the US-Mexico border in order to provide a deeper context and background for understanding the human rights crisis that occurs there.

REFERENCES

Alonso, A. M. (1994). The politics of space, time and substance: State formation, nationalism and ethnicity. *Annual Review of Anthropology, 23,* 379–405. DOI:10.1146/annurev.an.23.100194.002115.

Bonilla-Silva, E. (2010). *Racism Without Racists: Color-blind Racism and the Persistence of Racial Inequality in the United States.* 3rd edition. Lanham, MD: Rowman & Littlefield.

Brady, M. P. (2002). *Extinct Lands, Temporal Geographies: Chicana Literature and the Urgency of Space.* Raleigh: Duke University Press.

Buchanan, P. J. (2002). *The Death of the West: How Dying Populations and Immigrant Invasions Imperil Our Country and Civilization.* New York, NY: St. Martin's Press.

Canguilhem, G. (1989). *The Normal and the Pathological.* New York, NY: Zone Books.

Carbado, D., & Gulati, M. (2004). Race to the top of the corporate ladder: what minorities do when they get there. *Washington and Lee Review, 61,* 1645–1693.

Chavez, L. R. (2001). *Covering Immigration: Popular Images and the Politics of the Nation.* Berkeley: University of California Press.

Chavez, L. (2008). *The Latino Threat: Constructing Immigrants, Citizens, and the Nation.* Palo Alto: Stanford University Press.

Collins, P. H. (1998). It's all in the family: Intersections of gender, race, and nation. *Hypatia, 13*(3), 62–82.

Cunningham, H. (2004). Nations rebound? Crossing borders in a gated globe. *Identities: Global Studies in Power and Culture, 11,* 329–350.

Douglas, M. (1966). *Purity and Danger: An Analysis of Concepts of Pollution and Taboo.* Harmondsworth: Penguin.

Douglas, M. (1970). *Natural Symbols: Explorations in Cosmology.* New York, NY: Pantheon Books.

Dyer, R. (1997). *White: Essays on Race and Culture.* New York, NY: Routledge.

Fukuyama, F. (1995). Social capital and the global economy. *Foreign Affairs, 74*(5), 89–103.

Garner, S. (2007). *Whiteness: An Introduction.* Oxford: Taylor & Francis.

Graves, J. L. (2001). *The Emperor's New Clothes: Biological Theories of Race at the Millennium*. New Brunswick: Rutgers University Press.

Haney-Lopez, I. (1996). *White by Law: The Legal Construction of Race*. New York: New York University Press.

Haraway, D. J. (1989). *Primate Visions: Gender, Race, and Nature in the World of Modern Science*. New York, NY: Routledge.

Harris, C. (1993). Whiteness as property. *Harvard Law Review, 106* (June), 1709–1791.

Huntington, S. (2004). *Who Are We? The Challenge to America's National Identity*. New York, NY: Free Press.

Inda, J. X. (2000). Foreign bodies: Migrants, parasites, and the pathological nation. *Discourse: Journal for Theoretical Studies in Media and Culture, 22*(3), 46–62.

Jackson, J. L., Jr. (2010). *Racial Paranoia: The Unintended Consequences of Political Correctness*. New York, NY: Basic Civitas Books.

Kil, S. H. (2011). Immigration and "operations": The militarization and medicalization of the US-Mexico border. In P. P. Frassinelli, R. Frenkel, & D. Watson (Eds.), *Traversing Transnationalism: The Horizons of Literary and Cultural Studies* (pp. 75–93). Amsterdam: Rodopi.

Koff, H. (2009). Understanding "la contagion": Power, exclusion and urban violence in France and the United States. *Journal of Ethnic & Migration Studies, 35*(5), 771–790. DOI:10.1080/13691830902826178.

Kraut, A. M. (1994). *Silent Travelers: Germs, Genes, and the "Immigrant Menace."* New York, NY: Basic Books.

Kristeva, J. (1982). *Powers of Horror: An Essay on Abjection*. New York: Columbia University Press.

Marston, S. A. (2000). The social construction of scale. *Progress in Human Geography, 24*(2), 219–242. DOI:10.1191/030913200674086272.

Martin, E. (1992). The end of the body? *American Ethnologist, 19*(1), 121–140.

Martin, E. (1994). *Flexible Bodies: Tracking Immunity in American Culture from the Days of Polio to the Age of AIDS*. Boston: Beacon Press.

Miles, R. (1987). Recent Marxist theories of nationalism and the issue of racism. *British Journal of Sociology, 38*(1), 24–43.

Murray, C., & Herrnstein, R. (1994). *The Bell Curve: Intelligence and Class Structure in American Life*. New York, NY: Free Press.

Omi, M., & Winant, H. (1986). *Racial Formation in the United States: From the 1960s to the 1980s*. New York, NY: Routledge & Kegan Paul.

Ortner, S. B. (1972). Is Female to male as nature is to culture? *Feminist Studies, 1*(2), 5–31.

Rasmussen, C., & Brown, M. (2005). The body politic as spatial metaphor. *Citizenship Studies, 9*(5), 469–484.

Rozin, P., & Fallon, A. E. (1987). A perspective on disgust. *Psychological Review, 94*(1), 23–41. DOI:10.1037/0033-295X.94.1.23.

Rozin, P., Millman, L., & Nemeroff, C. (1986). Operation of the laws of sympathetic magic in disgust and other domains. *Journal of Personality and Social Psychology, 50*(4), 703–712. DOI:10.1037/0022-3514.50.4.703.

Said, E. W. (1978). *Orientalism.* New York, NY: Pantheon Books.

Santa Ana, O. (2002). *Brown Tide Rising: Metaphors of Latinos in Contemporary American Public Discourse.* Austin: University of Texas Press.

Sontag, S. (1978). *Illness as Metaphor.* New York: Farrar. Strauss and Giroux.

Smedley, A. (1993). *Race in North America: Origin and Evolution of a Worldview.* Boulder, CO: Westview.

Smith, N. (1992). Contours of a spatialized politics: Homeless vehicles and the production of geographical scale. *Social Text, 33,* 54–81. DOI:10.2307/466434.

Suárez-Orozco, M. (1996). California dreaming: Proposition 187 and the cultural psychology of racial and ethnic exclusion. *Anthropology and Education Quarterly, 27*(2), 151–167.

West, C. (1988). Marxist theory and the specificity of Afro-American oppression. In C. Nelson & L. Grossberg (Eds.), *Marxism and the Interpretation of Culture* (pp. 17–33). Urbana: University of Illinois Press.

Staff. Nation IN BRIEF: WASHINGTON, DC: Drug Chief Calls for Stress on Education April 12, 1996 | From Times Staff and Wire Reports http://articles.latimes.com/1996-04-12/news/mn-57865_1_drug-education-nation.

Wren, C. (1996). New drug czar is seeking ways to bolster his hand. *New York Times.* Retrieved from https://www.nytimes.com/1996/03/17/us/new-drug-czar-is-seeking-ways-to-bolster-his-hand.html.

Chapter 2

"Build that Wall!" Brutalizing Presidential Border War Policies and the Necropolitical Deathscape

"Build that wall" was a popular chant at political rallies when reality TV personality and real estate mogul Donald Trump ran for president (Bierman, 2016). He made the USA-Mexico border a centerpiece of his racialized presidential campaign. In his presidential announcement speech on June 16, 2015, he provided his rationale for the need for a more extensive border wall when he stated:

> When Mexico sends its people, they're not sending their best. They're not sending you. They're not sending you. They're sending people that have lots of problems, and they're bringing those problems with us. They're bringing drugs. They're bringing crime. They're rapists. And some, I assume, are good people. (Lee, 2015)

His rhetoric is a form of New Race Neutral Racism (NRNR) so that older, Jim Crow type racist logics that see people of color as criminally sexual are re-packaged in a new nativist way. His promise to build a border wall resonated with his voter constituency, which included many Whites who felt marginalized by the racial diversity of the nation especially in relation to immigration (Sides, 2017). The Southern Poverty Law Center (SPLC) who tracks hate groups documented the rise of racist Whites called the "alt right" who supported Trump and his presidential candidacy. SPLC defines the "alt right" below:

> The Alternative Right, commonly known as the Alt-Right, is a set of far-right ideologies, groups and individuals whose core belief is that "white identity" is under attack by multicultural forces using "political correctness" and "social justice" to undermine white people and "their" civilization. Characterized by heavy use of social media and online memes, Alt-Righters eschew "establishment"

conservatism, skew young, and embrace white ethno-nationalism as a fundamental value . . . . Trump is a hero to the Alt-Right. Through a series of semi-organized campaigns, Alt-Right activists applied the "cuckservative"[1] slur to every major Republican primary candidate except Trump, who regularly rails against "political correctness," Muslims, immigrants, Mexicans, Chinese and others. They have also worked hard to affix the Alt Right brand to Trump through the use of hashtags and memes. ("Alternative Right," n.d.)

Many decried Trump's border wall proposal as racist. However, this chapter will show that the nation's border enforcement policy in general is racist and Trump's proposal to add more walls to an already extensive border buildup is not an outlier, but part of an escalating attitude and policy stance that characterizes the militarization of the USA-Mexico border over the last several decades. By design, border enforcement of United States practices lead to at least one death per day of a border crosser and international bodies that govern human rights cannot constrain these deadly policies (Jimenez, 2009).

This chapter provides the setting of the study, the militarized USA-Mexico border. I offer two mechanisms that that help explain the escalating power of border militarization: Mbembe's (2003) Necropolitics and brutalization theory. I then provide a brief timeline of the history of the border militarization through an analysis of Presidential contributions to the present situation. I further argue that the border region is a Necropolitical Deathscape that affects immigrants' lives well beyond the border region, making them more vulnerable and exploitable.

MILITARIZATION, BRUTALIZATION, AND BORDER NECROPOLITICS

I use two frameworks together to describe the State's impulse for the brutality and death in this border region. First, I employ Mbembe's (2003) concept of Necropolitics and second, I add brutalization theory, borrowed from the death penalty literature, to describe how militarizing the border is a form of racial brutalization that encourages the public and policymakers to seek further militarization despite the deadly costs.

Mbembe (2003) uses the concept of Necropolitics to refer to the process of colonization that allows the colonizer to decide who will live and who will die. The Southwest region of the United States is a "double colonized" space, once by Spain and then by the United States (Gómez, 2008). Border militarization policies treat immigrant border crossings as controllable, and their life expendable in maintaining the U.S. American sovereign space against crossers who are constructed as "invading enemies."

Mbembe (2003) describes Necropolitics as follows:

> The ultimate expression of sovereignty [that] resides, to a large degree, in the power and the capacity to dictate who may live and who must die. Hence, to kill or to allow to live constitute the limits of sovereignty, its fundamental attributes. To exercise sovereignty is to exercise control over mortality and to define life as the deployment and manifestation of power." (pp. 11–12)

Necropolitics encompasses the State's right to kill as punishment or in war, but it also argues that this includes the right to expose people to death. In regard to the USA-Mexico border, the policy strategy of "prevention through deterrence" (described later in this section) is an example of Necropolitics, where the State *intentionally* pushed border crossers away from safer, urban crossing points like San Diego and El Paso into the harsh and deadly desert of Arizona through border militarization policies (Michaelwoski, 2007). "Colonial occupation itself was a matter of seizing, delimiting, and asserting control over a physical geographical area—of writing on the ground a new set of social and spatial relations" (Mbembe, 2003, p. 24). The "prevention through deterrence" strategy reflects the state's power to decide who dies so that others may live with less visible signs of sovereign violations/border crossings at more rural crossing sites. The use of the desert as a border-crossing deterrent is an exercise of state control over immigrant mortality. Like Necropolitics, Lisa Marie Cacho (2012) similarly contends that social death or "living nonbeings" (p. 6) is a form of racist rightlessness that applies to a wide range of marginalized groups including undocumented immigrants. Fueled by the neoliberal state and corporate capitalism, illegality reflects "permanently criminalized people" who are *"ineligible for personhood*—as populations subjected to laws but refused the legal means to contest those laws as well as denied both the political legitimacy and moral credibility to question them" (Cacho, 2012, p. 6).

I apply the concept of Necropolitics to brutalization theory in order to help explain why border policies have a negative and wide-ranging effect on the general public. Brutalization theory, which developed out of the long academic debate over capital punishment, posits that the public imitates the state as it metes out punishments on criminals, in that the public morally identifies with the state as it punishes (Bowers & Pierce, 1980). At central issue is the question over the state's moral message and how the public receives it. Advocates of the death penalty have and continue to argue that state executions have a deterrent effect on would-be murderers and communicate to the public that people who murder will be punished likewise. Opponents of the death penalty argue that it encourages violence in the society as the state conveys a brutal moral lesson to its citizenry that deadly violence is an acceptable solution for people who break the law. As Bowers and Pierce (1980) write, "Implicit in the brutalization argument is an alternative identification process, different from the one implied by deterrence theory. The potential murderer will not identify personally with the criminal who is executed, but will instead identify someone who has greatly offended him- someone he hates, fears, or both—with the executed criminal. We might call this the psychology of "villain identification" (p. 456). In this process of "villain identification," the potential murderer identifies with the state and punishes those seen as offending.

In a similar manner, the public follows the state in regard to border policy, which allows for the extralegal violence against immigrants to occur. Thus within a brutalization framework, it makes sense that vigilante groups along the border do not see themselves as violating the law, but instead mimic the state's position themselves as an additional but helpful "arm" of immigration enforcement and border patrol (which I detail later in the chapter). Roxanne Lynn Doty (2016) further argues that border vigilantes also affect the State where:

> their practices (which would include their rhetorical practices such as the slogans on the signs displayed at rallies) have the effect of *socially constructing* an enemy who presents a danger to the social order. This gives rise to and justifies practices (and policies) that otherwise would fly in the face of most of our notions of democracy and human/civil rights. (p. 12)

Thus, President Trump's support for building "that wall" is not an outlier but is part of the process of brutalizing border policies that results in necropolitical deaths in the border desert that is treated like a cost of US American exceptionalism. Weber and Pickering (2011) analyze and compare the various border death counting methodologies and contend that

> the counting of border-related deaths has given rise to estimates of future deaths. Based on numbers of apprehensions and estimates of numbers of unauthorized crossings, these future estimates mean that death becomes not only knowable and quantifiable but also predictable. In this regard, arguments for the alleged inevitability of deaths in illegalized border crossing can be seen to have parallels with arguments surrounding the inevitability of collateral deaths during wartime. (p. 56)

While Weber and Pickering (2011) do not offer any specific count of the USA-Mexico border deaths, Cornelius (2005) analyzed a peak period of border-militarized enforcement and says:

> to put this death toll in perspective, the fortified US [American] border with Mexico has been more than 10 times deadlier to migrants from Mexico during

the past nine years than the Berlin Wall was to East Germans throughout its 28-year existence. More migrants (at least 3,218) have died trying to cross the USA/Mexico border since 1995 than people—2,752—were killed in the World Trade Center attacks on 11 September 2001. (p. 783)

BI-PARTISAN PRESIDENTIAL BORDER WARS, NEOLIBERAL TRADE AGREEMENTS, AND VIGILANTES

I argue that bipartisan border policies that focus on "war" as a guiding principle brutalize the public and encourage violence against immigrants of color. While the mainstream media has focused on Trump's border wall proposals as extreme, in fact, his policies are a fruition of a long-standing trajectory of making the border the symbol of the racialized "war" where people who are basically economic refugees and asylum seekers are treated instead like "enemies." I demonstrate this with a brief timeline of bi-partisan presidential contributions to this "border war," neoliberal trade deals that impact borders, and modern border militarization policies, as well as its effect on border vigilantes.

Hernández (2010) notes that the border patrol was established in 1924 and traces its rise in the southern border region that "effectively Mexicanized the set of inherently and lawfully unequal social relations emerging from the legal/illegal divide" (p. 10) through its police practices. However, militarization of the border is a relatively recent phenomenon and Dunn's (1996) influential research focuses on the use of low intensity conflict doctrine in the late 1970s to early 1990s in regard to military tactics, strategies, equipment, and training on the USA-Mexico border by the Immigration and Naturalization Services. While the Posse Comitatus Act of 1978 prohibits the use of the military for domestic law enforcement, the "war on drugs" and the "war on the border" help to erode this federal statue (Kealy, 2003).

Neoliberal transformations also contribute to the border militarization and the criminalization of immigrants. While some scholars argue that the globalization process challenges and erodes the nation-state and its borders (Brown, 2010; Sassen, 1995), the necropolitical deathscape that is the USA-Mexico border is an ultimate expression of U.S. American sovereignty and demonstrate that borders matter in a globalizing world. Harvey (1995) contends that neoliberalism is a "theory of political economic practices that proposes that human well-being can best be advanced by liberating individual entrepreneurial freedoms and skills within an institutional framework characterized by strong private property rights, free markets, and free trade" (p. 2). He argues the role of the state has radically reconfigured its function to advantage and expand the power of corporations and to repress dissent through punitive practices like incarceration to manage marginalized communities (Harvey, 1995). Wacquant (2012) agrees yet focuses on punitive apparatuses as central to neoliberalism and articulates three aspects: (1) neoliberalism is a political project of state-crafting that puts liberal notions of individual responsibility at the service of commodification; (2) it is a "Centaur-state" that practices laissez-faire at the top and punitive paternalism at the bottom (for example, ending welfare with workfare), and (3) it relies on the growth and "glorification" of the prison industrial complex (p. 66). Ackerman (2011) argues that the neoliberal state uses a punitive border control apparatus as a claim of societal protection, in that the "insecurity opened up by liberalization is quelled by state 'protection' in the form of enforcement" (p. 55).

For example, in 1986, the United States formed a free-trade zone with Canada and Mexico through the General Agreement on Tariffs and Trade (GATT) that greatly affected the border situation. In effect, the United States would pursue what scholars call a "politics of contradiction—simultaneously moving toward integration while insisting on separation" (Massey, Durand, & Malone 2002, p. 73). Thus, globalization policies that liberalized trade and the flow of capital between these nations contributed to an increase in the movement of capital, goods, commodities, and information. These trade agreements effectively decoupled capital from the people's labor and, thus, while capital could flow more freely, people could not.

Such shifts in neoliberal economic policies—together with drug enforcement, immigration, national security, and customs concerns—would create an increasingly farraginous agency alliance along the USA-Mexico border with each subsequent presidential administration. For example, the Reagan administration (1981–1989) was concerned with the terrorist element among the Central American refugees seeking political shelter in the United States from U.S. American-sponsored regimes and this administration would first link immigration and cold-war concerns as a basis for the border buildup (Dunn, 1996). Under Reagan, the link between crime and immigration is set into motion when Congress passed the Immigration Reform and Control Act (IRCA) in 1986 that attempted (and failed) to reduce undocumented immigration through employee sanctions (Donato, Durand, & Massey, 1992), increased border enforcement, and offered the last amnesty program as a pathway to citizenship. IRCA also "contained a provision requiring the US Attorney General to deport noncitizens convicted of removable offenses as quickly as possible. This provision set in motion the practice of targeting immigrants convicted of crimes and expanded the mechanisms for policing immigrants" (Abrego, Coleman, Martínez, Menjívar, & Slack, 2017, p. 697). In addition, the Anti-Drug Abuse Act of 1988 created the crime of an "aggravated felony" to facilitate deportation of serious and violent criminals and the 1990 Immigration Act expanded the list of deportable offenses (Abrego,

Coleman, Martínez, Menjívar, & Slack, 2017). The Bush, Sr. Administration (1989–1993) further developed the massive buildup started by his predecessor and increased the paramilitary nature of the Immigration and Naturalization Service (INS) with equipment, forces, and training in tandem with an expansion of law enforcement authority (Dunn, 1996, p. 102). By the late 1980s, vigilantes began to patrol the California border area between San Diego and Tijuana. For example, citizens gathered in their cars and beamed their headlights on the border to put a spotlight on border crossers. This action became known and "Light Up the Border." (Doty, 2007; Kil, Menjívar, & Doty, 2009).

However, the proclivity for militarizing the border was not a partisan issue, for it was the Clinton administration (1993–2001) that answered the demand for even more to be done. His administration launched the INS offensive-border strategy called "prevention through deterrence." This strategy began with "Operation Hold the Line" (in El Paso, Texas in 1993; first called "Operation Blockade") and continued with "Operation Gatekeeper" (in San Diego, California in 1994), "Operation Safeguard" (in Nogales, Arizona in 1994), and "Operation Rio Grande" (in the Brownsville corridor that extends from the Lower Rio Grande Valley to Laredo, Texas in 1997; Andreas, 2000). Walls, stadium-style lighting, and ground sensors were placed in these border areas and border patrol staffing was increased dramatically. The goal was to move the migration path away from these safer urban areas into harsh, mountainous, and desert terrain, to deter people from crossing into the United States and make apprehension easier in the remote areas. Nevins (2002) argues this "Gatekeeping" deterrence strategy reflects the imagined geographical shift of the border as a zone of transition to a boundary/line of rigid demarcation which contribute to immigrant criminalization and normalize militarized enforcement practices (p. 10–11). Doris Meissner, Clinton's Commissioner of the Immigration Naturalization Serves under the Justice Department from 1993 to 2000, oversaw the initial implementation of this policy and stated, "We did believe geography would be an ally" (Davis & Chacón, 2017, p. 206).

Although it did successfully push the migration flow away from urban areas, it did not deter undocumented immigration, except that now immigrants are more likely to hire human smugglers as guides (Reyes, Johnson, & van Swearingen, 2002). Now, more than 90 percent of the million or more annual undocumented border crossers rely on human smugglers contributing to an $8 billion a year industry (Davis & Chacón, 2017). Additionally, immigrants are more likely to stay longer in the United States—because the return/reentry poses a far greater physical danger and monetary cost to them now than before the militarized-border buildup—thus increasing the number of undocumented immigrants residing in the United States (Massey et al., 2002; Reyes et al., 2002). Indeed, this border enforcement strategy has "backfired" in the sense it does not control the border, and now undocumented border crossers have settled with their families in all fifty states, eliminating the long-standing practice of circular migration by mostly men border crossers to three states (Massey, Durand, & Pren, 2016).

Many scholars agree that the sharp escalation in border patrol budgets and policing that yields low deterrent effects render the border enforcement strategy as a type of public spectacle or theater to show that serious things were being done about undocumented immigration (Andreas, 2000; Brownell, 2001; Nevins 2002; De Genova, 2013). Demo (2005) argues that the border spectacle or "look of deterrence" functions metonymically as both a symbol and an index of U.S. American sovereignty and:

> epitomizes how border imagery shapes national identity. As an expression of sovereignty, images of the border deterred both symbolize and legitimate the exercise of state power. At the most general level, the look of deterrence reconstitutes the spatial context within which U.S. national identity is defined. The fences and barricades that certify border integrity also provide a referent through which a public is constituted as national subjects. In addition, deterrence imagery institutionalizes particular ways of speaking about, seeing, and acting on the contemporary immigration context. The fences, barricades, and surveillance technology that define the look of deterrence are presented "as if they belonged to the natural order of things." As a result, border militarization functions as an unproblematic exercise of state independence, security, and strength. (p. 306, citing Camilleri & Falk, 1992)

In 1994, NAFTA liberalized trade policies among Canada, United States, and Mexico. This trade deal further decoupled labor from a freer flow of capital. In fact, Doris Meissner foresaw that NAFTA would increase undocumented immigration and would require increased border enforcement efforts (Nevins, 2007). Nevins (2007) notes that NAFTA intensified neoliberal policies that allowed the increased import of U.S. American corn into the Mexican economy leading to increased poverty rates and outmigration from rural Mexico to the United States. Nevins (2002) writes that

> the "NAFTA-ization" of the boundary thus dovetails with the "gatekeeper" state, the task of which is to provide extraterritorial opportunities for national territory-based capital (this intensifying the process of globalization) while, somewhat paradoxically, providing security against the perceived social cost unleashed by globalization—especially immigration. (p. 178)

Neoliberal economics feed into the punitive border apparatus, which requires legislative support to turn lesser crimes into "aggravated felonies" for undocumented immigrants, making their lives more easily removable.

In 1996 under the Clinton Administration, two pieces of legislation would further militarize the border and criminalize immigrants: the Illegal Immigration Reform and Immigrant Responsibility Act (IIRIRA) and the Anti-Terrorism and Effective Death Penalty Act (AEDPA). These laws expanded the definition of "aggravated felony" to include misdemeanors and minor offenses that are neither "aggravated" nor a "felony" thus allowing immigrants to be subjected to indefinite detention. Macías-Rojas (2016) argues that the explosion of the prison industrial complex reflected in a 500 percent population growth between 1980 and 1994 hastened the need for the deportations of non-citizens to free up prison beds. Before these laws, an undocumented immigrant had to receive a sentence of five years or more to be considered an "aggravated felony," now it only takes a year sentence and many misdemeanor crimes that carry a sentence of one year can be designated as an "aggravated felony." Both "AEDPA and the IIRIRA force judges to recharacterize misdemeanors and non-aggravated felonies as aggravated felonies solely for immigration purposes" (Johnson, 2001, p. 477). Torstveit Ngara (2016) notes that the term "aggravated felony" only exists in immigration law and contributes to a cognitive bias against immigrants that contributes to their criminalization by provoking fear, where the less harsh term "nonwaivable offense" would create less bias, less fear, and less injustice. AEDPA and the IIRIRA are particularly important for escalating the merger of crime and civil immigration matters because they establish the concept of the "criminal alien" making crime synonymous with an undocumented status (Abrego, Coleman, Martínez, Menjívar, & Slack, 2017; citing Ewing, Martínez, & Rumbaut 2015). IIRIRA targets "criminal aliens" as an enforcement priority and expanded deportation and detention powers with added infrastructure to accomplish that goal (Macías-Rojas, 2016). AEDPA criminalizes immigrants by mandating their detentions if convicted of a wide range of offenses that included minor drug offenses ("Analysis of Immigration Detention Policies," n.d.). IIRIRA also establishes the 287(g) program that provides a legal way to deputize state and local authorities to enforce immigration law (Abrego, Coleman, Martínez, Menjívar, & Slack, 2017).

In 1997, in an example of how Necropolitics not only apply to undocumented immigrants but to certain racialized U.S. American citizens as well, U.S. American Marines who had been performing a counterdrug and anti-terrorism operation called Joint Task Force 6 stalked and killed 18-year-old Esequiel Hernández, Jr. who was herding his family's goats near the border. The Marines did not provide immediate aid thinking he was a drug runner; consequently, the young teen bled out on the hill overlooking his home. Esequiel Hernández, Jr. became the first U.S. American citizen killed by U.S. American military forces on native soil since the 1970 Kent State massacre (Verhovek, 1997). No one was convicted of his murder.

Under the Bush, Jr. Administration (2001–2009) and after the tragedy of 9/11 terrorist attacks on New York and D.C., immigration-policy enforcement focused more on threats to national security signaled by the creation of the Department of Homeland Security (DHS) eleven days after the 9/11 attack. Ackleson (2005) analyzes the social construction of USA-Mexico border in relation to security prior to 9/11 and notes that elite border patrol officials often emphasized the "disorder" and "chaos" due the newly defined threat of border crossers, which calls for remedies of "control" in the form of technology and manpower. This discourse of control/disorder helps to construct the southern border through the securitization of migrants as a threat that has an impact on U.S. American identity by encouraging the idea of separation and associating it with crime and security concerns. These types of discourses help to construct immigrants as a security threat with criminal intent, which helps to justify and expand border patrol operations. Post 9/11, this threat was magnified by the concerns over terrorism and border crossings (Ackleson, 2005). However, the only confirmed terrorist border crossing was pre-9/11 and occurred at the USA-Canada border when Ahmed Ressam, the "Millennium Bomber," planned an Al-Queda attack on the Los Angeles International Airport in 1999 and crossed the northern border by ferry with a fraudulent Canadian passport (Salter & Piché, 2011). In addition to the magnification of terrorism at the border, "policies that followed in the 2000s, moreover, cast an increasingly wider net which continually re-determined who could be classified as a 'criminal alien,' such that the term is now a mostly incoherent grab bag" (Abrego, Coleman, Martínez, Menjívar, & Slack, 2017, p. 695). If punishment is central to neoliberal statecraft (Wacquant, 2012), then border and immigration enforcement increasingly punishes border crossers (as well as those who make it far past the border) by magnifying security concerns over the terrorism and crime which expand the border enforcement apparatus that brutalizes the general public to treat Brown border crossers as invaders.

The "prevention through deterrence" policy and the aftermath of 9/11 not only affected where immigrants cross, but it also affected the geographic strategies of militia-style, vigilante groups. Since Arizona has seen the increase in traffic, resulting from redirecting migration flows caused by border patrol operations, vigilante groups moved from California and Texas into Arizona to be near their perceived "ground zero." In April 2005, many of these groups converged to form a super group called the "Minutemen Project" lead by Jim Gilchrist and included Chris Simcox (Civilian Homeland Defense), Jack Foote (Ranch Rescue), and Glen Spencer (American Border Patrol). As part of my scholar-activist approach, I trained as a human rights legal observer and took shifts along the border of Cochise County in Arizona ("ACLU of Arizona to Provide Legal Observers during Controversial 'Minuteman' Border Watch Program," 2005). The vigilantes brought weapons, detection technologies, training, and expertise honed in their home states and deployed in Arizona. For instance, Ranch Rescue, headed by Texan Rancher Jack Foote, is an "armed volunteer organization" interested in protecting private landowners' property rights from "criminal trespassers." At the time, they claimed to have branches in Washington, Oregon, Arkansas, Illinois, Georgia, New Mexico, Arizona, Texas, California, and an international branch. They boasted of a membership base composed of Border Patrol agents, military personnel, law enforcement officers, and Soldier of Fortune mercenaries (www.ranchrescue.com). In 2000, Ranch Rescue circulated a flier in Arizona calling for recruits to "hunt" immigrants and "to help keep trespassers from destroying private property" (Rotstein, 2000).

Another group, the American Border Patrol, moved operations from California (where this organization was called Voices of Citizens Together/American Patrol and recognized by the Southern Poverty Law Center as a hate group) to Arizona, and began "operations" in 2002 with a focus on high-tech detection equipment installed along the border (Hammer-Tomizuka & Allen, 2002). Its founder, Glenn Spencer, believes these extra precautions are necessary since he is convinced that the Mexican government purposefully sends undocumented immigrants for a "Reconquista," or the retaking of the Southwest by Mexico. He states, "Mexico, which has been hostile toward the U.S. for over 100 years, is invading us with the intent of conquering the [U.S.] American Southwest. There is no question of this" (Grigg, 1996). Since moving his operations to Arizona, Spencer has established his group as a grassroots organization, garnering an incorporated, nonprofit status (Banks, 2003). Two of the organization's officers are former Border Patrol sector chiefs (Hammer-Tomizuka & Allen, 2002). Chavez (2008) notes a conservative White anxiety about this re-conquest theory and cites academic Samuel Huntington who warned that the United States will follow the model of Quebec and lead to a separate state with Spanish as an official language since immigrants are somehow perceived as refusing to assimilate.

Chris Simcox—another former California resident and now a convicted pedophile—led the Civilian Homeland Defense and openly described his group as a militia and wants the U.S. American government to deputize his members in the interest of national security (Hammer-Tomizuka & Allen, 2002). Members are openly armed and "operate on public lands, patrol routes leading to water stations set up by humanitarian groups to aid immigrants and have volunteers apply for concealed weapons permits" ("Tombstone Militia Will Operate on Public Land," 2002). In a fact card distributed by the group Civil Homeland Defense, it claims to be a "community service volunteer neighborhood watch group who has answered the call of the President of the United States to report suspicious, illegal activities." They assume that "illegal immigration allows terrorists, criminals, people with disease into our country" (Civil Homeland Defense fact card, Cochise County, Arizona).

These are just a few of the vigilante groups that have felt compelled to move to Arizona because of the rise in border traffic and death in the Tucson border sector (Kil & Menjivar, 2006). They are motivated by the immigration and drug policies that have made this state's border a "war zone," and they thus mimic the government's military border paradigm in rhetoric and strategy. Many of these groups have quasi-governmental names, similar to those of governmental agencies, and wear uniforms that are hard to distinguish from those of the official Border Patrol. Importantly, they see themselves as necessary supplements to the current militarized-border effort, which they see as too soft and inadequate. Therefore, it is not surprising that they see immigrants as criminals, enemies, and threats to national security. Many of these groups have current or past affiliations with national, racist-hate groups, and despite their self-perception as supplementing border-enforcement efforts, they contributed to an atmosphere of brutalization, violence, and racial hate. Fortunately, the Minutemen project crumbled quickly under the spectacle of its own celebrity. The movement fractured with many splinter groups bearing some version of the Minuteman name (Murphy, 2014). In 2016, the Southern Poverty Law Center counts only two nativist extremist groups in Arizona: Arizona Border Recon and Minuteman Civil Defense Corp ("Once again, Number of 'nativist extremist' group falls," 2017).

The urge to militarize continued under the Bush, Jr. administration with the Secure Border Initiative in 2005, which increased funds to hire more border patrol agents, build more fortified fencing, and acquire more helicopters and planes to monitor the border (Hagen & Philips, 2008). In 2005, Operation Streamline implemented mass trials for those who reenter after deportation where undocumented border crossers face charges in federal district courts for a felony violation of a prior deportation order as well as a misdemeanor for unauthorized entry, where most accept a plea deal with imprisonment but also "marks them as criminals, a status that places them at greater risk the next time they attempt to cross the border" and contributes to a growing deportation to prison pipeline (Macías-Rojas, 2016, p.125). That same year there was a peak in deaths with 492 bodies recovered in the SW border region by border patrol records (United States Border Patrol, 2016). In 2006, the Secure Fence Act was passed by a Republican Congress and signed by the president. It was also supported by then senators Obama and Clinton (Graves, 2017). This act secured an additional 700 miles of fence that "if completed, could make it the most heavily fortified international boundary in the industrialized world" (Hagan & Philips, 2008, p. 91). At this point, the USA-Mexico border then figuratively "travels" to the interior (Ono, 2012) with an escalating focus on deportations while deaths on the border also escalate.

For example, the conservative and official number of immigrant deaths, particularly in Arizona, peaked four times in 2005, 2007, 2009, and 2010 at over 200 deaths per fiscal year in Tucson Border Sector between 1998–2016 (U.S. Border Patrol SW border deaths by fiscal year). See Figure 2.1.

United States Border Patrol

Southwest Border Sectors

Southwest Border Deaths By Fiscal Year (Oct. 1st through Sept. 30th)

Fiscal Year	Big Bend (formerly Marfa)	Del Rio	El Centro	El Paso	Laredo	Rio Grande Valley (formerly McAllen)	San Diego	Tucson	Yuma	Southwest Border Total
2017	1	18	2	8	83	104	4	72	2	294
2016	2	14	9	6	68	132	7	84	7	329
2015	4	12	4	2	57	97	6	63	6	251
2014	5	17	6	0	54	116	5	107	3	313
2013	3	18	3	2	62	156	7	194	6	451
2012	1	29	11	1	91	144	5	180	9	471
2011	2	18	5	6	65	66	15	195	3	375
2010	0	23	14	4	35	29	8	251	1	365
2009	3	29	27	5	58	68	15	212	3	420
2008	3	22	20	8	32	92	32	171	5	385
2007	0	20	12	25	52	61	15	202	11	398
2006	4	34	21	33	36	81	36	169	40	454
2005	4	28	30	28	53	55	23	219	52	492
2004	0	21	36	18	22	35	15	142	39	328
2003	0	23	61	10	17	39	29	137	22	338
2002	4	29	64	8	15	30	24	134	12	320
2001	3	41	96	10	28	37	21	80	24	340
2000	3	48	72	26	47	40	34	74	36	380
1999	0	30	56	15	37	36	25	29	21	249
1998	3	28	90	24	20	26	44	11	17	263

*Data may be subject to change based on new discoveries of remains and possible dates of death as determined by a medical examiner

Figure 2.1   Southwest Border Deaths by Fiscal Year.

Between FY 2004 through 2008, Congress dramatically increased ICE's Criminal Alien Program (CAP) from $6.6 million to $180 million (Cantor, Noferi, & Martinez, 2015). CAP is a "massive enforcement program administered by U.S. Immigration and Customs Enforcement (ICE) and has become the primary channel through which interior immigration enforcement takes place. Between two-thirds and three-quarters of individuals removed from the interior" of the United States are removed by CAP and relies on cooperation with state and local law enforcement for its effectiveness (Cantor, Noferi, & Martinez, 2015, p. 1). Cantor, Noferi, and Martinez (2015) examine the CAP program between fiscal years 2010 and 2013 and their:

> data shows that through CAP's enormous web, ICE has encountered millions and removed hundreds of thousands of people. Yet, CAP is not narrowly tailored to focus enforcement efforts on the most serious security or safety threats—in part because CAP uses criminal arrest as a proxy for dangerousness and because the agency's own priorities have been drawn more broadly than those threats. As a result, the program removed mainly people with no criminal convictions, and people who have not been convicted of violent crimes or crimes the Federal Bureau of investigation (FBI) classifies as serious. CAP also has resulted in several anomalies, including that it appears biased against Mexican and Central American nationals. (p.1)

CAP "has become one of the chief mechanisms driving federal criminal prosecution and imprisonment for immigration offenses" (Macías-Rojas, 2016, p. 4). For example, under the Bush, Jr's administration of CAP, deportations peaked at 359,795 in 2008 (Office of Immigration Statistics, 2016). Hing (2019) notes that Bush's gun-toting ICE raids at employment sites like factories and farms would turn into silent raids under Obama's early presidency.

The Obama Administration (2009–2017) greatly expanded the momentum the Bush Jr. administration put into CAP by increasing the deportations to numbers unmatched by any prior president. His administration would pursue the "carrot and stick" approach toward immigration issues with effects mostly on the "stick." For example, pro-immigration activists characterized President Obama as "Deporter-in-Chief" for his efforts in deporting not just immigrants with prior criminal records but also immigrants with no prior criminal record ("Obama Leaves Office As 'Deporter-in-Chief,'" 2017). Based on the most recent yearbook (2015) of immigration statistics published by the Department of Homeland Security, Obama has deported more than 3 million people (US Department of Homeland Security, 2017), which is more than the combined effort of every U.S. American president of the twentieth century (Hasan, 2017). Hing (2019) notes that Obama's deportation policies focus on those with a criminal record and who crossed the border recently without documents. He further argues that Obama's silent raids, that sent federal workers to examine company files for undocumented workers instead of to farms and factories, gave way to more Bush-style raids later in Obama's presidency that even targeted immigrant civil rights leaders (Hing, 2019). Slack (2019) argues that these immigrants are "deported to death," dropped on the Mexican side of the border and exposed to extreme drug violence due to the growth of drug cartels with many deportees killed as a result of their immigration removal.

Additionally, in 2010, in a rare showing of bipartisanship, Obama signed into law a bill that would provide $600 million to deploy some 1,500 new Border Patrol agents and additional unmanned aerial surveillance drones ("Obama Signs $600M Bill to Increase Militarization of U.S.-Mexico Border," 2010). In 2011, the Consequences Delivery System (CDS), a program that guides Border Patrol agents to apply a risk-based metric to an individual immigrant in order to evaluate the penalty that will deter that person from re-crossing the border, allows the Border Patrol to "wield the full force of the carceral state against migrants" (Slack, Martinez, & Whiteford, 2018, p. 6).

In 2012, however, the Obama Administration did provide a carrot to "Dreamers," or undocumented people who arrived in the United States as youth, with the Deferred Action for Childhood Arrivals (DACA) program, which did not provide a pathway to citizenship but did confer two important privileges: temporary suspension of deportation and work authorization. As of FY 2016, the Citizenship and Immigration Services of the United States approved 741,546 total initial applicants from these "Dreamers" (U.S. Citizenship and Immigration Services, 2016). But then in 2013, forcible removals peaked under the Obama Administration at 434,015 people, far surpassing Bush, Jr.'s record in 2008. In 2013, the federal program Secure Communities that permitted more communication and shared databases between local law enforcement, ICE and the Federal Bureau of Investigation, was fully implemented in all states (https://www.ice.gov/secure-communi ties). Inaugurated in 2008, the Secure Communities program is a "287(g) lite," where an immigration status check is part of the jail intake process and greatly increases the chances of law enforcement encounters with undocumented people and "by the time Secure Communities was shelved in 2014, the program had identified an astounding 2.4 million people as deportable" (Abrego, Coleman, Martínez, Menjívar, & Slack, 2017, p. 703). Hing (2019) argues that Secure Communities was intended to focus on serious criminals but actually removed people with no criminal record or people with low-level offenses by capturing all fingerprints of people not born in the United States "whether or not they pose criminal risk" (p. 31). In 2014, DHS replaced the Secure Communities program with Priority Enforcement Program (PEP), through which ICE continues to obtain booking data from state and local law enforcement agencies, but limits the transfer of undocumented immigrants in custody to the conviction of specific crimes or the "demonstrable risk to national security" (U.S. Department of Homeland Security, 2014, para. 3). In the same month, Obama also sought to expand DACA and implement some protections for the parents of citizens and lawful permanent residents to request deferred action and employment authorization for three years, in a new Deferred Action for Parents of Americans and Lawful Permanent Residents (DAPA; U.S. Citizenship and Immigration Services, 2015). The Obama Administration began to prioritize the deportation of unaccompanied minors after a spike in FY 2014 of 73,700 apprehensions, mostly Central American children fleeing crime, violence, and poverty, who were sent to detention facilities before their expediated, "rocket dockets"/court removal, with many children lacking counsel, which contributed to many deaths upon their forced return home (Hing, 2019, p. 68).

President Trump took office in January 2017 and signed two immigrant-related Executive Orders (EOs) that month. The first EO titled, "Border Security and Immigration Enforcement Improvements":

> reinstitutes and expands the 287(g) program, allowing local law enforcement agents in certain western and southwestern states to enforce immigration law, as outlined in IIRIRA, and named after §287(g) of the Immigration and Nationality Act, for which the program was named. It allows for sheriffs and police departments, as well as state-level policing agencies—to investigate immigration cases, make immigration-related arrests, and among other things, take custody of immigrants on the basis of both criminal and civil immigration violations. The EO also expands the use of expedited removals in the border region, calls for an additional 5,000 Border Patrol agents, mandates the detention of immigrants apprehended for unlawful entry, and prioritizes criminal prosecutions for immigration offenses committed at the border. (Abrego, Coleman, Martínez, Menjívar, & Slack, 2017, p. 698)

The second EO titled, "Enhancing Public Safety in the Interior of the United States" terminates the Obama's PEP program and restores his harsher Secure Communities program with an additional hiring of 10,000 ICE agents (Abrego, Coleman, Martínez, Menjívar, & Slack, 2017).

On June 15, 2017, the Trump Administration rescinded the Deferred Action for Parents of Americans plan. The following summer, the news media reported on the separation of children from parents seeking asylum at the border that sparked a national outcry. It was intended to "send a message" that if immigrants do not want to be separated from their children, they should not cross the border because they would be treated as criminals, even if they seek asylum and the Department of Health and Human Services would take custody of their children (Rosenberg, 2018). A federal judge ordered the reunification of over 2,500 children affected by this zero-tolerance policy by July 2018, with 400 children still left separated from their parents after that deadline passed. In addition, the Department of Homeland Security announced that it would allow the government to detain migrant families for longer periods of time, which would reduce the current standards of care of immigrant children in detention (Barajas, 2018). In January 2019, the Inspector General for the U.S. Department of Health and Human Services determined:

> the total number of children separated from a parent or guardian by immigration authorities is unknown. Pursuant to a June 2018 Federal District Court order, HHS has thus far identified 2,737 children in its care at that time who were separated from their parents. However, thousands of children may have been separated during an influx that began in 2017, before the accounting required by the Court, and HHS has faced challenges in identifying separated children. (U.S. Department of Health and Human Services, 2019)

In December 2018, Trump shut down the federal government for a record-breaking thirty-five days when he did not get the budget he desired for his border wall (see Introduction chapter). Congress approved 1.375 billion for his wall and Trump signed the bill, but declared a national emergency the same day in order to access additional billions in funds for the "virtual invasion" he cited as the nation's emergency (Paschal, 2019, para. 32). President Trump's $4.7 trillion budget proposal for 2020 calls for $8.6 billion in new border wall funding (Horsley, 2019). Trump's demand for a greater border wall revitalizes the border militia groups' efforts to mobilize for an invasion in the border region (Grant & Miroff, 2018).

So far it seems President Trump wants to break Obama's record as Deporter-in-Chief and militarize the border more than both the Clinton and Bush, Jr.'s Administrations combined. However, much like border vigilantes deny their blatant racism, President Trump also denies that his border wall is racist:

> I can never apologize for the truth. I don't mind apologizing for things. But I can't apologize for the truth. I said tremendous crime is coming across [the border]. Everybody knows that's true. And it's happening all the time. So, why, when I mention, all of a sudden I'm a racist. I'm not a racist. I don't have a racist bone in my body. (Lee, 2015, para 2)

Recall in the Introduction chapter that a unique feature of contemporary nativist discourse is that it is not directly and honestly racist. The covert, invisible, nonracial articulations of NRNR that occur in nativist discourse allow Whiteness to reproduce itself without much challenge. If NRNR is the method of nativist discourse, then Whiteness is the result. This allows Trump to offer a racist border policy in an attempt to protect the Whiteness of the nation while denying any racist intentions.

NECROPOLITICAL DEATHSCAPE AT THE BORDER AND BEYOND

The militarized border region is a necropolitical deathscape shaped by presidential border war policies, neoliberal transformations, and racist nativism that create a new set of social relations and spatial arrangements. Necropolitics cultivate these social and spatial arrangements that put people in daily contact with the possibility of death, thus acquiring the status of the "living dead," a space between life and death that makes the deathscape easier to manage and the "living dead" in it, easier to dispose of (Peoples & Vaughan-Williams, 2015, citing Mbembe, 2003). Deathscapes are "new and unique forms of social existence in which vast populations are subject to conditions of life conferring upon them the status of the living dead" (Mbembe, 2003, p. 40).

However, these strategies not only affect Mexicans who cross, but undocumented Brown border crossers in general, as well as entire groups who live in the Southwest region of the United States who do not "look" White, regardless of citizenship status as evidenced by the Chandler, Arizona example in the Introduction chapter. Using war rhetoric and deploying low-intensity conflict methods to enforce border policies increase the social and racial polarization, while encouraging a climate of abuse and violence toward undocumented immigrants and those who racially or ethnically resemble them. The present border paradigm promotes hate and fear toward the border and mistreats border communities. The militarization of the border diminishes the human rights and quality of life in these communities—composed mostly of people of color—primarily through racial profiling by the Border Patrol who are looking for drug and immigrant smugglers but treat as potential criminals Brown U.S. American citizens (Macías-Rojas, 2016). Thus, the borderlands become a hostile place for the human rights of both residents and crossers (Allen, 2003). The "war on the border" imagery shapes a racial national identity that contributes to Whiteness.

And this necropolitical deathscape is not just contained at the USA-Mexican border. The deathscape follows immigrants well past crossing the border. For example, immigrants live a life of "legal nonexistence" where undocumented immigrants are physically present and socially active in civil society, but lacking legal recognition (Coutin, 2000). Placing undocumented people outside the legal order into a realm of lawlessness supports extreme actions and exempts authorities from obligations to them and, thus, the rights of those who are legally nonexistent are ambiguous (Coutin, 2000). This precarious existence of undocumented immigrants of color works like a caste system that places them outside of citizenship, social legitimacy, and the imagined national community (Ngai, 2014). Thus, the criminalization of immigrants constitutes a systematic legal violence by permitting violence against immigrants as acceptable, which negatively impact their work, family, and school lives and produces human suffering (Menjívar and Abrego, 2012). The right of "due process," which is considered inherent in the criminal justice system toward any person—even undocumented immigrants—eventually gives way to the militarized construction of the enemy "other," an entity with dubious access to rights (Kil & Menjívar, 2006). Thus, fears about geographic contagion and its threat to the Whiteness of the nation take on dramatic symbolic and material form with the militarization of the USA-Mexico border that also follow immigrants into the interior of the nation.

In conclusion, President Trump contributes to an "Us vs. Them" border war frame that makes immigrants into symbolic national enemies that public officials, the media, and the general public also echo. However, bipartisan, presidential policies of prior administrations also contribute to a "border war" that brutalize the public and encourage violence against immigrants. Mbembe's (2003) concept of Necropolitics and brutalization theory—to note, borrowed from the death penalty literature—describe how militarizing the border is a form of racial brutalization that encourages the public and policymakers to seek further militarization despite the deadly costs. This has led the Clinton administration to adopt "prevention through deterrence," a steep escalation in the militarized border policy that directly resulted in the rise of border deaths in the region and occurred in conjunction with neoliberal trade policies like NAFTA and passage of IIRIRA and AEDPA, that further militarized the border and criminalized immigrants. Under the Bush administration, the creation of the Department of Homeland Security in response to the 9/11 and the "war on terror," refocused terrorist concerns about the border. Bush, Jr. also began the CAP program the dramatically increase interior enforcement and passed the Secure Fence Act that bolstered the border buildup. Obama would not only provide a carrot to immigrants with the passage of DACA but also provide a stick in the form of record-breaking numbers of deportations of any U.S. American president in history while still contributing a militarized border buildup. President Trump's motivation for building a border wall is in line with the trajectory of public policy and public discourse that dehumanizes immigrants who cross the USA-Mexico border using a blurred war/crime/disease discursive frame that come from "racist dirt fixations." The only departure is that this president uses rape as a specific crime that he accuses undocumented people of committing, tapping into an old racist logic that see people of color as immorally and abnormally sexual, and repackages in a new nativist way within a crime framework.

The next chapter provides the analysis of these newspaper articles beginning with the scale of the body as a "Vulnerable Body." "Racist dirt fixations" arise out of anxieties about borders that reflect discursively in scales and the physical body is the most significant and foundational scale in relation to the prosperity of these covert fixations in the news reporting. I analyze three dominant themes that compose this "vulnerable body" scale: "body aches," "body functions," and "body parts." An analysis of racist dirt fixations reveals a fear of disability that intersects with racist, classist, gendered, and sexualized ideas about the immigration disorder and its impact on the health of body politic and its association with Whiteness. Analyzed within an embodied and scaled framework of the "vulnerable body," the border news discourse reveals an "othering" process that associates Whiteness with nation via the use of bodily imagery in a highly nuanced rhetorical way. This seemingly race neutral rhetoric, when taken together within the scale of the body and "dirt," communicate deeply, racialized phobias about a permeable border and its potential impact on the imagined White body politic.

NOTE

1. "The term 'cuckservative'—a combination of 'cuckold' and 'conservative,' coined to castigate Republican politicians who are seen as traitors to their people who are selling out conservatives with their support for globalism and certain liberal ideas. The phrase has a racist undertone, as some of its backers have suggested, implying that establishment conservatives are like white men who allow black men to sleep with their wives. It received widespread media attention . . . ." (Southern Poverty Law Center, 2018).

REFERENCES

Abrego, L., Coleman, M., Martínez, D. E., Menjívar, C., & Slack, J. (2017). Making immigrants into criminals: Legal processes of criminalization in the post-IIRIRA era. *Journal on Migration and Human Security*, 5(3), 694–715.

Ackerman, E. (2011). NAFTA and Gatekeeper: A theoretical assessment of border enforcement in the era of the neoliberal state. *Berkeley Journal of Sociology*, 55, 40–56.

Ackleson, J. (2005). Constructing security on the U.S.–Mexico border. *Political Geography*, 24(2), 137–266.

Allen, J. (2003). Justice on the line: The Unequal impacts of the border patrol activities in Arizona Border Communities. Retrieved from www.borderaction.org.

American Civil Liberties Union. (n.d.). Analysis of immigration detention policies. Retrieved from https://www.aclu.org/other/analysis-immigration-detention-policies.

American Civil Liberties Union. (2005). ACLU of Arizona to provide legal observers during controversial "Minuteman" border watch program. Retrieved from https://www.aclu.org/news/aclu-arizona-provide-legal-observers-during-controversial-minuteman-border-watch-program.

Andreas, P. (2000). *Border Games: Policing the U.S.-Mexico Divide.* Ithaca: Cornell University Press.

Associated Press. (2002). Tombstone militia will operate on public land, leader says. *Associated Press*, December 3, 2002.

Banks, L. W. (2003). Crossing the line: Tensions escalate on the border. *Tucson Weekly*, December 19–25, 2003, 14–17.

Barajas, J. (2018). More than 400 migrant children remain separated from their parents: Here's what we know. *PBS.org*. Retrieved from https://www.pbs.org/newshour/nation/more-than-400-migrant-children-remain-separated-from-their-parents-heres-what-we-know.

Bierman, N. (2016) A new favorite chant has overtaken Donald Trump's rallies. *The Los Angeles Times*. Retrieved from http://www.latimes.com/nation/politics/trailguide/la-na-trailguide-updates-there-s-a-new-favorite-chant-at-donald-1476745635-htmlstory.html.

Bowers, W. J., & Pierce, G. (1980). Deterrence or brutalization? *Crime and Delinquency, 26*(4), 453–84.

Brown, W. (2017). *Walled States, Waning Sovereignty.* Cambridge Mass: MIT Press.

Brownell, P. B. (2001). Border militarization and the reproduction of Mexican migrant labor. *Social Justice, 28*(2), 69–92.

Cacho, L. M. (2012). *Social Death: Racialized Rightlessness and the Criminalization of the Unprotected.* New York: NYU Press.

Cantor, G., Noferi, M., & Martinez, D. E. (2015). Enforcement overdrive: A comprehensive assessment of ICE's Criminal Alien Program. *AmericanImmigrationCouncil.org*, November 1, 2015. Retrieved from https://www.americanimmigrationcouncil.org/research/enforcement-overdrive-comprehensive-assessment-ice%E2%80%99s-criminal-alien-program.

Demo. A. (2005) Sovereignty discourse and contemporary immigration politics. *Quarterly Journal of Speech, 91*(3), 291–311. DOI:10.1080/00335630500350319.

Doty, R. L. (2007). States of exception on the Mexico-U.S. border: Security, "decisions," and civilian border patrols. *International Political Sociology, 1*(2), 113–137.

Doty, R. L. (2016). *The Law into their Own Hands: Immigration and the Politics of Exceptionalism.* Tucson: University of Arizona Press.

Donato, K., Durand, J., & Massey, D. (1992). Stemming the tide? Assessing the deterrent effects of the immigration reform and control act. *Demography, 29*(2), 139–157.

Dunn, T. (1996). *The Militarization of the U.S.-Mexico Border, 1978–1992: Low Intensity Conflict Doctrine Comes Home.* Austin: University of Texas Press.

Gómez, L. E. (2005). Off-White in an age of White supremacy: Mexican elites and the rights of Indians and Blacks in nineteenth-century New Mexico. *Chicana/o Latina/o Law Review, 25*(1), 9–60.

Grant, M. L., & Miroff, N. (2018, November 3). U.S. militia groups head to border, stirred by Trump's call to arms. *The Washington Post*. Retrieved from https://www.washingtonpost.com.

Graves, A. (2017). Fact-check: Did top Democrats vote for a border wall in 2006? *Politifact*, April 23, 2017. Retrieved from http://www.politifact.com/truth-o-meter/statements/2017/apr/23/mick-mulvaney/fact-check-did-top-democrats-vote-border-wall-2006/.

Grigg, W. N. (1996, August 19). Race and revolution. *New American*. Retrieved from http://thenewamerican.com/tna/1996/vo12no17/no12no17_revolution.htm.

Hagan, J., & Phillips, S. (2008). Border blunders: The unanticipated human and economic costs of the US approach to immigration control, 1986–2007. *Criminology & Public Policy*, 7(1), 83–94.

Hammer-Tomizuka, Z., & Allen, J. (2002). Hate or heroism: Vigilantes on the Arizona-Mexico border" [online]. Tucson: Border Action Network. Retrieved from http://www.borderaction.org/BAN-Vigilante.pdf.

Hasan, M. (2017, January 14). Barack Obama: The deporter-in-chief. *Aljazeera*. Retrieved from http://www.aljazeera.com/programmes/upfront/2017/01/barack-obama-deporter-chief-170113105930345.html.

Harvey, D. (2007). *A Brief History of Neoliberalism*. Oxford, UK: Oxford University Press.

Hernández, K. L. (2010). *Migra!: A History of the US Border Patrol*. Berkeley, CA: University of California Press.

Hing, B. O. (2018). *American Presidents, Deportations, and Human Rights Violations: From Carter to Trump*. Cambridge UK: Cambridge University Press.

Horsley, S. (2019, March 11). Trump seeks more border wall funding in new budget. *National Public Radio*. Retrieved from https://www.npr.org.

Jimenez, M. (2009). Humanitarian crisis: Migrant deaths at the US–Mexico border, American Civil Liberties Council of San Diego and Imperial Counties, Mexico's National Commission of Human Rights.

Johnson, D. M. (2001). The AEDPA and the IIRIRA: Treating misdemeanors as felonies for immigration purposes. *Journal of Legislation*, 27(2), 477–492.

Kealy, S. J. (2003). Reexamining the Posse Comitatus Act: Toward a right to civil law enforcement. *Yale Law & Policy Review*, 21, 383–442.

Kent A Ono. (2012). Borders that travel: Matters of the figural border. In D. Roberts DeChaine *Border Rhetorics: Citizenship and Identity on the US-Mexico Frontier* (pp. 19–32). Tuscaloosa: University of Alabama Press.

Kil, S. H., & Menjívar, C. (2006). "The 'War on the border': The criminalization of immigrants and militarization of the USA-Mexico border." In R. Martinez, Jr. & A. Valenzuela, Jr. (Eds.), *Immigration and Crime: Race, Ethnicity, and Violence* (pp. 164–188). New York: New York University Press.

Kil, S. H., Menjívar, C., & Doty, R. L. (2009). Securing borders: Patriotism, vigilantism and the Brutalization of the US American public. In W. F. McDonald (Ed.), *Immigration, Crime and Justice: Sociology of Crime, Law and Deviance* (Vol. 13, pp. 297–312). Bingley, UK: Emerald/JAI Press. DOI:10.1108/S1521-6136(2009)0000013019.

Lee, M. Y. H. (2015). Donald Trump's false comments connecting Mexican immigrants and crime. *The Washington Post*. Retrieved from https://www.washingt onpost.com/news/fact-checker/wp/2015/07/08/donald-trumps-false-comments-con necting-mexican-immigrants-and-crime/?utm_term=.37e9cb6eecc3.

Macías-Rojas, P. (2016). *From Deportation to Prison: The Politics of Immigration Enforcement in Post-civil Rights America*. New York: NYU Press.

Massey, D. S., Durand, J, & Malone, N. J. (2002). *Beyond Smoke and Mirrors: Mexican Immigration in an Era of Economic Integration*. New York, NY: Russell Sage Foundation.

Massey, D. S., Pren, K. A., & Durand, J. (2016). Why border enforcement backfired. *American Journal of Sociology*, *121*(5), 1557–1600.

Mbembe, J. A. (2003). Necropolitics. *Public Culture*, *15*(1), 11–40.

Menjívar, C., & Abrego, L. (2012). Legal violence: Immigration law and the lives of Central American immigrants. *American Journal of Sociology*, *117*(5), 1380–1421.

Michalowski, R. (2007). Border militarization and migrant suffering: A case of transnational social injury. *Social Justice*, *34*(2), 62.

Murphy, T. (2014, August 4). The meltdown of the anti-immigration Minuteman militia: Why the self-appointed border patrollers are nowhere to be seen. *Mother Jones*, August 4, 2014. Retrieved from http://www.motherjones.com/politics/2014 /08/minuteman-movement-border-crisis-simcox/.

Ngai, M. M. (2014). *Impossible Subjects: Illegal Aliens and the Making of Modern America-Updated Edition*. Princeton, NJ: Princeton University Press.

Nevins, J. (2007). Dying for a cup of coffee? Migrant deaths in the US-Mexico border region in a neoliberal age. *Geopolitics*, *12*(2), 228–247.

Nevins, J. (2002). *Operation Gatekeeper: The Rise of the "Illegal Alien" and the Remaking of the US–Mexico Boundary*. New York, NY: Routledge.

Torstveit Ngara, E. C. (2016). Aliens, aggravated felons, and worse: When words breed fear and fear breeds injustice. *Stanford Journal of Civil Rights & Civil Liberties*, *12*(2), 389–431.

Obama leaves office as "Deporter-In-Chief." (2017). *NPR.org*, January 20, 2017. Retrieved from http://www.npr.org/2017/01/20/510799842/obama-leaves-office-as-deporter-in-chief.

Obama signs $600M bill to increase militarization of US-Mexico border. (2010). *DemocracyNow.org*, August 19, 2010. Retrieved from https://www.democrac ynow.org/2010/8/19/obama_signs_600m_bill_to_increase.

Office of Immigration Statistics. (2016). 2015 yearbook of immigration statistics [PDF file]. Retrieved from https://www.dhs.gov/sites/default/files/publications/Ye arbook_Immigration_Statistics_2015.pdf.

Once again, Number of "nativist extremist" group falls. (2017, February 19). Retrieved from https://www.splcenter.org/fighting-hate/intelligence-report/2017/ once-again-number-nativist-extremist-groups-falls.

Paschal, O. (2019). *The Atlantic*, February 15. Retrieved from https://www.theatlan tic.com/politics/archive/2019/02/trumps-declaration-national-emergency-full-text /582928/.

Peoples, C., & Vaughan-Williams, N. (2015). *Critical Security Studies: An Introduction* (2nd ed.). New York, NY: Routledge.

Reyes, B. I., Johnson, H. P., & van Swearingen, R. (2002). *Holding the Line?: The Effect of the Recent Border Build-up on Unauthorized Immigration.* San Francisco, CA: Public Policy Institute of California.

Rosenberg, E. (2018). Sessions defends separating immigrant parents and children. *The Washington Post.* Retrieved from https://www.washingtonpost.com/news/post-politics/wp/2018/06/05/sessions-defends-separating-immigrant-parents-and-children-weve-got-to-get-this-message-out/?utm_term=.b07986a25b7f.

Rotstein, A. H. (2000). Vigilante recruiting brochure aimed at deterring illegal crossers sparks protest. *Associated Press*, April 26, 2000.

Salter, M. B., & Piché, G. (2011). The securitization of the U.S.–Canada border in American political discourse. *Canadian Journal of Political Science/Revue Canadienne de Science Politique, 44*(4), 929–951.

Sassen, S. (1995). *Global City.* New York, London, Tokyo: Princeton University Press.

Sides, J. (2017). Race, religion, and immigration in 2016: How the debate over American identity shaped the election and what it means for a Trump presidency. *Voterstudygroup.org.* Retrieved from https://www.voterstudygroup.org/reports/2016-elections/race-religion-immigration-2016.

Slack, J. (2019). *Deported to Death: How Drug Violence is Changing Migration on the US-Mexico Border.* Oakland CA: University of California Press.

Slack, J., Martínez, D. E., Whiteford, S., & Peiffer, E. (2015). In harm's way: Family separation, immigration enforcement programs and security on the US-Mexico border. *Journal on Migration and Human Security, 3*(2), 109–128.

Southern Law and Poverty Center. (2018). Alternative Right. *SPL Center.* Retrieved from https://www.splcenter.org/fighting-hate/extremist-files/ideology/alternative-right.

U.S. Border Patrol. (2016). Southwest border deaths by fiscal year (Oct. 1st through Sept. 30th) [PDF file]. Retrieved from https://www.cbp.gov/sites/default/files/assets/documents/2017-Dec/BP%20Southwest%20Border%20Sector%20Deaths%20FY1998%20-%20FY2017.pdf.

U.S. Citizenship and Immigration Services. (2015). 2014 executive actions on immigration. Retrieved from https://www.uscis.gov/immigrationaction.

U.S. Citizenship and Immigration Services. (2016). Number of I-821D, consideration of Deferred Action for Childhood Arrivals by fiscal year, quarter, intake, biometrics and case status: 2012–2016 (June 30) [PDF file]. Retrieved from https://www.uscis.gov/sites/default/files/USCIS/Resources/Reports%20and%20Studies/Immigration%20Forms%20Data/All%20Form%20Types/DACA/daca_performancedata_fy2016_qtr3.pdf.

U.S. Department of Health and Human Services. (2019). Office of Inspector General: Separated Children Placed in Office of Refugee Resettlement Care. Retrieved from https://www.oig.hhs.gov/oei/reports/oei-BL-18-00511.pdf.

U.S. Department of Homeland Security. (2014). The Secure Communities program, as we know it, will be discontinued. Retrieved from https://www.dhs.gov/sites/defa ult/files/publications/14_1120_memo_secure_communities.pdf.

U.S. Department of Homeland Security. (2017). Yearbook of immigration statistics 2015. Retrieved from https://www.dhs.gov/immigration-statistics/yearbook/2015.

Verhovek, S. H. (1997). After Marine on patrol kills a teen-ager, a Texas border village wonders why. *The New York Times*, June 29, 1997. Retrieved from http://www .nytimes.com/1997/06/29/us/after-marine-on-patrol-kills-a-teen-ager-a-texas-bord er-village-wonders-why.html.

Wacquant, L. (2012). Three steps to a historical anthropology of actually existing neoliberalism. *Social Anthropology*, *20*(1), 66–79. DOI:10.1111/j.1469-8676.2011.00189.x.

Weber, L., & Pickering, S. (2011). *Globalization and Borders: Death at the Global Frontier*. Hampshire: Palgrave Macmillan.

Chapter 3

The Scale of the Vulnerable Body

This chapter lays out the empirical foundation for how the nation is discursively constructed as a body and how the scale of the body plays into notions of a nation at risk of an immigrant disorder. Recall from chapter 1, "Dirt, Scales, and the White Body Politic," I offer a two-part theoretical framework for this study. First, I describe how "racist dirt fixations" work in a new race neutral racist (NRNR) manner to make sense of the wide range of dissimilar images deployed by the media in nativist discourse. This framework draws on West's (1998) genealogies and justifications for racism that are historically suggestive and derive from religious, scientific, and sexual ordered systems, as well as Douglas' (1966) "dirt" concept, which ontologically represents disorder. Second, these "racist dirt fixations" work with geographic scales that "nest" within larger scales, beginning with the body, then house, region, and the nation, with each scale possessing embodied qualities that can be violated and breached in unique ways to that particular scale. This embodied, nested, and scaled nativist discourse creates a naturalized portrait of a White national body in danger from the criminal immigrant who represents dirt, disgust, abjection, and disorder in a symbolic, material, metaphoric, and ideological ways depending on the scale.

Each of these bodily scales—the body, house, region, and nation—insinuates "dirt" or disorder by employing intersectional associations with race, class, gender, sexuality, and disability in order to communicate a racialized threat by geographic contagion. This novel theoretical framework explains how the news media socially constructs immigration and USA-Mexican border into these nested scales that produce racial tensions, anxieties, and nightmares about borders and crossings at each level of representation. This chapter focuses on the first scale, the "Vulnerable Body."

47

Table 2.1   Racist Dirt Fixations at the Body Scale

Tier 1 Theory	Racist Dirt Fixations		
Tier 2 4 Scales	Body		
Tier 3 Themes	"Body Aches"	"Body Functions"	Body Parts"
Tier 4 Concepts	Cross (3,669 references)	Secure (3,332 references)	Face (1,498 references)
	Death (3,378 references)	Services (3,149 references)	Hand (1,007 references)
	Help (2,940 references)	Jobs (2,985 references)	Arm (565 references)
	Problem (2,163 references)		Foot (434 references)
			Heart (320 references)

The chapter is thematically divided into three parts that compose this "Vulnerable Body" scale: "Body Aches," "Body Functions," and "Body Parts." "Body Aches" is the most dominant theme and constitutes four concepts ordered by frequency: "Cross," "Death," "Help," and "Problem." "Body Functions," while not as prevalent as "Body Aches," offer striking imagery about how key issues are imagined as threats to the functions and capacities of the body politic. Concepts of "Secure," "Services," and "Jobs" lead this theme. The final theme that makes up the "Vulnerable Body" scale includes references to physical organs or appendages of "Body parts." While not as frequently used by the news media in its coverage, when deployed, the result is vivid bodily geography. Together, "Face," "Hand," "Arm," "Foot," and "Heart" exemplify the "Body Parts" theme. Using the framework of "racist dirt fixations," I analyze the ways that the body is geographically imagined as the nation in scaled and intersectional ways (table 2.1).

BODY ACHES: CROSS, DEATH, HELP, AND PROBLEM

In her epochal book *Borderlands/La Frontera*, Anzaldúa (1987) uses cultural theory to describe her own personal experience growing up in the borderlands:

> The U.S-Mexican border *es una herida abierta* where the Third World grates against the first and bleeds. And before a scab forms it hemorrhages again, the lifeblood of two worlds merging to form a third country—a border culture. Borders are set up to define the places that are safe and unsafe, to distinguish *us* from *them*. A border is a dividing line, a narrow strip along a steep edge. A borderland is a vague and undetermined place created by the emotional residue of an unnatural boundary. It is in a constant state of transition. The prohibited

and forbidden are its inhabitants. Los atravesados live here: the squint-eyed, the perverse, the queer, the troublesome, the mongrel, the mulato, the half-breed, the half dead; in short, those who cross over, pass over, or go through the confines of the "normal." (p. 25)

Her poetic and political writings point to the paradoxical state where the Global North meets the Global South at the USA-Mexico border "like an open wound" that affect the lives of people in the borderlands. And while both countries are considered North American, the difference in power, economies, and people are distinct as well as culturally and territorially marked. The academic work of Border Studies adopts an interdisciplinary Cultural Studies perspective and tends to focus on the "crossings" of this border as a metaphorical icon of analysis (Alvarez, 1995). The image of the border crossed is important because it opens up theoretical fields of mixing, blending, and hybridity that create localized cultures not as fixed, bounded communities but as constantly in flux (Rosaldo, 1989) due to unequal and dual state powers that interact with culture, traditions, and social identities (Anzaldúa, 1987).

Other border scholars critique the use of the border as image or icon (Cunningham, 2004; Heyman, 1994). Heyman (1994) argues that this type of Border Studies perspective does not critique the deterritorialization of neoliberal policies like NAFTA that affect labor and capital of both countries in this region. He further argues that more attention must focus on power holders and the coercive modes of territorial control, rather than on the experiences of borderland hybridity (Heyman, 1994). Likewise, Cunningham (2004) and Vila (2000) eschew the critique of hybridity because they claim it fails to forcefully analyze the political nature of crossing borders, especially where crossings can reinforce difference rather than hybridize.

To note, though, Border Studies have contributed political critiques to the dynamics of Borderlands culture, in particular, its critique of Whiteness and its modes of territorial supremacy that use terrorizing methods. For example, Anzaldúa (1987) writes:

Gringos in the U.S. Southwest consider the inhabitants of the borderlands transgressors, aliens—whether they possess documents or not, whether they're Chicanos, Indians or Blacks. Do not enter, trespassers will be raped, maimed, strangled, gassed, shot. The only "legitimate" inhabitants are those in power, the whites and those who align themselves with whites. Tension grips the inhabitants of the borderlands like a virus. Ambivalence and unrest reside there and death is no stranger.

Anzaldúa's poetic analysis becomes prophetic and describes the rise of racist, nativist vigilantes in the region that would peak in Arizona in April 2005 with the Minutemen Civil Defense Corps convergence on the border.

Below are two examples of the concept "Cross" (3,669 references). The concept "Cross" dominates the "Body Aches" theme of the body scale. The social construction of "crossing borders" here contributes to both camps of Border Studies. The first is from the *Arizona Republic* daily newspaper. The fact that this excerpt was published in 1997 offers helpful context here. So, after the defeat of Prop. 189 in California, the architects of Prop. 187 looked to other states for a successful replication. Arizona's "Save our State" attempted to replicate Prop. 187, but it failed to make the ballot in 1995. It was eventually successful, though, with "Protect Arizona Now," or Prop. 200 in 2004 (McDonnell, 1996). I will detail Prop. 200 further in this chapter.

Arizona Republic: "Border Deaths on Rise: Illegals'
Risk-Taking Reaches 'Epidemic' Levels"

When six Mexican illegal immigrants drowned while trying to *cross* a flooded ditch in Douglas last week, law officers said risky behavior by immigrants was a problem that had reached epidemic proportions.

That was spelled out Monday in a study by the University of Houston's Center for Immigration Research, which documented the deaths of almost 1,200 illegal immigrants from 1993 through 1996 on the U.S. border with Mexico.

Nestor Rodriguez, the center's director, said the study, "Death at the Border," is the first to attempt to count the number of people who died while trying to traverse the 1,600-mile boundary that separates Mexico from California, Arizona, New Mexico, and Texas.

"It's something like a plane crash full of people every year," Rodriguez said of the deaths of the 1,185 illegal immigrants. Of that total, 72 percent drowned and Mexico's border with Texas was by far the most deadly, accounting for 71 percent of the deaths [....] (Shaffer, 1997, p. A1)

This "blame the Brown victim" approach overlooks the political policy like "prevention through deterrence" and its deadly policy outcomes. Recall in the earlier chapter that this strategy began with "Operation Hold the Line" (in El Paso, Texas in 1993) and continued with "Operation Gatekeeper" (in San Diego, California in 1994), "Operation Safeguard" (in Nogales, Arizona in 1994), and "Operation Rio Grande" (in the Brownsville corridor that extends from the Lower Rio Grande Valley to Laredo, Texas in 1997; Andreas, 2000). Border Patrol staffing increased dramatically as walls and stadium-style lighting were placed in these border areas. To both deter people from crossing into the United States and to make apprehension easier in the remote areas, the "prevention through deterrence" approach pushed the migration path away from these safer urban areas into remote, mountainous, and desert terrain. So, in 1997, when this news article was published, the outcomes of this policy would affect Arizona's rise in crossings and deaths while the death toll was still high in Texas as well. Later, the full effect of this policy would make Arizona the center of the necropolitical deathscape among the border states.

Additionally, the use of the words "epidemic levels" in the headline raises the alarm on the number of crossings and deaths while also deprioritizing the human rights crisis inherent in these deaths by using a "disease" frame. "Racist dirt fixations" deploys science to justify racialization and frame these deaths as an "epidemic" like a contagious disease rather than a human rights crisis. Furthermore, it insinuates that the body politic has a social illness in the "risky behavior by immigrants" that results in fatalities when crossing.

Finally, in this news excerpt, Nestor Rodriguez, the director of the Center for Immigration Research, attempts to humanize the problem by comparing a commercial airplane crash in order to commensurate the disaster of these border deaths. Rodriguez states that border deaths are "something like a plane crash full of people every year." Most middle- and upper-class people have access to commercial planes as a means of transportation, so this example attempts to translate the plight of poor and working poor border-crossers into a scenario that is more relatable to middle-class or upper-class readers. Fatal airplane crashes, however, generally receive more sympathetic media coverage than any deaths in the border deserts.

The second example of the concept "Cross" is from the *Los Angeles Times* a few years before the Minuteman Civil Defense Corps convergence in 2005 in Arizona.

> *Los Angeles Times*: "Up in Arms at Mexico Border: A Newspaper Editor's Militia fulfills what He calls His Patriotic Duty to Thwart Illegal Immigrants. Some Fear Lawsuits or Even Deaths Could Result."
>
> If these were the days of frontier justice, newspaper editor Chris Simcox would fit right in. With a .45-caliber handgun strapped to his side, he rustles through river-bottom oaks and reeds, looking for outlaws.
>
> His prey: foreigners, and maybe terrorists, who illegally *cross* into the United States from Mexico. His posse: 600 citizens who share his frustration about the porous border.
>
> Simcox, owner and editor of the *Tombstone Tumbleweed*, has formed an armed militia to patrol the U.S.-Mexico border, fulfilling what he says is his patriotic duty to thwart illegal immigrants by placing them under citizen arrest. About a dozen members of the militia held their first strategy meeting Saturday at the O.K. Cafe, a sourdough biscuit's throw away from the corral where Marshal Virgil Earp, brothers Wyatt and Morgan, and buddy John "Doc" Holliday shot and killed three cowboys for carrying guns in town. [....] (Gorman, 2002, p. A19)

This passage describes planning for animalistic human roundups under the guise of a "citizen arrest," "frontier justice," and defense of land using a "posse" of "600 [White] citizens" all frustrated about a "porous border."

As I mentioned in the earlier chapter, Chris Simcox is a convicted pedophile and former California resident who moved to Arizona and published a newspaper, in the historic city of Tombstone, called the *Tombstone Tumbleweed*, which he used as an organizing platform for anti-immigrant militia patrols in 2002. This example demonstrates his efforts of using the Wild West Tombstone history as a media platform for White vigilantism that allows this journalist to associate "illegal immigrants" with "outlaws," "foreigners," "terrorist," and as Simcox's "prey" while describing his gun "strapped to his side." It is this type of uncritical White supremacy, veiled in Wild West romantic, nostalgic tropes in news media reporting that made him a cause célèbre of such news media venues as Fox News' Sean Hannity and CNN's Lou Dobbs (Lemons, 2013) before his incest pedophile conviction. Indeed, he was so popular that he made a brief attempt in 2010 to challenge Senator John McCain's U.S. senate seat in the Arizona Republican Primary (Cassidy, 2016).

But essentially, this type of romanticized reporting attempt to rewrite the Southwest history as a White history by ignoring that much of the Southwest has been intergenerationally Brown and Red because it was historically indigenous and part of Mexico until the Treaty of Guadalupe Hidalgo in 1848. This romanticism also revives issues of Manifest Destiny that helped to depopulate the native peoples in the Western frontier. "Gringos in the U.S. Southwest consider the inhabitants of the borderlands transgressors, aliens—whether they possess documents or not, whether they're Chicanos, Indians or Blacks" (Anzaldúa, 1987, p. 25). The brutalization framework makes sense of vigilante activities along the border (see chapter 2). Chris Simcox and other vigilantes do not see themselves as violating the law, but instead mimic the State's militarized posturing at the border that brutalizes both immigrant border-crossers and the general public alike. Thus, the militarized border mentality dehumanizes the public even beyond the border states, which can also be seen in the rise of the "alt-right"/neo-Nazi's support of Trump's border wall proposal.

The media, politicians, and public tend to treat the border deaths as the ultimate cost of personal risk-taking. However, that view is shortsighted and does not focus on power holders and the coercive modes of boundary maintenance. The "deterrence through prevention" policy (1993–2000) that pushed border-crossings from safer, urban locations to the harsh, deadly deserts was a type of premediated murder, justified as a cost of progress in defending the border.

In 1994, the U.S. Border Patrol acknowledged that Operation Gatekeeper would force migrants to take routes that placed them in "mortal danger" due to "extremes of heat and colds." For the immigration policy planners behind

Gatekeeper, the death and injury of migrants were not something to be avoided, but rather a useful "deterrent" to other potential border crossers. (Michaelwoski, 2007, p. 66, citing U.S. Border Patrol Strategic Plan: 1994 and Beyond)

Essentially, the militarization of the border created "killing deserts," which direct a "large percentage of migrants into the treacherous geography of the 'killing deserts' [that] constitute managed forms of violence that are inextricably linked to the racialization processes of American empire" (Rosas, 2006, p. 1).

Below is an example full of the concept "death" (3,378 references, that includes an aggregate of stemmed word die, dead, and death),

Arizona Republic: "MIGRANT *DEATHS* NEAR RECORD PACE"

Illegal immigrants are embarking on more *deadly* crossings through the Arizona desert than anywhere else along the U.S.–Mexican border. In fact, while other well-known border-crossing areas report substantial drops in immigrant *deaths*, Arizona is close to keeping up with last year's record-setting pace. The U.S. Border Patrol said 81 immigrants have *died* crossing the 350-mile Arizona-Mexican border so far this fiscal year, which ends Sept. 30. At the same time last year, the agency had recovered 82 bodies and closed out the year with 102 *deaths* [....] (Rozemberg, 2002, p. B1)

Allusions to a "record-setting pace" raise an alarm to the increase in deaths. "More deadly crossings though the Arizona desert than anywhere else" flags Arizona as a bottleneck of immigrants' crossings due to policy premeditations like "detention through deterrence" policies. "Closed out the year with 102 *deaths*" and "82 bodies" tally the shocking numbers of humans who died and who are reduced to bodies or numbers. And the lack of a human rights framework in the headline speaks to the reduction of immigrants to their dead bodies.

Border militarization policies treat immigrant border crossings as controllable and their lives expendable in maintaining the racialized national space. Recall from the prior chapter that Mbembé (2003) concept of Necropolitics, which refers to the process of colonization that allows the colonizer to decide who will live and who will die, helps to explain the use of the "killing deserts" (Rosas, 2006) as a border-crossing deterrent which is an exercise of state control over immigrant mortality. The militarized border region is a necropolitical deathscape that placed immigrants crossing the border in constant contact with the possibility of death that they become the "living dead" (Mbembé, 2001, p. 179).

Here, "Help" (2,940 references) comes in the form of 4,700 National Guard Troops, detention cells, and security technology.

Houston Chronicle: "Chertoff Calls Guest Worker Plan Key"

[....] Chertoff [Homeland Security Chief] said his staff has calculated that rounding up merely a tenth of the 12 million illegal immigrants in the United States would cost $9 billion to $10 billion a year.

"The round 'em up and detain 'em method is astronomically expensive," Chertoff said. Lawmakers sought assurances Thursday that the nearly $2 billion in supplemental funding for the border security passed by Congress last month would have a direct effect on stemming illegal immigration.

Chertoff said the money would *help* pay for the National Guard troops on the Southern border, add thousands of detention cells that would *help* immigration authorities end the "catch and release" of illegals from countries other than Mexico detained near the border, and pay for 40 miles of fence and 140 miles of vehicle barriers on the border.

The money would *help* speed the development of the ambitious Secure Border Initiative, which would use cameras, motion detectors, unmanned aerial vehicles, and other technology to keep the entire border under constant scrutiny, he said. Chertoff said there are signs that the deployment of 4,700 National Guard troops to the border area, to free up border patrol agents, is changing border activity.

In most sectors of the Southwest, arrests of people making illegal crossings have fallen 45 percent, an indicator that fewer people were trying to enter the United States, Chertoff said. (Hedges, 2006, p. A21)

The concept of help is again entangled with animal metaphors of "round ups" and "catch and release" discourse painting law enforcement like cowboys and anglers in this region (see chapter 4). Round ups have a specific meaning in the Southwest region as they evoke either public performances like rodeos and calf-roping or ranching purposes that drive cattle into a herd for branding, inspection, or shipment.

While "catch and release" imagery evoke angling or fishing using conservation methods, which implies this "astronomically expensive" policy is conserving immigrants rather than expelling or deterring immigrants from crossing the border. In regard to immigration, political conservatives claim "catch and release" as a racialized pejorative that critiques the release rather than detention of immigrants after apprehension. Conservatives see this as a way for immigrants to go underground once released from detainment on their own recognizances (Macías-Rojas, 2016). The program ended in August 2006 (Jordan, 2006). Either way, immigrants are portrayed as animals and law enforcement as hunters and wranglers. While "billions" have been spent on apprehending and releasing immigrants in this "astronomically expensive" policy, an additional $2 billion will help "stem" the problem with National Guard Troops, detention cells, and security technology.

In addition to seeing immigrants as terrorists, criminals, corpses, cattle, fish, prey, and a social disease, news reporting on the border also constructs immigrants as the "enemy" or a problem (2,163 references).

Albuquerque Journal: "U.S. PLANS TO PATCH BORDER GAPS: Some in N.M. Question Merit of Repairing Fence"

COLUMBUS—Portable lights, concrete barriers and a refurbished barbed-wire fence are the latest weapons planned in the war against illegal drug trafficking and immigration on New Mexico's border with Mexico. But some area residents question whether the improvements will be an effective deterrent along the vast stretch of desert.

"We have a *problem*. We're being invaded by Mexico," said Ralph Johnson, 71, whose family runs a 100,000-acre ranch along the border west of Columbus and farms chile, onions, and corn.

"They need the Army in here, that's the only solution." [. . .] (Romo, 1997, p. A1)

The immigrant invasion metaphor is a paradox in that it is simple and complicated at once (see chapter 5). There is an anxiety about immigration in relation to geographic contagion—immigrants are seen as intruders that will take over the nation. This relates to a complicated, racialized disgust complex where boundary violation is both bodily and territorial, an ideology that I detailed in chapter 1. At the heart of feelings of disgust is the violation between the boundary of animal and human (Rozin & Fallon, 1987) and immigrants are seen as animals, among other violating things. Since immigrants reside and work in the nation, magical thinking permits imagined contagion to spread through this contact. Chavez (2008) uses what he terms the "Quebec Model" to make sense of this fear of immigrant invasion. He notes that this invasion theme arose in the 1970s and has evolved to fear immigrants who maintain socially and linguistically separate lives from the rest of U.S. American Society, much like French-speaking Quebecers seeking independence in Canada. For Chavez, the invasion theme is based on the racial assumption that Spanish speaking Mexican immigrants do not want to integrate but instead want to reconquer the region that was once Mexico through immigration.

Pushing this argument a little further, this is much like how White settler colonialism conquered the Southwest during Manifest Destiny, but now it is imagined in reverse: immigrants are somehow like settler colonialists who conquer by residing and inhabiting the land through a process of geographic contagion. Santa Ana (2002) also notes the robust use of "invasion" metaphors to describe immigrants in the media coverage about Proposition 187 in California. The war metaphor used in the news coverage of that campaign stresses a violent aggression that simultaneously ignores the nation's over-all immigration experience of simply seeking the "American Dream" and reduces the immigrants' intent to warfare. This simplification ignores history, empirical evidence, and reason. The rancher Ralph Johnson's quote above reflects this simplification and expresses disgust to boundary violations and the "patching of gaps" in fences and barriers by offering the "only solution" to the problem: an "army."

BODY FUNCTIONS: "SECURITY," "SERVICES," AND "JOBS."

"Body Functions," while not as prevalent as "Body Aches," offer strik-ing imagery of both the nation and immigrants and refers to functions and capacities of the body. Concepts of "Security," "Services," and "Jobs" lead this theme.

To better understand this White nativist fear of immigrants taking social services, background on how neoliberal reform policies changed the nation's economy and citizen reactions to those changes is needed. Calavita (1996) offers the idea of "Balance Budget Conservatism" as a way to understanding of how national public attention was directed away from austere realities of neoliberalism in shaping the nation's economic and job structures and placed upon immigrants as the source of all evils in a type of scapegoating scenario. Calavita (1996) argues that between World War II and the mid-1970s, a "Cri-sis of Fordism" arose for most advanced industrial countries that operated on Fordist principles of production and factory work. As profits for big compa-nies began to fall in the 1970s, management responded by cutting labor costs. Jobs were thus eliminated or exported to poorer countries and annual average wages began to drop. "Contingent workers" who work part-time or for short contracts became a central cost-cutting measure, making up one-third of the workforce around the time of Prop. 187 (Calavita, 1996) and currently make up 20 percent of job force (Noguchi, 2018).

"Balance Budget conservatism" helped to dismantle the welfare state, which forced workers to sell their labor on market terms (Calavita, 1996). Corporations then turned their profit-making toward financial transactions, which drained investment from the already faltering industrial sector. Merg-ers, acquisitions, and hostile takeovers in the 1980s also helped to financialize the economy that created increased worker uncertainty. Wealth polarization increased and the middle class dwindled. The public was angry and focused on the size of the federal deficit and rising tax rates, which led to "deficit-mania." Based on these observations from past eras, "Balance Budget con-servatism" is anti-government, suspicious of government spending, resistant to taxes, and focused on the taxpayer over citizen as a central agent to civic life. Furthermore, it deflects responsibility from the corporations' cost-cutting mania that led the economy into the post-Fordist crisis and instead focuses on pressuring the government to adopt austerity measures that impact the most economically vulnerable (Calavita, 1996).

Calavita (1996) contends that this was the political and economic context for Proposition 187 (1994), the "Save our State" initiative. In addition, California in particular experienced a recession, defense cutbacks, and race riots, and the state's mechanism of ballot box initiatives all contributed to the context in which undocumented immigrants targets received citizens' blame. Calavita argues that Prop. 187—a ban against undocumented immigrants accessing health and educational services—was an example of symbolic law and a political statement that allowed the public to express nativist discontent not only to undocumented immigrants but also to the federal government for failing to stop border crossings. Five years later, after several lawsuits challenged the proposition, it was voided by a court-approved mediation. The public rhetoric of Prop. 187 constructed immigrants as an illness, particularly the image of the parasite, to describe immigrants' role in relation to its "host" (Inda, 2000). For example, public discourse used parasitic images to describe immigrants' use of social services (Suárez-Orozco, 1996). These lines of thinking continue in news discourse and issues related to "security" for terrorism and crime, as well as social services.

Following is an example of the leading concept "secure" (3,332 references), where the focus is not on crime and terrorism but on securing state resources from undocumented immigrants.

Albuquerque Journal: "Border Governors Blast Illegals:
Three Ask Congress to Repay State Costs"

Washington, Border-state governors appealed to Congress Wednesday to stop the flow of illegal immigrants into the country and repay states for billions spent to educate, medically treat and incarcerate them.

Florida Gov. Lawton Chiles told the Senate Appropriations Committee that the influx of illegal immigrants "is battering our shores today, unleashing yet another crisis" just as Hurricane Andrew did two years ago.

The federal government, said California Gov. Pete Wilson, "Must *secure* our borders, and it must pay the bill for illegal immigration." [....] (Abrams, 1994, p. A9)

The two border governors offer some interesting rationales in "blasting" undocumented immigrants. Then Florida Governor Chiles likens immigration to a natural disaster in "battering our shores" and "unleashing yet another crisis." He alludes to the damage caused by Hurricane Andrew in 1992.

"Unleash" implies releasing an animal like a dangerous dog or setting a powerful force into motion from its constraints. One of the tropes of "racist dirt fixations" is religious justification for racial hierarchy that refers to immigration like biblical plagues. The nation is imagined as an inhabited, cultured geographic area that suffers immigration as destructive forces of nature, either by animals (see chapter 4) or climate (see chapter 5).

Former California Governor Pete Wilson was a strident advocate of Prop. 187. "California Governor Pete Wilson deserves as much credit as anyone for framing immigration as an exclusively federal responsibility. He has effectively depicted his state as the helpless victim of a failed federal effort to control U.S. borders" (Skerry, 1995, p. 73). He frames security as a federal government issue and the federal government "must pay the bill for illegal immigration . . . for billions spent to educate, medically treat and incarcerate" immigrants. Mehan (1997) explains some of the rationale of supporters of Prop. 187:

> Proponents of the initiative made statements such as "While our own citizens and legal residents go wanting, those who choose to enter our country illegally get royal treatment at the expense of the California taxpayer," and "[The People of California] have suffered and are suffering economic hardship caused by the presence of illegal aliens in this state," and "illegal immigrants take jobs away from law abiding citizens," and "illegal aliens are an overwhelming drain on the State's social services." (p. 259)

The next section elaborates on his notion that immigrants are a burden to state public services.

Calavita (1996) argues that the goal of Balanced Budget conservatism was the protection of the taxpayer interests, but this prioritization "'stigmatizes poorer, property-less people as somehow less than fully citizens' (citing Plotkin & Scheuerman, 1994, p. 31). Those who are not even citizens—indeed, are not legal residents—are the ideal target of blame, more undeserving even than the traditional "undeserving poor" (p. 296). Immigrants then become ideal targets for stealing social "services" (3,149 references) that "hurt" the nation:

Arizona Republic: "MIGRANTS HURTING NATION,
SOME SAY TAKING TOO MUCH"

> And most poll respondents said illegal immigrants are taking more in terms of government *services* than they are giving back by paying taxes and strengthening the economy.
> The newcomers are straining the system by committing more crime and demanding more schooling, health care and other social *services* than this country would otherwise have to supply, some respondents said.

Glendale resident Curtis Pruitt, 63, a retired welder, thinks law enforcement is hard put to deal with illegal immigrants.

"They're stealing everything they can get their hands on," Pruitt said. "There's a lot more crime since they started letting them across the border . . . . They're the ones who are getting this drive-by shooting started and keeping it going." (Kelly, 2001, p. A6)

The preceding news article shows a concern that immigrants do not "give back" by paying taxes and this crime of "stealing" weakens the economy and "hurts" the nation. The sentiments that drove the popularity of Prop. 187 did not die when it was voided in California and continues to influence the border region and the nation long after the proposition's defeat. The focus on White suffering of middle-class Californians would continue to reverberate to Arizona as a "ground zero" in the "border war" as well as to the current national climate. However, this White suffering continues to subordinate undocumented immigrants then and now.

Ideologically, the rhetoric of white injury has played its part in the maintenance of larger economic, political, and cultural structures. When dislocated from these informing contexts, the rhetoric of white injury serves to legitimate the containment, exploitation, and surveillance of communities of color. Undocumented immigrants are represented as criminal and parasitic, while white middle-class citizens are cast as the only ones capable of feeling injury and suffering. What is masked, as a result, is the way the rhetorical construction of "the people of California" as white, middle-class and "suffering" is connected to the on-going injury and subordination of other aggrieved groups. (Cacho, 2000, p. 415)

Prop. 187 inspired copycat initiatives across the nation. Additional nativist concerns that immigrants impersonate voters to gain services would materialize with Arizona's Proposition 200, the "Arizona Taxpayer and Citizen Protection" supported by a citizen's group called Protect Arizona Now in 2004 (Campbell, 2011). It attempted to prevent undocumented immigrants from voting in elections and receiving public benefits, which is ironic given it is against the law for undocumented citizens to vote in the first place. But again, this speaks to the "symbolic" nature of nativism in that White nativism imagines that undocumented immigrants are impersonating citizens in order to gain access to privileges like voting and social services, in which the citizen taxpayer is portrayed as the ultimate victim. President Trump would also make these claims when he created and then disbanded a panel to study the alleged voter fraud based on his belief that he lost the popular vote in 2016 to Democrat Hillary Clinton due to millions of illegally cast ballots (Wagner, 2018). Maine Secretary of State Matthew Dunlap served on the disbanded panel and described his experience "bizarre" after reviewing 8,000 documents that contained no evidence of widespread voter fraud (Rosenburg, 2018).

Public attitudes like Pruitt, the retired welder quoted above, would eventually lead to Arizona's SB 1070 (2010), the "Support Our Law Enforcement and Safe Neighborhoods Act" that proposed the use of racial profiling by law enforcement against immigrants. This wave of nativism attempts to formalize a *petit apartheid* system by driving immigrants further underground. Indeed, Archbishop Desmond Tutu (2011), a freedom fighter against South Africa's apartheid policy, stated, "Abominations such as apartheid do not start with an entire population suddenly becoming inhumane. They start here [with Arizona's SB1070]."

Jobs are treated like another property that immigrants "steal." Like the debates in California over Prop. 187, these accusations depict social life as a zero-sum game, framing immigration as an issue in which immigrant gain is the nation's loss, that is based on an *us versus them* relationship (Mehen, 1997). Following is an example of the concept "jobs" (2,985 references):

Arizona Republic: "HOUSE OKS 2 BILLS ON IMMIGRANTS"

Cracking down on illegal immigrants, the House passed two bills Wednesday: one that focuses on law enforcement and another that would let states deny public-school education to children in this country illegally.

Only the first is believed to have a chance of being signed into law by President Clinton.

The Senate is expected to reject the second bill, which passed 254-175, and Clinton has said that he would veto the measure, which would exempt children who are already enrolled in school.

Supporters in the House said the bill would remove one incentive that foreigners have for coming here illegally, and it would allow voters to decide whether they want to bear the expense of educating children who should not be in the country.

"This bill secures America's borders, penalizes alien smugglers, expedites the removal of criminal and illegal aliens, prevents illegal aliens from taking American *jobs* and ends non-citizens' abuse of the welfare system," said Rep. Lamar Smith, R-Texas, who introduced the legislation. [....] (Associated Press, 1996, p. A1)

These two 1996 bills refer to President Clinton's Illegal Immigration Reform and Immigrant Responsibility Act (IIRIRA) and the Anti-Terrorism and Effective Death Penalty Act (AEDPA) that further militarized the border and criminalized immigrants making them easier to deport (see chapter 2). IIRIRA also included a measure that prevented undocumented immigrants from in-state residency tuition rates for postsecondary education, unless the same benefit is provided to all eligible U.S. America citizens regardless

of their state residency, forcing many to pay out of state tuition rates even
if they resided in the that state for many years (Villarraga-Orjuela & Kerr,
2017). Ultimately, the nation and its resources are treated like White private
property that Brown criminal aliens steal, "take, and "abuse." Cacho (2012)
writes:

> The everyday conduct of "illegal" but law-abiding immigrants is often made
> intelligible as "criminal" by likening immigrants' actions to "property crimes,"
> which are characterized as the theft, fraudulent use, and/or depreciation of
> someone else's entitlement. When immigration opponents appeal to concerns
> over resources by portraying immigration as an infringement on rightful own-
> ership (e.g., immigrants take jobs that belong to American citizens), they are
> appealing to the expectation of white entitlement. (Cacho, 2012, p. 26)

In addition, Cheryl Harris's (1992) groundbreaking work on Whiteness as
property analyzes the historical and legal coevolution of White supremacy
and property rights that justified the enslavement of Blacks and the seizure of
Native American lands. "Whiteness and property share a common premise—
a conceptual nucleus—of a right to exclude. This conceptual nucleus has
proven to be a powerful center around which whiteness as property has taken
shape" (p. 1714). Blacks were excluded from owning their bodies and labor
with slavery and Whites seized indigenous lands by defining White uses of
land (agriculture, foundations, buildings, etc.) over indigenous uses (hunting and gathering) to claim first ownership by law. Lipsitz (1998) similarly
argues that there is *Possessive investment in Whiteness* today that impacts
housing, education, wealth accumulation, and employment. "Whiteness has
a cash value…[and] is…a social fact, an identity created and continued with
all-too-real consequences for the distribution of wealth, prestige, and opportunity" (Lipsitz, 1998, p. vii). Thus, Lipsitz (1998) echoes Harris' exclusion
principle where the "whiteness has been characterized, not by an inherent
unifying characteristic, but by the exclusion of others deemed to be 'not
white'" (p. 1736).

Thus, when then presidential hopeful Donald Trump called Mexicans who
cross the border without proper papework "rapists" (Lee, 2015, citing Donald
Trump), he tapped into a racialized fear about crime and also metaphorical,
imagined nightmares about the future of the Whiteness of the nation. The
image of a rapist aligns with the pillaging imagery that public discourse
generates about nation at "war" with undocumented immigration. The White
nation is raped by a Brown border-crosser when the nation's nurturing
resources and social services are not secured from immigrant criminality. The
news often portrays the border as a "vulnerable place in danger of being violated" (Ono & Sloop, 2002, p. 50) that Trump's use of rape helps to amplify

in his justification for his border wall. Trump's rape accusation also expresses a nativist fear of miscegenation and race mixing. While Trump's comment echo long-standing racial fears that men of color rape White women, the stark truth is that the victims of rape in the militarized border region are mostly undocumented immigrant women (Falcon, 2006).

BODY PARTS

The final theme that makes up the "Vulnerable Body" scale is not frequently used by the border news coverage but demonstrates vivid imagery on how the body is geographically imagined within the "Body Parts" theme. Here the body politic metaphor, which had originated in classical political thought and reached its zenith in medieval and premodern times, still succeeds in contemporary times in a more literal form with "body parts."

The imagery of a racially changed face (1,498 references) expresses the anxiety of Whiteness, its challenged supremacy, and its future. The following article offers an extended analysis of these troubling feelings Whiteness expresses about Brownness.

Albuquerque Journal: "ETHNIC SHIFTS STOKE ANXIETY CHANGING
FACE OF U.S. STIRS DOUBTS ABOUT MELTING POT"

WASHINGTON—They come in ways that are ordinary, desperate and mundane—jetting into New York aboard commercial airliners, scrambling off boats on the Florida shore, and trudging into New Mexico across the desert border.

But no matter how they get here, those who come, both legally and illegally, arrive in an environment that ranges from anxious to alarmed: 53 percent of Americans favor denying public education to children of the nation's 3 million to 5 million illegal immigrants, according to a recent CNN poll. (Parker, 1996, p. A1)

Chavez (2001) notes the "changing face" image in his research that analyzes popular magazine covers. His example is a visual depiction of many faces (*Time* magazine cover "Changing Faces of America" July 8, 1985) with mostly Yellow, Brown, with one White face populating the cover. He contends that it is a way to communicate that the nation's changing face is non-White, non-European. He argues that this subtle message about the changing demographics of the nation is not overtly alarmist.

In contrast, this news article above is highly alarmist, admitting that immigrants arrive to national attitudes that "ranges from anxious to alarmed." The discourse about the "face" of the nation naturalizes Whiteness as the default race and the "change" as racial one. The notion that "face" of the United

States can change also taps into ableist feelings of disfigurement and disability. The lead headline "Ethnic Shifts Stoke Anxiety" helps to frame the "changing face" concept in that it "stirs doubts about the melting pot" model of assimilation and acculturation. Bonilla-Silva (2003) clarifies the "melting pot" concept:

> The idea of the melting pot has a long history in the American tradition, but it really was a notion that was extended exclusively to white immigrants. That pot never included people of color: Blacks, Chinese, Puerto Ricans, etc., could not melt into the pot. They could be used as wood to produce the fire for the pot, but they could not be used as material to be melted into the pot.

Under an additional sub-headed section titled, "Whites as a minority," the news article focuses on "changing the color of the country":

> [....] But to many White Americans, the *face* of America is changing too fast.
> "It's simply shifting the ethnic balance of the country very radically," says Peter Brimelow, author of last year's best-selling book, "Alien Nation," which argued for suspending all immigration, in part to keep Whites from being outnumbered.
> Brimelow, a naturalized U.S. citizen from Britain, argues that the country is experiencing "an ethnic transformation without precedent in the history of the world."
> But Americans are too squeamish to confront the racial and ethnic dimensions of immigration. Whites, he says, don't hate the newcomers, but they are locked in a struggle for both identity and power.
> "They see their country transformed and they're deeply alarmed by it," Brimelow says. "They want to know, 'Whose country is this?' " [....] (Parker, 1996, p. A1)

The Southern Poverty and Law Center, which tracks and fights hate groups and extremists, describes Peter Brimelow as "a leading anti-immigration activist and author of the bestselling anti-immigrant tome Alien Nation, is the president of the VDARE Foundation, a nonprofit that warns against the polluting of America by non-Whites, Catholics, and Spanish-speaking immigrants." The fear that the face of nation is no longer White but now non-White is based on fear, disgust, and abjection. It speaks of both racial and geographic contamination within embodied imagery of a White national "face" changing into a non-White face. It also speaks for perceiving this change as disfigurement and disability. Haney-Lopez (2006) argues that "whiteness possesses a fundamental, inestimable value for whites" (p. 142). White identity and power are threatened by demographic shifts that "pollute" the White body politic.

The next most frequent "body parts" concept is the "hand" (1,007 references). The following is an example of this concept:

Albuquerque Journal: "COLUMBUS ON BORDER OF TOLERANCE"

Town residents form group to uphold their rights in area thick with Border Patrol agents, history of tension
COLUMBUS—Tension between residents and green-clad federal agents has eased over the past year in this tiny border town. Since last year, several residents said, it appears that Border Patrol checkpoints are less frequent and that agents have been less aggressive.
But while some locals say they welcome warmer relations with the U.S. Border Patrol, others quietly fume over what they see as the agency's sometimes heavy *hand*.
"They have the attitude that we are slaves on a plantation or something, and we should just be grateful, no matter how they treat us," said 66-year-old Marilyn Steffen, an 18-year Columbus resident who refers to Border Patrol agents with loaded terms such as "bullies" and "Gestapo."
Former Columbus Mayor Carlos Ogden said the Border Patrol's relationship with the community grew more tense as the agency beefed up its presence in the area in recent years.
Agents and their surveillance equipment became more visible, and many new agents did not know local residents, Ogden said.
But in mid-1999, a group of residents, fed up with frequent highway checkpoints and questioning by the Border Patrol, formed a group called Citizens United for Rights on the Border, or CURB, aimed at protecting their constitutional rights.
Longtime residents chafed at Border Patrol questions "Where are you coming from? Where are you going?" that agents use to sniff out potential drug traffickers and immigrant smugglers.
CURB put up signs around town informing residents about their rights and urging them to call a hot line with complaints. [....] (Romo, 2000, p. A1)

In the prior chapter, I argued that a necropolitical deathscape not only exists at the border but also beyond into the interior of the nation and affects not just undocumented immigrants but also citizens and legal residents especially those imagined to racially resemble them. The Chandler incident described in the introduction chapter is an example of this. The example above is another example of this. "Locals" and "residents" "fume" over "frequent" "checkpoints" and "aggressive" "agents" who use a "heavy *hand*." Rasmussen and Brown (2005) analyze the body politic as a spatial metaphor that link citizens to particular geographic relationships. They argue that historically, the king's body holds a central place in this organic metaphor and both his hands and arms tend to represent the royal military. Rasmussen and Brown continue, "Heavy hand" here represents the Border Patrol's enforcement efforts (not the king's but the nation's hand) and reduce residents to "slaves on a planta-tion" and in need of "uphold[ing] their rights in area thick with Border Patrol agents" who act like "bullies" and "Gestapo." Former Columbus Mayor noted the relationship between the community and Border Patrol "grew more tense as the agency beefed up." The use of "beef" is an interesting term (see chapter 5). Beef, muscle and masculinity tend to be associated with each other in popular culture (Stibbe, 2004) and seems to compliment the mas-culinized, "heavy hand" association with enforcement in this example. In response, residents created CURB to protect "their constitutional rights" from "frequent highway checkpoints and questioning" like "'Where are you com-ing from? Where are you going?' that agents use to sniff out potential drug traffickers and immigrant smugglers."

The next most frequent "body parts" concept is "Arm" (565 references). Below is an example of this concept:

Arizona Republic: "BORDER BUILDUP TO BE SLOW ARIZONA
WON'T GET EXTRA AGENTS FOR 4–7 MONTHS"

The buildup of Border Patrol personnel and equipment announced Monday amid hopeful fanfare won't happen quickly and may not make much difference anyway.

Even supporters of the latest federal effort control illegal immigration in Arizona acknowledge that 100 more Border Patrol agents, two helicopters and heavy-steel fencing through Nogales isn't enough.

The border won't be getting the new agents for another four to seven months, Border Patrol spokesman Rob Daniels said, adding that it takes that long to recruit, hire and train them.

The Border Patrol, the enforcement *arm* of the Immigration and Naturaliza-tion Service, agrees that the additional resources are not enough to stop people from coming in, but anything helps, Daniels said.

"It's not quite as much as we had hoped for, but it's going to make a differ-ence," Daniels said from his Tucson offices, which oversee operations along 281 miles of border from the New Mexico line to west of Nogales. The Yuma sector covers the remaining 97 miles of Arizona's border.

Daniels said he hopes the agency's increased visibility, called "Operation Safeguard," will prevent at least some entries, and reduce crime in border towns like El Paso's "Operation Hold the Line" has done.

Hold the Line, which began in September 1993, positioned 400 Border Patrol agents along a 20-mile stretch of the Rio Grande, along with helicopter surveil-lance. In the first few months, apprehensions of illegal immigrants dropped 81 percent. [....] (Medrano Leslie, 1994, p. A1)

This is an example of the Clinton administration's (1993–2001) INS offen-sive-border strategy called "prevention through deterrence." This strategy

began with "Operation Hold the Line" (in El Paso, Texas in 1993) and continued with "Operation Gatekeeper" (in San Diego, California in 1994), "Operation Safeguard" (in Nogales, Arizona in 1994), and "Operation Rio Grande"
(in the Brownsville corridor that extends from the Lower Rio Grande Valley
to Laredo, Texas in 1997; see chapter 2). While the headline claims the "Border buildup will be slow," this is in stark contrast to the study's finding (see
chapter 5) that the border and its buildup is imagined and reported as growing and active phenomenon. So while "supporters of the latest federal effort
to control illegal immigration in Arizona" lament that the "100 more Border
Patrol agents, two helicopters and heavy-steel fencing through Nogales isn't
enough," compared to the "400 Border Patrol agents" for Operation Hold the
Line, Border Patrol spokesman Rob Daniels states, "It's not quite as much as
we had hoped for, but it's going to make a difference." Rasmussen and Brown
(2005) argue that historically the king's hands and arms tend to represent the
royal military in the body politic and in this example, the Border Patrol is "the
enforcement *arm* of the Immigration and Naturalization Service." In this and
the prior example, "arm" and "hand," respectively, represent the border law
enforcement of the contemporary body politic.

The next most frequent "body part" concept is "foot" (434 references). The
following is an example of this concept:

Arizona Republic: "7-DAY ORDEAL LEAVES
ILLEGAL HURTING, BROKE"

Juan Carlos Bernal never knew what he was in for when he left his native
Mexico City, hoping to steal easily across the border. Instead, he was led into
a desolate desert and abandoned. Alone for nearly seven days, he survived by
drinking rainwater from puddles and finally by surrendering to the Border Patrol
he'd hoped to evade.

The 22-year-old bus driver began his journey easily enough on Aug. 17 when
he caught a flight from Mexico City to Tijuana. Determined to earn money to
support his family, he put his life in the hands of a smuggler who took him by
bus to the border across from southern Arizona.

In exchange for $500 at the border and $500 on arrival in Los Angeles, the
coyote promised to guide him through the desert.

Instead, the man abandoned Bernal in the wilderness on the first day out,
leaving him to crisscross the gulches, hills and flatlands of the unforgiving land
by *foot*.

Almost a week later, Bernal was lost and alone, some 1,500 miles from home.
His stomach and pockets empty, Bernal's hopes were gone. Now he stood at the
side of the road, his black hair matted into wet spikes by a monsoon soaking,
ready to turn himself in.

"I came with the dream of earning some money. But this is as far as I got,"
he said, surveying the prickly terrain surrounding the two-lane highway.

Ironically, it was the Border Patrol that came to Bernal's rescue. Agent Kevin Liles pulled over when Bernal flagged him down on Arizona 86 about 9 a.m. on Aug. 27.

"Do you want a ride? Are you hungry?" Liles asked in Spanish as he approached.

"Si," Bernal said, relief washing over his tired face. "Tengo hambre y sed (I'm hungry and thirsty)."

Liles dug into his lunch box and offered an apple and a bottle of cold water to a grateful Bernal before starting his paperwork. Bernal answered questions calmly and unemotionally until he was asked how much money he had with him.

"I don't have even one peso," he said. As he emptied his pockets, Bernal pulled out a small stack of snapshots, wet from the rain. ' 'This is my nephew and my 3-year-old daughter," he managed to say before tears of defeat overwhelmed him. [....] (Sevilla, 1999, p. A1)

This example shows the struggles of crossing the Arizona border without documents. Juan Carlos Bernal is portrayed as a victim of human smugglers who "abandoned" him (this is repeated twice) in the "unforgiving land." And while he started his trek from his home in Mexico City by plane and then by bus, he hired a smuggler to take him across the desert terrain of Arizona "by *foot*," all the while showing how he lost more and more money and became hungrier and thirstier as his trek continued. Rasmussen and Brown (2005) further argue that peasants are historically associated with feet in the body politic since the body is naturally hierarchical and the "internal spatial structure and orientation are key to conveying a normative order within the space of the polity" (p. 473). Thus, the head

being the highest point on the body suggests superiority and greater significance that all other parts of the body, while lower organs like the belly or appendages like the feet connote worse or less important parts of the body politic . . . . The peasants are embodied in the feet, the lowest point in the image that is furthest from the head. (p. 473)

Walking or being a pedestrian is a sign of poverty in Arizona. "Middle and upper classes rarely walk or bike in Arizona heat unless they are engaged in exercise and dressed in special 'work-out' clothes. They might be observed walking if a leashed dog is attached to their bodies" (Romero, 2006, p. 462). Bernal's working-class status as a "bus driver" in Mexico is reduced to abject poverty in the Arizona desert where "Bernal was lost and alone, some 1,500 miles from home. His stomach and pockets empty, Bernal's hopes were gone." The news framing of Bernal's tale helps to deflect any premeditation of the "prevention through deterrence" border policy that attempted to use this deadly desert as a deterrent to border crossing, and "ironically" portrays "the Border Patrol that came to Bernal's rescue" as the hero of his tale who asked him in Spanish "Do you want a ride? Are you hungry?" and "offered an apple and a bottle of cold water" from his "lunch box."

The next leading "body parts" concept is "heart" (320 references). The following is an example of the concept:

> *Albuquerque Journal*: "'FLOOD' OF ILLEGALS WASHES INTO N.M."
>
> [....] Dona Ana County Sheriff's Lt. West Gilbreath said that deputies have also reported increased numbers of illegals making their way north.
>
> "This whole area is like an interstate for them," Gilbreath said. "This is the way they go because they can stick to the roads and stay near civilization instead of going through the mountains or the desert."
>
> Border Patrol agents also say that a different type of illegal immigrant is trying to head north.
>
> Border Patrol agent Cruz said that more Mexicans from central and southern Mexico are making their way to the United States.
>
> Cruz said that most have never tried crossing the border, so they are easier to catch. However, he said, because they have traveled much farther, they are more determined to keep trying to make it north.
>
> "They're from the interior and want to go farther north to the very *heart* of America," Cruz said. (Gonzalez, 1995, p. A1)

Rasmussen and Brown (2005), in their analysis of the body politic, argue that the spiritual "heart" of the body polity is the priesthood (p. 473). In this example, the heart is not reflecting any modern version of religion here, though the "flood" imagery in the headline does contain biblical meaning (see chapter 5). Instead, the discourse suggests that immigrants are a type of blood clot or virus/bacteria that use the nation's roadways "like an interstate" much like veins and arteries carry blood, nutrients, or illness through a body. A "different type of illegal immigrant is trying to head north," where more people from central and southern Mexico attempt to cross the border and "because they have traveled much farther, they are more determined to keep trying to make it north." So while the headline starts with "flood" imagery, it switches to describing immigrants like determined agents of harm intent on making it "farther north to the very *heart*" of the United States, supposedly for negative intentions. In this sense "heart" is not used in the more medieval sense of the body politic that we still find with the "hand," "arm," and "foot" concepts, instead we see a more modern understanding of the body in relation to veins, arteries, clots, bacteria, and viruses. Chapter 6 explores the more modern understanding of the body politic in relation to contemporary understanding of medical disease and immunology.

In conclusion, the foundational scale of the body shows the success of the body politic and its persistence as a spatial metaphor into contemporary times. "Racist Dirt Fixations" construct border-crossing as "dirt," a racial violation of religious, scientific and sexual ordered systems. Within this "Vulnerable Body" scale, the most dominate theme is "Body Aches," with the leading concepts of "Cross," "Death," "Help," and "Problem" that reveal the necropolitical deathscape at the border and the fear of racialized geographic contagion the drives the border policies that shape this landscape. Immigrants are either reduced to their deaths and their dead bodies, or they are imagined as wild animals that need capture or "rounding up." Vigilantes, brutalized by the militarized border posture, mimic this violence by "hunting" immigrants in an attempt to stop what they imagine is an "invasion."

In the second most frequent theme, "Body Functions," the concepts "Secure," "Services," and "Jobs" show how the public blamed immigrants for the neoliberal transformations to the national economic order that created more social inequality and economic insecurity. The public imagined immigrants as agents intent on diminishing the nation's function and capacity by draining social services that creates injury both to the taxpayer and the nation. Immigrants are racially seen as natural disaster, thieves, and rapists to the nation that is constructed as injured, suffering, and White. While "Body Parts" theme of this body scale was the least frequent theme, "Face," "Hand," "Arm," "Foot," and "Heart" concepts show that body politic metaphor still persists in more literal ways that speak to a fear of disability or disfigurement with the "changing face" of the nation. "Hand," "Arm," and "Foot" concepts show how border enforcement is seen either as a "heavy hand" or "arm," while immigrants who must cross the border by "foot" are poor and associated with the lowest valued part of the body politic. "Heart" shows a medicalized understanding of the body politic that is more modern and imagines immigrants as a type of blood clot or virus/bacteria that travels to the "heart" of the United States. I demystify NRNR to show how the body scale is geographically imagined as a White nation in intersectional ways.

The next chapter will review the scale of the house.

REFERENCES

Abrams, J. (1994). Border governors blast illegals: Three ask Congress to repay state costs. *Albuquerque Journal*, June 23, 1994, A9.

Alvarez, R. R., Jr. (1995). The Mexican-US border: The making of an anthropology of borderlands. *Annual Review of Anthropology*, 24(1), 447–470.

Andreas, P. (2000). *Border Games: Policing the US-Mexico Divide*. Ithaca: Cornell University Press.

Anzaldúa, G. (1987). *Borderlands: La frontera*. San Francisco: Auntie Lute.

Associated Press. (1996). House OKS 2 bills on immigrants. *Arizona Republic*, September 26, 1996, A1.

Bonilla-Silva, E. (2003). Me, my race & I: Slideshow transcripts. *www.pbs.org*. Retrieved from https://www.pbs.org/race/005_MeMyRaceAndI/005_01-transcripts-04.htm.

Cacho, L. M. (2000). "The people of California are suffering": The ideology of white injury in discourses of immigration. *Journal for Cultural Research, 4*(4), 389–418.

Calavita, K. (1996). The new politics of immigration: "Balanced-budget conservatism" and the symbolism of Proposition 187. *Social Problems, 43*(3), 284–305.

Campbell, K. M. (2011). The road to SB 1070: How Arizona became ground zero for the immigrants' rights movement and the continuing struggle for Latino civil rights in America. *Harvard Latino Law Review, 14*, 1.

Cassidy, M. (2016). Chris Simcox sentenced in child sex abuse case. AZ Central, July 11, 2016. Retrieved from https://www.azcentral.com/story/news/local/phoenix/2016/07/11/chris-simcox-sentenced-child-sex-abuse/86948200/.

Chavez, L. (2008). *The Latino Threat: Constructing Immigrants, Citizens, and the Nation.* Palo Alto: Stanford University Press.

Cunningham, H. (2004). Nations rebound? Crossing borders in a gated globe. *Identities: Global Studies in Culture and Power, 11*(3), 329–350.

Douglas, M. (1966). *Purity and Danger.* New York: Routledge.

Falcon, S. (2006). "National security" and the violation of women: Militarized border rape at the U.S.-Mexico border. In Incite! Women of Color Against Violence (Eds.), *Color of Violence: The INCITE! Anthology* (pp. 119–129). Cambridge, MA: South End Press.

Gonzalez, R. C. (1995). "Flood" of illegals washes into N.M. *Albuquerque Journal*, February 19, 1995, A1.

Gorman, T. (2002). Up in arms at Mexico border: A newspaper editor's militia fulfills what he calls his patriotic duty to thwart illegal immigrants. Some fear lawsuits or even deaths could result. *Los Angeles Times*, December 8, 2002, A19.

Haney-López, I. (2006). *White by Law 10th Anniversary Edition: The Legal Construction of Race.* New York: NYU Press.

Harris, C. I. (1992). Whiteness as property. *Harvard Law Review, 106*, 1707–1791. DOI:10.2307/1341787.

Hedges, M. (2006). Chertoff calls guest worker plan key: A multifaceted approach can solve immigration woes, DHS chief says. *Houston Chronicle*, July 28, 2006.

Heyman, J. M. (1994). The Mexico-United States Border in Anthropology. *Journal of Political Ecology, 1*(1), 24.

Inda, J. X. (2000). Foreign bodies: Migrants, parasites, and the pathological body politic. *Discourse, 22*(3), 46–62.

Jordan, L. J. (2006). U.S. ends "catch and release" at border. *Washington Post*, August 23, 2006. Retrieved from http://www.washingtonpost.com/wp-dyn/content/article/2006/08/23/AR2006082301082_pf.html U.S. Ends 'Catch-And-Release' at Border.

Kelly, C. (2001). Migrants hurting nation, some say taking too much. *Arizona Republic*, August 26, 2001, A6.

Lee, M. Y. H. (2015). Donald Trump's false comments connecting Mexican immigrants and crime. *The Washington Post*, July 8, 2015. Retrieved from https://www

.washingtonpost.com/news/fact-checker/wp/2015/07/08/donald-trumps-false-co
mments-connecting-mexican-immigrants-and-crime/?utm_term=.37e9cb6eecc3.
Lemons, S. (2013). Chris Simcox's life arc mirrors the nativist movement's demise. *Phoenix New Times*, September 5, 2013. Retrieved from http://www.phoenixne
wtimes.com/news/chris-simcoxs-life-arc-mirrors-the-nativist-movements-demis
e-6459748.
Lipsitz, G. (1998). *The Possessive Investment in Whiteness: How White People Profit from Identity Politics*. Philadelphia: Temple University Press.
Macías-Rojas, P. (2016). *From Deportation to Prison: The Politics of Immigration Enforcement in Post-civil Rights America*. New York: NYU Press.
Mbembé, J. A. (2001). *On the Postcolony*. Berkeley: University of California Press.
Mbembé, J. A., & Meintjes, L. (2003). Necropolitics. *Public Culture*, *15*(1), 11–40.
McDonnell, (1996). Plan similar to Prop. 187 falls flat in Arizona immigration: Lack of organization, funds and interest thwart bid to place it on November ballot. *Los Angeles Times*, July 14, 1996. Retrieved from http://articles.latimes.com/1996-07
-14/news/mn-24167_1_illegal-immigrants.
Medrano Leslie, L. (1994). Border buildup to be slow: Arizona won't get extra agents for 4–7 months. *Arizona Republic*, October 19, 1994, A1.
Mehan, H. (1997). The discourse of the illegal immigration debate: A case study in the politics of representation. *Discourse & Society*, *8*(2), 249–270.
Michalowski, R. (2007). Border militarization and migrant suffering: A case of trans-national social injury. *Social Justice*, *34*(2, 108), 62–76.
Noguchi, Y. (2018). Freelanced: The rise of the contract work force [audio]. *Heard on All Things Considered*. Retrieved from https://www.npr.org/2018/01/22/5788
25135/rise-of-the-contract-workers-work-is-different-now.
Parker, R. (1996). Ethnic shifts stoke anxiety: Changing face of U.S. stirs doubts about melting pot. *Albuquerque Journal*, August 4, 1996, A1.
Rasmussen, C., & Brown, M. (2005). The body politic as spatial metaphor. *Citizenship Studies*, *9*(5), 469–484.
Romero, M. (2006). Racial profiling and immigration law enforcement: Rounding up of usual suspects in the Latino community. *Critical Sociology*, *32*(2–3), 447–473.
Romo, R. (1997). U.S. plans to patch border gaps. *Albuquerque Journal*, August 8, 1997, A1.
Romo, R. (2000). Columbus on border of tolerance. *Albuquerque Journal*, November 19, 2000, A1.
Rosaldo, R. (1989). *Culture & Truth: The Remaking of Social Analysis*. Boston, MA: Beacon Press.
Rosas, G. (2006). The managed violences of the borderlands: Treacherous geographies, policeability, and the politics of race. *Latino Studies*, *4*, 401–418.
Rosenberg, E. (2018). "The most bizarre thing I've ever been a part of": Trump panel found no widespread voter fraud, ex-member says. *Washington Post*, August 3, 2018. Retrieved from https://www.washingtonpost.com/news/politics/wp/2018/08
/03/the-most-bizarre-thing-ive-ever-been-a-part-of-trump-panel-found-no-voter-fr
aud-ex-member-says/?utm_term=.518701ede585.

Rozemberg, H. (2002). Migrant deaths near record pace. *Arizona Republic*, July 13, 2002, B1. Retrieved from https://www.aclu.org/news/cas-anti-immigrant-propo sition-187-voided-ending-states-five-year-battle-aclu-rights-groups.

Rozin, P., & Fallon, A. E. (1987). A perspective on disgust. *Psychological Review*, *94*(1), 23.

Santa Ana, O. (2002). *Brown Tide Rising: Metaphors of Latinos in Contemporary American Public Discourse*. Austin: University of Texas Press.

Sevilla, G. (1999). 7-day ordeal leaves illegal hurting, broke. *Arizona Republic*, September 7, 1999, A1.

Shaffer, M. (1997). Border deaths on rise: Illegals' risk-taking reaches "epidemic" levels. *Arizona Republic*, August 12, 1997, A1.

Skerry, P. (1995). Many borders to cross: Is immigration the exclusive responsibility of the federal government? *Publius: The Journal of Federalism*, *25*(3), 71–85.

Stibbe, A. (2004). Health and the social construction of masculinity in Men's Health magazine. *Men and Masculinities*, *7*(1), 31–51.

Suárez-Orozco, M. M. (1996). California dreaming: Proposition 187 and the cultural psychology of racial and ethnic exclusion. *Anthropology & Education Quarterly*, *27*(2), 151–167.

Tutu, D. (2011). Arizona: The wrong answer. *Huffington Post*, May 25, 2011. Retrieved from https://www.huffingtonpost.com/desmond-tutu/arizona----the-w rong-answ_b_557955.html.

Vila, P. (2000). *Crossing Borders, Reinforcing Borders: Social Categories, Metaphors, and Narrative Identities on the US-Mexico Frontier*. Austin: University of Texas Press.

Villarraga-Orjuela, A., & Kerr, B. (2017). Educational effects of banning access to in-state resident tuition for unauthorized immigrant students. *Educational Evaluation and Policy Analysis*, *39*(4), 620–643. DOI:10.3102/0162373717704303.

Wagner, J. (2018). Trump abolishes controversial commission studying alleged voter fraud. *Washington Post*, January 4, 2018. Retrieved from https://www.washingt onpost.com/politics/trump-abolishes-controversial-commission-studying-voter -fraud/2018/01/03/665b1878-f0e2-11e7-b3bf-ab90a706e175_story.html?utm_ term=.8f3dd77b858c.

West, C. (1988). Marxist theory and the specificity of Afro-American oppression. In C. Nelson & L. Grossberg (Eds.), *Marxism and the Interpretation of Culture* (pp. 17–33). Urbana: University of Illinois Press.

Chapter 4

A Ranch in the Wild (House Scale)

On June 19, 2018, President Trump (2018c) tweeted to his Twitter followers, "Democrats are the problem. They don't care about crime and want illegal immigrants, no matter how bad they may be, to pour into and infest our Country, like MS-13." A few days later on June 24, Trump (2018e) also tweeted, "We cannot allow all of these people to invade our Country. When somebody comes in, we must immediately, with no Judges or Court Cases, bring them back from where they came. Our system is a mockery to good immigration policy and Law and Order. Most children come without parents . . . " And on July 5, 2018, President Trump (2018f) continued to tweet that Congress needed to pass immigration laws that would allow greater legal authority to remove undocumented immigrants from the United States: "Tell the people 'Out,' and they must leave, just as they would if they were standing on your front lawn." President Trump's use of deeply nativist and racist rhetoric against immigrants is part of the most recent trajectory of contemporary nativism that began with Prop. 187 in California (1994) and continues today (see Introduction chapter).

The real difference is that the rhetoric of fringe White supremist groups and border militias are now being used by a person who occupies the highest office in the nation. His use of water metaphors such as "pour into . . . our country," animal and animal-disease comparisons like "infest," war imagery in the form of "invade our Country," and finally the image of a criminal home invader "standing on your front lawn" all demonstrate the paradox and irony of New Race Neutral Racism. President Trump proclaimed to reporters: "I am not a racist. I'm the least racist person you have ever interviewed." He said this to defend his comments describing African nations as "shitholes" and instead suggested that the United States offer temporary residency to migrants from countries like Norway (Trump, 2018j).

Table 4.1   Racist Dirt Fixations at the House Scale

Tier 1 Theory	Racist Dirt Fixations	
Tier 2 4 Scales	House	
Tier 3 Themes	"Home on the Ranch"	"Immigrants as threatening fauna"

Tier 4
Concepts
	"home" (3391 references)
	"citizen" (2881 references)
	"resident" (2,348 references)
	"fence" (2,119 references)
	[includes fence (1,307
	    references), "wall" (518
	    references) and "barrier" (294
	    references)]
	"enter" (1203 references)
	"guest" (1059 references)
	"English" (1003 references)
	"ranch" (797 references)
	"door" (548 references)
	"owner" (504 references)
		"worker" 5,764 references
		    [includes worker (4,420
		    references) "laborer" (1,344
		    references)]
		"family" (3,201 references)
		"child" (2996 references)
		"Fear" (2,700 references)
		    [includes fear (952 references),
		    worry (538 references),
		    trouble (329 references),
		    afraid (190 references),
		    stress (158 references), scare
		    (154 references), alarm
		    (112 references), nervous
		    (73 references), anxiety
		    (62 references), distress
		    (41 references), panic (38
		    references), horror (29
		    references), and uneasiness (24
		    references)]
		Catch (2,247 references)
		    [including catch (998), track
		    (574), pursue (246), chase
		    (162), hunt (143), and round
		    up (124)]
		Threat (1,593 references)
		    [includes threat (724), danger
		    (645), peril (82), risk (53),
		    hazard (50), and jeopardy (22)]
		"Spanish" (1,138 references)

In July of 2018, a Quinnipiac University National Poll (2018) that interviewed self-identified, registered voters nationwide showed that 49 percent of survey respondents said President Trump is racist, while 47 percent said he is not. And 50 percent said the main motive for Trump's immigration policies is "a sincere interest in controlling our borders," while 44 percent said the main motive is "racist beliefs." The poll had a margin of sampling error of +/−3.7 percentage points making the question over whether Trump is a racist with a statistical tie among respondents. This shows the power of race neutrality in that the President of the United States can use an "infestation" metaphor against immigrants in a similar manner to Hitler when he persuaded the German people that Jews were "infesting" Germany in order to implement the Holocaust (Perry, 1983). The power of the infestation metaphor can not only de-humanize but the metaphor also provides a vivid explanation of the small or invisible social threat that can cause disease and destruction to the national body (Perry, 1983). At the same time, Trump can profess that he is the "least racist person" and can seem to convince half the nation of it.

This chapter offers an empirical analysis of the second larger nested scale: house. The border newspaper coverage ascribes imaginings to immigrants that renders them as less-than-human abstractions by portraying them as home intruders and wild animals. I analyze the scale of the house in a bifurcated way by not only showing the social construction of the house scale with a focus on home and property features, where the border is like an "revolving door" into the national home but also showing how immigrants are socially constructed as threatening fauna and as external threats to the house scale for which the home provides a haven and refuge. The house scale is best exemplified by the symbol of the "ranch" in the Southwest border region, under siege by wildlife and criminals that threaten its safety and economic vitality. Immigrants at the house scale are both criminal home invaders and frightening wild animals that reflect scripts of a White, middle-class, heteropatriarchal home under threat by security breaches to their national house and property.

HOME ON THE RANCH

The last chapter revealed how the scale of the body reflects body aches, body functions, and body parts that possess "dirt" hidden within the narratives of the scale's imagined vulnerability. After the body, the scale of the house or home is the next most powerful extension of the human psyche. "The desire to act upon and modify the dwelling and to express one's ideas and values is interpreted as a subconscious expression of self" (Després, 1991, p. 100). Indeed, Santa Ana (1999) notes that the "nation as house" metaphor was used quite extensively in the Prop. 187, "Save our State" news discourse. The home is seen as a refuge or haven from the outside world and plays a crucial role in self-identity as it contains meaningful material possessions within, as well as communicating to the larger community through a manipulation of a home's external appearance. One meaning of home is the ability to act upon and modify a dwelling, which provides a sense of control, achievement, and self-expression with an aim toward defining territory (Després, 1991). Thus, President Trump's mandate to "Build that Wall!" creates a home for Whiteness within the national house scale with a fortified shelter from the dangers of the racialized, outside world. Sarah Ahmed (2007) argues that borders can produce "stranger danger" toward bodies of color within a "politics of mobility, of who gets to move with ease across the lines that divide spaces, can be re-described as the politics of who gets to be at home, who gets to inhabit spaces" (p. 162). Thus, whiteness is a "form of positive residence: as if it were a property of persons, cultures, places" (Ahmed, 2007, p. 154).

The concept of "home" (3,891 references) leads the House Scale. After the 9/11 terror attacks of 2001, the INS (Immigration and Naturalization Services) under the Justice Department was reorganized into the new cabinet called the Department of Homeland Security (DHS) in 2003. Not only were immigration matters moved from a "justice" to a "security issue" (prior to 1940, the Department of Labor oversaw immigration matters), but the invocation of "homeland" in the title of the new cabinet, coupled with "security," signaled an aggressive territorialization but also an ethnic assertion of who belongs in this "homeland." Thus, "homeland" leads the "home" concept in the data. Kaiser (2002) argues:

> Nationalists mobilize myths and images of a primordial homeland to reinforce the depiction of the nation as an ancient community of belonging; an organic singularity "rooted" to a particular place. An alternative nationalistic narrative represents the homeland as a sacred place set aside by God for the nation, now represented as God's "chosen people." Narrating nation and homeland in this way naturalizes the linkage between blood and soil, and so strengthens the legitimacy of nationalist claims to the land itself, at least among in-group members. The ancestral homeland is not only portrayed as the geographic cradle of the nation, it is also depicted as the only place where the nation truly belongs, as the one place where it can survive and thrive in the future. The homeland thus tends to be perceived by members of the nation as exclusively theirs, consigning all non-members to the status of foreigners or outsiders who do not properly belong. (p. 230)
>
> Although homelands are most often depicted as politically neutral, cultural spaces that are both "natural" and "eternal," in reality homelands are politically constructed places toward which the population is territorialized. Homelands are constructed to instill not only a sense of spatial identity or emotional attachment to an ancestral homeland among the population being territorialized but also a sense of exclusiveness. (Kaiser, 2002, pp. 230–231, citing Kaiser, 1994)

The creation of DHS politically recolonizes the nation under the image of an exclusive community shaped by race, gender, class, disability, and citizenship particularly in the border region. Yet this border cuts through lands that were formerly Mexico, prior to the 1848 Treaty of Guadalupe Hidalgo, along with other annexations, wars, and occupations that characterized the mandate of Manifest Destiny. The use of "homeland" by DHS also helps to mystify the national colonial legacy in that the United States is an ancestral homeland to Native Americans, and like DHS, the United States is also a relatively new creation compared to other Global North nations.

Below is an example of the concept "home" (3,891 references):

The Arizona Republic: "ARIZ. BORDER 'WEAKEST SPOT'"

Calling Arizona the weakest portion of the Southwestern border and warning that terrorists may try to exploit its vulnerability, top *Home*land Security officials on Wednesday pledged to add 534 Border Patrol agents and to more than double the number of aircraft within six months.

Robert Bonner, U.S. Customs and Border Protection commissioner, said officials have a "comprehensive strategy" designed to secure Arizona's border, a goal that has remained elusive despite record manpower increases in recent years. Department of *Home*land Security plans include increasing the number of agents in the state to more than 2,900 by the end of September and adding 23 helicopters and fixed-wing aircraft and targeting popular smuggling corridors controlled by organized-crime networks.

But some border security experts and academics said they doubt the increase, although widely recognized as significant, will be enough to stem illegal immigration through Arizona. The state shares 389 miles of border with Mexico and includes remote, treacherous expanses of desert, and well-established smuggling corridors.

Arizona remains the most popular illegal-crossing corridor in the nation, last year accounting for 52 percent of the 1.1 million arrests along the entire length of the 1,950-mile border with Mexico.

"This is a national security issue and *home*land security issue, and nowhere is that more apparent than in Arizona," Bonner said, adding that the data clearly show it is the "weakest spot in our border right now." (Carroll, 2005, p. A1)

Again, notions of body politic vulnerability are communicated in the headline "Arizona Border Weakest Spot" that help to justify a fortification with aircrafts and agents for securing the border at this "most popular" location. "Well-established smuggling corridors" and almost 400 miles of shared border with Mexico that are "remote and treacherous" paint the high stakes involved in Homeland Security. This contributes to the notion that immigrants are criminal home intruders when they cross the border, entering the Homeland that does not belong to them (or no longer belongs to Mexican nationals who cross). The home is a desire and concept that expresses a secure and bounded identity (Young, 2005). And the idea of home as territory is closely associate with family (Fox, 2002). Moreover, as nativism progresses over time the imagined family becomes more White, privileged, patriarchal, and able-bodied.

Feminists are divided over the concept of home. Chandra Talpade Mohanty (2004) argues that home, identity, and community tend to be racialized and sexualized in a White, heteronormative manner. She critiques White feminists' investments in home comforts and security bought in a capitalistic way that excludes marginalized people and can even sexualize them as rapists and threats to home/body. Thus, Mohanty (2004) argues that feminists should transgress and decolonize the ideal of a safe home. Iris Marion Young (2005) disagrees and argues that there are four normative values of home that should be accessible to all and not just the White and privileged: safety, individuation, privacy, and preservation. Hence, the home should ideally be a safe place from dangers, a person without a home is deprived of individual existence for a home is an extension of the body (individuation), to own space/home is to possess autonomy over that space and the contents within (privacy), and home is a place of construction and re-construction of the self (preservation). Young agrees with some feminists that the comforts of house and home tend to historically be at a woman's expense in patriarchal society. However, she does not reject wholesale the ideal of home for feminists. But Young does acknowledge the pitfalls of home projected onto a larger scale and that "[n]ationalism is an important and dangerous manifestation of this temptation, in romanticizing 'homeland' . . . Nationalism attempts to project such a local feeling of belonging onto a huge territory and 'imagined community' of millions, and in doing so creates rigid distinctions between 'us' and 'them' and suppresses the differences within 'us.' Other attempts to project an ideal home onto a large political unit are just as damaging." (pp. 150–151, as cited in Anderson, 1983).

The recent use of the "homeland" by the United States is curious. Kaplan (2003) notes that before President George W. Bush, no president had ever used the word "homeland" to describe the United States. She finds it odd because the term is typically used by ethnic groups who are struggling against great odds for their sovereignty, like Palestine, Basque or Kurds; which is quite unlike the USA situation. She also notes a fascist connotation of the "homeland" concept:

> [when] the newly appointed Texas homeland security chief, David Dewhurst, made a revealing faux pas in October 2001, when he purchased a full-color, four-page advertisement in Texas Monthly magazine that depicted a military officer standing in front of an unfurled American flag. The caption read, "As chairman of the Governor's Task Force on Homeland Security, David Dewhurst encourages you to support President Bush and the brave men and woman of our Armed Forces as they fight to eliminate terrorism and work to restore confidence in our economy." Controversy erupted over the ad, though, when people noticed that the officer in the photograph was not an American general, but very clearly a German *Luftwaffe* officer—complete with military decorations, insignias, and a name tag bearing the German flag. (p. 85)

The next most frequent concepts of the house scale are "citizen" (2,881 references) and "resident" (2,348 references). Following is an example of both concepts since the news tends to treat the terms interchangeably:

Los Angeles Times: "Border Battle Is New Turf for Costa Mesa Mayor"

Allan Mansoor once focused on potholes. Now he's hailed by activists, including the Minutemen, for fighting illegal immigration.

The mayor of Costa Mesa looked sheepish when he appeared before a cheering crowd of anti-illegal immigration activists in January.

The son of Egyptian and Swedish immigrants, Allan Mansoor was being named "an honorary Minuteman" by members of the *citizen* border patrol.

"You are a dream come true, mayor," said Minuteman Project cofounder Jim Gilchrist as he paid tribute.

"I was humbled by the honor," the mayor said later.

The event illustrated how Mansoor, once more concerned about his neighborhood's potholes, has morphed into a darling of border activists. Now he's best known for persuading the City Council to allow local police to enforce some immigration laws. To the mayor, the effort, approved in December, fits into his goal of reducing crime.

Immigrants' rights advocate are alarmed, but the mayor and his longtime supporters say he's doing nothing more than acting on campaign promises to fight crime, fix roads and reduce public funding of social service agencies.

"He is just doing what he said he would do in his campaign. It's just getting a lot of attention," said city *resident* and supporter Judi Berry. (Delson, 2006, p. B5)

In this example, citizens and residents praise Costa Mesa Mayor Allan Mansoor (in office 2005–2010) for his anti-immigrant stance. His 2005 proposal to allow police to check a person's immigration status would predate SB 1070 in Arizona in 2010 that similarly wanted police to racially profile for immigration status. In April 2005, Jim Gilchrist and Chris Simcox (Civilian Homeland Defense) helped to start the citizen vigilante group called the "Minutemen Project" in Arizona that patrolled the border in paramilitary gear in order to detain undocumented immigrants (see chapter 2). This "border battle" in "fighting illegal immigration" is "new turf" for this mayor, who Gilchrist calls a "dream come true." Gilchrist promotes the idea of a reconquest of lands that formerly belonged to Mexico through undocumented Mexican immigration in his book titled "Minutemen: The battle to secure America's borders" coauthored with Jerome Corsi (Chavez, 2013, citing Gilchrist & Corsi, 2006). In 2005, Gilchrist capitalized on his fame with the Minuteman Project and ran (and lost) as a third-party candidate for the 48th Congressional district in Orange County, CA (Chavez, 2013). Gilchrist also encouraged the idea that Central American children immigrating to the United States are the "vanguard" of a "Trojan-horse invasion," and even sympathized with the idea of gassing these children to death at the border (Neiwert, 2014, para 2; also see Family and Children concept in the following section). Ironically, President Obama began using tear gas on immigrants at the border in 2010, and it has been used 126 times since 2012. The Border Patrol's use of tear gas reached a seven-year record high under the President Trump. The Chemical Weapons Convention bans the use of tear gas by International law (Democracy Now, 2018). Santa Ana (1999), in his study of news media coverage of immigration, documented that "immigrants correspond to citizens as animals correspond to humans" (p. 203) and Gilchrist is a strong promotor of this racist logic. Part of this "animalization" of immigrants is to see them all with criminal intentions. Thus, in this example, the mayor is "hailed" for his "campaign promises" to "fight crime" and "reduce public funding of social service agencies" that immigrants are accused of abusing (see prior chapter).

The next frequent concept for the house scale is "fence" (2,119 references) that includes the word stem for "fence" (1,307 references) as well the stemmed synonyms "wall" (518 references) and "barrier" (294 references) for a total of 2127 references for this synonym group. Following is an example of this concept.

Los Angeles Times: "Senate Toughens Border
Stand, Approves Miles of New *Fence*"

> The Senate overwhelmingly approved a measure Wednesday to build at least 370 miles of double- and triple-layered *fencing* along the U.S.-Mexico border, moving its immigration bill closer to the enforcement-focused approach favored by conservatives.
>
> The provision would also replace and extend **fenc**ing along parts of the border in Arizona where illegal crossings have surged to the nation's highest levels.
>
> Should the illegal entries increase in other places, the measure authorizes *fence* construction in "areas that are most used by smugglers." That could include California and Texas, where *fences* already exist.
>
> The measure also calls for 500 miles of vehicle *barriers* where needed along the border.
>
> Sen. Jeff Sessions (R-Ala.), the provision's sponsor, said building the *fencing* would send "a signal to the world that our border is not open, it is closed. . . ."
>
> He added: "Good *fences* make good neighbors; *fences* don't make bad neighbors." (Gaouette, 2006, p. A1)

Attorney General Jeff Sessions was the Attorney General for the Trump Administration (2017–2018) and has dodged accusations of racism throughout his career (he was National Senator for Alabama from 1997–2017). Recently, in July of 2018, Sessions gave a speech to the National Sheriffs Association where he made an association with policing and Whiteness: "The office of sheriff is a critical part of the *Anglo*-American heritage of law enforcement. We must never erode this historic office" (Sit, 2018, para 2 [emphasis added]). In the summer of 2018, news media reported on the separation of immigrant families seeking asylum at the border that sparked a national outcry. Asked to comment on the situation on a conservative radio program, Sessions stated, "If people [undocumented immigrants] don't want to be separated from their children, they should not bring them with them [across the border] . . . . We've got to get this message out. You're not given immunity" (Rosenberg, 2018, para 3). Session's use of the quote from Robert Frost's "Mending Wall" (1914) poem—that "good fences make good neighbors"—overlooks that the poem was actually a critique of boundary versus hospitality as well as privacy (Kohn, 2004). So, for Sessions, building "double- and triple-layered" fencing with a more "enforcement-focused approach" with the passage of the 2006 Secure Fence Act "toughens [the] border stand" and is a "signal to the world that our border is not open, it is closed." Both the "message" of the additional fencing and the "signal" of separating parents from children sent to undocumented immigrants is part of the necropolitical, brutalization process that I describe in chapter 2. Both convey the United States as colonizer who decides who will live (including separating parents from their children) and who will die (by attempting to cross border fences and barriers in remote areas) by treating immigrants as abusable, expendable and less than human.

The next most frequent concept to the house scale is "enter" (1,203 references). The following is an example of this concept:

The Albuquerque Journal: "CONSTRUCTION JOBS
DRAW HOST OF ILLEGAL WORKERS"

> Still, there are no easy solutions to the immigration problem, Petty said. Until the Mexican economy revives, thousands of immigrants will continue to illegally *enter* the United States in hopes of better paying jobs, he said.
> On the last day of Operation Hard Hat, 32 workers were arrested during one morning's work. When a Border Patrol agent asked how many workers planned to try to later re-*enter* illegally, a show of hands went up.
> At least half of the workers arrested indicated they will try to return. (O'Neill, 1995, p. 1)

The "Prevention through Deterrence" (1993–1997) strategy implemented by former President Clinton (see chapter 2) moved the migration path away from these safer urban areas along the border into more mountainous and desert terrain in order to deter people from crossing into the United States and make apprehension easier in the rural and remote areas. The result was a dramatic increase in border-crossing deaths that encouraged many immigrants to stay and establish communities in the United States, rather than work seasonally and travel back and forth to their native country as immigrants had done before when border crossing was less deadly and militarized. The motivation (economic, family reunification, political asylum, etc.) to successfully cross the border can frequently entail multiple attempts. When "at least half" of the "workers" in this example indicated that they would "re-enter" and "return" to recross the border, and that "constructions jobs draw host of illegal workers," these suggest that immigrants are endless multitudes and masses (Chavez, 2001).

This complements the next most frequent concept of "guest" (1,059 references). But first, a bit of historical background is needed to understand this peculiar concept. During World war II, the *Bracero* Program between United States and Mexico allowed almost five million Mexican men to "guest" or contract farm work in California and Texas under abusive and exploitive conditions for over twenty years, until the program's end in 1964 (Calavita, 1992; Kil, Menjívar, & Doty, 2009; Rodrigúez, 1997). "The bracero program is a strategy designed to transport indentured labor from an underdeveloped country to the most powerful nation in history and, as such, comprises a labor policy whose contemporary parallels can be found in colonial labor systems such as those implemented by the British in India and the French in Algiers" (Gonzalez, 2016, p. 10). Moreover, the *Bracero* Program was historically bookended between two massive deportation programs. During the Great Depression era, the first but lesser-known massive deportation program forcibly repatriated about a half a million Mexican *and* U.S. American citizens of Mexican-origin to Mexico (Chavez, 1996; Kil et al., 2009). The second massive deportation program was the highly publicized called "Operation Wetback" of 1954 and may have removed nearly one million people, again including Mexican-American citizens (García, 1980; Kil et al., 2009). During former President Bush, Jr.'s administration, he attempted to work with then President of Mexico Vicente Fox to introduce a new guest worker program, but to no avail. "In general, Americans tend to be divided in their attitudes toward a guest worker program, although support for temporary worker policies is stronger when legalization for unauthorized immigrants is conditioned on certain requirements, and when the program is coupled with enhanced border security" (Ilias, Fennelly, & Federico, 2008, p. 741).

Following is an example of the concept "guest." This news article reports on the immediate aftereffects of the historic 2006 May Day marches that also called for an immigrant labor boycott or "A Day without Immigrants/Día sin Inmigrantes." The event described underneath was called, "A Rumble at the Ranch," since it took place not far from Bush, Jr.'s Crawford ranch estate in Texas. The Texas Minutemen and Latino Americans for Immigration Reform co-organized the gathering.

Houston Chronicle: **"500 Protest Immigrant 'Invasion' in Crawford/
Minutemen Join a Latino Group to Show Disfavor with Current Policy"**

The speakers were cheered when expressing frustration with current policies and the discussion in Washington, D.C., about allowing illegal immigrants to work toward citizenship or be allowed to remain as *"guest"* workers."

Others decried the dangers of unsecured borders during an era of increased vigilance against terrorism. "All of the United States is feeling it," said Gayle Nyberg of Murrieta, Calif., who has spend [*sic*] the last several months traveling in a caravan along the southwestern border with Mexico.

She voted for President Bush in 2000, but now calls him a "traitor" who ought to be "impeached," though she concedes that's unlikely. "Our country is in crisis. Time is short. We all need to fight to band together to save our country," said Nyberg, who wore a black-and-white, early-American outfit. [....]
(Stiles, 2006, p. B)

There is a wide divide between the use of "invasion" in the headline and the concept of "guest." Post-9/11 concerns about "increased vigilance against terrorism" and the nation "in crisis" and "feeling" "dangers," motivate the "fight" to "save" the nation from immigrants, even potential "guest workers." The alarmist rhetoric peaks in this example when Gayle Nyberg asserted that Former President Bush, Jr. is a "'traitor' who ought to be 'impeached'" for his advocacy of a guest worker program. Hostility toward guest worker programs are a reflection of magical thinking, an emotional reaction to boundary violations that lead to feelings of racial disgust and abjection, which are the foundation for fantasies of geographic contagion in the form of invasions (see chapter 1). That the event was co-organized by "Latino Americans" shows the power of new race neutral racism and its effect on people of color by internalizing NRNR and lashing out at undocumented immigrants in a rally with racist border vigilantes. Nyberg was wearing a "early-American outfit" that harkens to more openly racist time where the genocide of Native Americans and the enslavement of Black people were signs of progress.

The next leading concept is "English" (1,013 references).

The Arizona Republic: "LAWMAKERS SIFT THROUGH 21 SURVIVING REFERENDUMS"

English Only

One issue that stirs strong opinions and could make it to the polls is a proposal by Rep. Russell Pearce, R-Mesa, to make *English* the state's official language. Arizona voters agreed to an "*English* only" measure in 1988, but the Arizona Supreme Court declared much of it unconstitutional. Pearce pushed the issue again last year in a bill that made it through the Legislature before being rejected by Napolitano.

Pearce said last year that he didn't want to crowd the 2006 ballot with a referendum on the issue. He's changed his mind.

Pearce introduced House Concurrent Resolution 2036, which mandates that government services, programs and publications be provided in *English* "to the greatest extent possible." All official government actions would be taken in *English*.

>Pearce said this measure meets constitutional muster because it does not
>prohibit the use of languages other than *English*, except in official actions and
>on documents like state Web sites.
>
>"It's simply the right thing to do. *English* is one of those things that bind us
>together as a nation and it's what this is about," he said. [....] (Watters, 2006,
>p. B1)

A group called U.S. English that began in 1983 advocates for a constitutional amendment to make English the official language of the United States
through the English-Only movement and as a consequence, several states
have passed English-only laws (Lucas & Katz, 1994). Macedo (2000) argues
that the English-Only Movement is a form of colonialism: "The position of
U.S. English Only proponents is not very different from the Portuguese colonialism that tried to eradicate the use of African languages in institutional life
by inculcating Africans through the educational system in Portuguese only
with myths and beliefs concerning the savage nature of their cultures" (p.
16). In addition, Chicana feminist and border studies scholar Gloria Anzaldúa
(1987) writes: "So, if you want to really hurt me, talk badly about my language. Ethnic identity is twin skin to linguistic identity—I am my language"
(p. 81). Russell Pearce, who is featured in this example, was a former Arizona
senator and was a primary sponsor of SB 1070. He later served as vice chair
of the Republican Party of Arizona. He resigned that position in 2014 when
he suggested that forced sterilization be applied to poor women on Arizona
public assistance. Pearce stated, "You put me in charge of Medicaid, the first
thing I'd do is get Norplant, birth-control implants, or tubal ligations . . . .
Then we'll test recipients for drugs and alcohol, and if you want to [repro-
duce] or use drugs or alcohol, then get a job" (Sullivan, 2014, para. 5). This
is a eugenic logic and reflects a long history of "national hygiene" (Ordover,
2003). In the early twentieth century, U.S. American "eugenicists helped to
pass sterilization laws in many states, and before 1933, German racial hygien-
ists cited this experience to buttress their own proposals for a sterilization
law" (Bachrach, 2004, p. 418). Pearce's claim that "English is one of those
things that bind us together as a nation" really reflects Whiteness and English
as a "twin skin" of identity.

The next most frequent example of the house scale is the concept "ranch"
(797 references). I added the concept "owner" (504 references) here with
"ranch" even though the following house scale concept of "door" has
more references (548 references) than "owner." The "ranch" and "owner"
concepts possess similar characteristics for "ranch" as an ideal example
of house scale in this region and owning a border ranch provides property
rights to the "owner" against immigrants who trespass on property. I analyze
them together for efficiency reasons. The image of the home as a refuge or

haven from the dangers of the outside world has historical roots in the ranch and expresses a pioneer image. Edward Said (1993) argues that the house derives its comfort from empire and "what assures the domestic tranquility and attractive harmony of one is the productivity and regulated discipline of the other" (p. 87). The image of the ranch depends on both material and discursive ownership and exploitation of the colonized land of the Western frontier. It has a domestic economic meaning in that it is a space that merges both home and work (like cattle ranches), a settlement that depended on the nationalist practices of empire in the form of Manifest Destiny. Hence, the concept of home projected unto this border region is the symbolized in owning and protecting a ranch.

Houston Chronicle: "Volunteers plan armed border patrols
Leader says: 'We go where we are invited'"

A group of North Texas volunteers has announced plans to mount armed patrols near the Mexican border next spring, less than a year after an immigrant was killed there, allegedly by a land*owner*. Arlington-based *Ranch* Rescue produced a flier calling for "volunteers from all over the USA" to congregate in Kinney County, a desolate stretch of rolling hills and mesquite just north of Eagle Pass. The group already has traveled to Arizona, where volunteers ran patrols with controversial *ranchers* along the border there last month.

Ranch Rescue leader Jack Foote said his property-rights group did not choose Kinney County because a Mexican immigrant was shot there last May after asking a land*owner* for water. Instead, he said the group selected the area because **ranch**ers have complained about the damage caused by the flow of illegal migrants across the land.

"We go where we are invited," said Foote, a former U.S. Army captain.

The group will help mend fences and protect private property from the trespassing immigrants, he added. He did not say whether the armed volunteers in their khaki uniforms and combat boots would try to capture immigrants. [...] (Hegstrom, 2000, p. A37)

Recall in chapter 2 that Ranch Rescue is an armed vigilante group interested in protecting private landowners' property and "hunting" immigrants to stop them from trespassing and causing "damage" to border ranchland. They claim to be composed of Border Patrol agents, military personnel, law enforcement officers, and mercenaries (Ranch Rescue, 2018). The Southern Poverty Law Center filed a lawsuit with the Mexican American Legal Defense and Educational Fund and obtained a pair of judgments totaling $1 million against Jack Foote and Casey Nethercott, a member of Ranch Rescue. The case centered on two Salvadorans: Fatima Leiva and Edwin Mancia. After Texan rancher Joe Sutton invited the Ranch Rescue to his property in 2003, they terrorized and assaulted Fatima Leiva and Edwin Mancia by capturing them and holding them at gunpoint. They struck Edwin Mancia in the head and their dog also attacked him. The $1 million settlement included Nethercott's 70-acre Arizona property, which was Ranch Rescue's paramilitary training headquarters and was deeded to the Salvadoran victims (Southern Poverty Law Center, 2018).

In the "ranch" example, "We go where we are invited" is repeated both in the headline and in the third paragraph. The news article downplays his hate-motivated purpose in the area by denying they were there "because a Mexican immigrant was shot there last May after asking a landowner for water." Rather, he repeats the mission of Ranch Rescue in that they protect private property and "mend fences" caused by the "flow" of border immigration as "armed" "volunteers." NRNR enables White supremacy by hiding racial animus behind neutral and right-based discourse about property and harm. In addition, Foote is given legitimacy as "a former U.S. Army captain." Ranch Rescue claims they "rescue" ranches in a defensive, militaristic manner from the danger of border crossers in their "uniforms and combat boots." They are "invited" guests to the ranch.

The final concept of the house scale is "door" (548 references). There have been many metaphors that describe immigration in U.S. American history, but "door" and "gate" stand out in the ability to allow in and keep out, unlike the "melting pot" metaphor that was losing in popularity in the early twentieth century (Prchal, 2007). The Chinese exclusion act made the "gate" metaphor into an ideology of "gate keeping" and "legalized and reinforced the need to restrict, exclude, and deport 'undesirable' and excludable immigration" (Lee, 2002, p. 37). Ericka Lee (2003) argues that there are three elements that make up the "gatekeeping ideology": (a) racializing Chinese immigrants as permanently alien and inferior in a race, classed, gendered manner, (b) controlling them as a danger by impacting their economic viability and geographic mobility and barring them from citizenship, and (c) protecting the nation by restricting new immigration, as well as applying surveillance and deportation to those residing within the gates. The metaphor of the "closed gate" was combined with rhetoric of "unwelcome invasion" and applied to the Chinese immigrants (p. 43). This sharply contrasts to "The New Colossus" (1883) poem written by Emma Lazarus, found on the pedestal of the Statue of Liberty, "Give me your tired, your poor, your huddled masses yearning to breathe free, the wretched refuse of your teeming shore. Send these, the homeless, tempest-tossed to me. I lift my lamp beside the golden door!" The difference between "gate" and "door" is that gate can connote protection against intruders, while the door image presents something "homier" (Prchal, 2007, p. 41). While the popularity of "gate" reigned even with its most recent use by INS with "Operation Gatekeeper" in 1994 (see chapter 2), the use of door seems to be making a comeback. The use of "gate" (148 references) was much less frequent in this study's data than "door" (549 references). Beneath is an example of the concept "door," specifically a "revolving door" to describe the launch of Operation Gatekeeper.

Los Angeles Times: "U.S. weighing controversial border crossing fee, Reno says: Checkpoints: In Beverly Hills speech, she unveils program to close 'revolving door for illegal immigrants'"

U.S. Atty. Gen. Janet Reno announced Saturday that a controversial proposal to impose fees for crossing the Mexican border is under serious consideration by the Justice Department.

Reno's comments came during a Beverly Hills address in which she unveiled a federal program designed to close California's "revolving *door* for illegal immigrants." Dubbed Operation Gatekeeper, the program will:

- Use hundreds of new and redeployed federal officers to patrol the Mexican border—a move that will result in at least temporary closure of a busy inland immigration checkpoint at San Clemente.
- Institute an automated fingerprinting system to catch criminal immigrants and track habitual illegal immigrants.
- Increase fencing and lighting at the San Diego border.

"The days when the border served as a revolving *door* for illegal immigrants are over," Reno told a receptive Town Hall audience at the Beverly Hilton Hotel. (Hurst & Rotella, 1994, p. A3)

Attorney General Janet Reno, who held that office between 1993 and 2001 under President Clinton, could have chosen to use the "gate" metaphor and emphasized, like the nation had done before with the Chinese, that the U.S. American gate is closed to "illegal immigrants." However, she instead chose to use a "revolving door" image that is repeated several times in the news article, including the headline. The "revolving door" image is a highly racist, sexualized crime metaphor. In 1986, George Bush, Sr. ran a television ad featuring a revolving door that suggested his opponent, then Governor of Massachusetts Michael Dukakis was procrime because he supported prison furloughs. A Black convicted murderer named Willie Horton was serving a life sentence and was released from a Massachusetts prison on such a program, did not return and instead traveled to another stated, raped a White woman and assaulted her fiancé. Though Horton was never mentioned by name in the original attack ad, the connection was clear and *TIME* (2018) magazine named it the fourth-most effective campaign ad of all time. Thus, Attorney General Janet Reno applied this highly popular, "revolving door" crime narrative, but in this example, the attackers are Brown "illegal immigrants" and the implied victim is the Whiteness of the nation and those that defend it. In addition, she "unveiled" plans of Operation Gatekeeper to "a receptive Town Hall audience at the Beverly Hilton Hotel," which is a luxury setting associated with elite Whiteness. So, when President Trump argues that "When Mexico sends its people . . . They're rapists," it both physically and symbolically re-affirms this type of crime script that fears White rape, both psychically and symbolically, by people of color.

National space can become a type of national possession through a fusion of "place, property, and heritage," a compound "whose perpetuation is secured by the state" (Alonso, 1994, p. 383). However, this is a "territorial trap" that relies on the assumptions that states are fixed units that function as natural containers of societal space (Agnew, 1994). This state-centered concept of space allows for the naturalization of borders and hides the socially constructed and contestable nature of these divides. Thus, transnational crossings by capital or migrants are deterritorializing nation states while stimulating issues of national security and sovereignty especially in relation to migrants. Nations of the global North are turning more toward a "gated globe" concept, where immigration is restricted and highly regulated (Cunningham, 2004). Political and economic structures as well as global racial inequalities shape this new "gated" landscape.

In the next section, I offer analysis of the scale of the house by moving away from the focus on home and property features and instead show how the news media constructs immigrants as wild, threatening fauna to the house or home that acts as a safe haven.

Immigrants as Threatening Fauna

Mohanty (2004) argues that "stable notions of self and identity are based on exclusion and secured by terror" (p. 91). In order to stabilize the concept of a national "White" house as a protective container for a "vulnerable" body politic, the outside needs to be terrifying, dangerous, and filled with wild animals in which the struggle for survival is about keeping threatening fauna outside and not allowing it inside. The house scale is the only scale that I analyze in a bifurcated manner because of the salience of the inside/outside themes, I observe in my data with the outside associating immigrants with animals. Santa Ana (2002) notes in his analysis of immigrant discourse in the *Los Angeles Times* that animal metaphors are "uniquely associated with immigrants" (p. 94). President Trump also espouses this view when he said at a Cabinet meeting attended by journalist that "'You wouldn't believe how bad these people are. These aren't people, these are animals, and we're taking them out of the country at a level and at a rate that's never happened before" (Davis, 2018, para. 4).

I begin this theme "immigrants as threatening fauna" with the most frequent concept "worker" (5,764 references), which includes the stemmed word "worker" (4,420 references) and its stemmed synonym "laborer" (1,353 references). While both worker and laborer are referring to human beings, I place them in my analysis in the "threatening fauna" theme because they stand outside the national imaginary of belonging, thus border newspapers tend to portray immigrants as sub-human/animals. The following two examples illustrate my point:

The Arizona Republic: "ILLEGAL CROSSERS JEERED AT RALLY CALIF. GROUPS HELP STAGE FORUM IN RANCH COUNTRY"

The volume of the debate over ranchers detaining illegal immigrants rose another couple of notches Saturday as the California Coalition for Immigration Reform rallied here with local residents. The group arrived loaded with quote-laden videotapes, rhetoric-filled books and fliers comparing Roger Barnett, a media-friendly local rancher who has detained thousands of immigrants on his property, to an early American minuteman.

"CCIR lauds Roger Barnett and the many equally courageous ranchers who have taken an active position in defense of not only their own property but also the protection of their fellow American neighbors from the violent and vicious acts committed by illegal aliens who enter the United States across their property in violation of federal immigration law," the fliers announced.

Inside the packed meeting room at the Windemere Hotel, with about 250 people and many TV cameras present, the sentiment was similar.

California-based Rick Oltman, a member of the Federation for American Immigration Reform, listed crime statistics in several major cities that he linked to illegal immigration.

"Phoenix is Cocaine Central," he said, also blaming that problem on illegal immigrants.

Oltman then introduced the main speaker, Glenn Spencer, a California radio commentator and president of the Voice of Citizens Together, who began by accusing an Arkansas-based chicken processing plant of advertising in Mexico to lure low-wage immigrant *workers*. [....] (Borden, 2000, p. B1)

This first example shows a lot of the spectacle and grandstanding that characterizes these racist, border vigilante groups. Roger Barnett stands out because while many vigilante groups tend to claim they defend ranchland without being a rancher, Barnett is one of the few that is both vigilante and a ranger. Barnett is credited with saying, "Humans. That's the greatest prey there is on earth" (Grandin, 2013, para 4). In 2004, on leased federal land northeast of Douglas, Arizona near the USA-Mexico border, local Rancher Roger Barnett and his brother Donald stopped and detained a family hunting party, taking out an AR-15 assault rifle, chambering the weapon, and saying: "My fucking name is Roger Barnett! If you don't get off my property, I'm gonna shoot you and shoot you and shoot you!" Local law enforcement officials refused to file criminal charges against the Barnett brothers even though the Mexican-American family was hunting on federal land that Barnett leases (Kil et al., 2009). "In 2006, a state jury in Arizona, ruling in a lawsuit sponsored by the Southern Poverty Law Center, ordered Barnett to pay $98,570 to a family of Mexican-Americans, including two young children and their friend, who he mistook for undocumented immigrants and held at gunpoint" (Southern Poverty Law Center, 2009a, para 3). Again in 2004, he detained four Mexican women on his property where he "drew a pistol and pointed it at them, kicking and threatening to kill them before finally turning them over to the Border Patrol" (Southern Poverty Law Center, 2009a, para 5). A federal civil jury in 2009 found Barnett liable for assault and infliction of emotional distress and ordered him to pay the women $77,804 in damages, $60,000 of them punitive (Southern Poverty Law Center, 2009a). In this example, California Coalition for Immigration Reform (CCIR) "lauds" Barnett and his racist activates given that CCIR (now called National Council for Issue Reform) is an extremist group tracked by the Southern Poverty Law Center (2009b). Glenn Spencer, the "main speaker" of this rally, then moved his group "Voices of Citizens Together" to Arizona in 2002 and subsequently rebranded it "American Border Patrol" (see chapter 2). His rhetoric that U.S. American jobs "lure low-wage immigrant workers" reduces immigrants to prey animals like fish or game.

Beneath is another example that uses the concept "laborer" (1,344 references).

The Arizona Republic: "QUESTIONS TRUMP ANSWERS IN WAR ON DRUGS LOTS OF CASH, LITTLE TO SHOW FOR ALL OF IT"

The lure of fast American cash is nearly irresistible in a country where much of the workforce is unemployed and *laborers* earn only about $25 a week.

Even those at the bottom of the chain, the human mules who risk their own hides to deliver loads into the United States earn wages they couldn't hope to match in Mexico's legal economy. [....] (Wagner & Flannery, 2000, p. A14)

Again, "lure" is used in addition to a "chain" image that suggests immigrants are placed at the "bottom" as "human mules who risk their own hides" for "fast American cash." This image suggests a type of food chain where immigrants are unthinking animals and beasts of burden and occupy a link in the chain below humans, where humans "lure" immigrants in order to capture their labor that deliver "loads" of goods and services into the United States.

The next two most frequent concepts are "family" (3,201 references) and "children" (2,996 references). Since the two concepts are so closely related and follow each other in frequency I will analyze them together for efficacy purposes. In his June 24, 2018, tweet provided in the introduction of this chapter, Trump (2018a) tweeted, "Most children come [over the border] without parents . . ." and seems to suggest that Brown immigrants are bad parents and send their children across the border alone. However, on April 6, 2018, his administration ordered a "zero tolerance policy" on the border. On May 7, 2018, Trump's then-Attorney General Jeff Sessions spoke to law enforcement in Arizona and essentially threatened the public at large: "If you are smuggling a child then we will prosecute you, and that child will be separated from you as required by law . . . If you don't like that, then don't smuggle children over our border" (Jenkins, 2018, para 2). The implication of this statement is that if a family crosses the border without documents, then those parents are trafficking their children and thus "child smuggling." The media firestorm and public outcry over this policy would rattle the administration given that about 1,995 children were separated from roughly as many adults between April 19 to May 31, 2018 (Rhodan, 2018, para. 9). Chavez (2001) analyzed popular magazine covers about immigration and noted that images of women and children tend to be powerful because of the shared universality of the mother-child dyad. "Images of helplessness and dependency, however, are gendered touchstones in a society still characterized as patriarchal . . . therefore, [these images] are emotional and persuasive symbols that can be used to galvanize public opinion in favor of refugee assistance and international aid" (p. 73).

Despite his refusal to own his zero-tolerance policy and its destructive aftermath on particularly children, Trump (2018d) signed an executive order that directed the DHS to "maintain custody of alien families" on June 20, 2018, which would reverse the policy of separation and begin detaining families together. Trump (2018g) would further tweet the following month and try to "blame the victim" again by stating, "Please understand, there are consequences when people cross our Border illegally, whether they have children or not—and many are just using children for their own sinister purposes." In light of this timeline, Trump's tweet that "most [immigrant] children come without parents . . . " and "many are just using children for their own sinister purposes" is a hollow deflection of presidential responsibility for his racist, classist border policy. These are intentional and brutal policy decisions. Just like "prevention through deterrence" policy under former President Clinton, immigrants are blamed for their plight and not the border or neoliberal policies that motivate economic migration. President Trump chose to punish immigrants by using the harshness of forced separation of parents and their children as "a signal to the world." Former slave and leading abolitionist Frederick Douglas analyzed the brutality of a system that separates children from parents. He writes: "freedom does not reside primarily in individual or collective forms of ownership or control . . . freedom lives or dies in the relations forged between persons . . . the practice of separating children from their mothers . . . is a marked feature of the cruelty and barbarity of the slave system. But it is in harmony with the grand aim of slavery, which, always and everywhere, is to reduce man [sic] to *a level with the brute*" (Willett, 2001, p. 197; emphasis added).

Underneath is an example of the concept "family" (3,201 references) and "child" (2,996 references):

> *The Arizona Republic*: "COUPLE FOUGHT WAY TO SUCCESS
> IMMIGRANTS 'MUST STRUGGLE A LOT,' THEY SAY
> IMMIGRATION EL OTRO LADO—THE OTHER SIDE PROFILE
> OF UNDOCUMENTED MEXICAN IMMIGRANTS"

When hunger pangs would awake Pablo and Dolores Felix late at night, they'd lie in bed forging plans for success in their illegally adopted country.

For hours, they'd talk of owning a business, perhaps a restaurant featuring traditional dishes from their native Mexico.

But morning would bring reality to the couple and their infant son, who barely survived on Pablo's minimum-wage earnings as a construction worker. And Dolores was pregnant again.

On weekends, Pablo would play his accordion in Phoenix-area nightclubs and restaurants for extra cash. He'd earned a modest living doing that in Nogales, Sonora, where he was better off economically than many of Mexico's poor. But Pablo could not resist the lure of the U.S. pay scale.

Twenty-four years ago, Pablo and Dolores crossed the border using their local passports. They boarded a Greyhound bus in Nogales, Arizona, carrying a small suitcase, his old accordion and their 6-month-old son. With $5 to their names, the couple fixed their thoughts on the riches they would find in the Promised Land.

"We thought everyone here had a nice car and earned plenty of money," Pablo said recently, now smiling about their innocence. "We soon found out that people, and perhaps immigrants more, must struggle a lot to accomplish their dreams."

Pablo, 63, a native of Torreon, Coahuila, is a small man whose bushy mustache curls at the ends. Dolores, 49, is short and full of smiles. She hails from Magdalena, Sonora, and the couple met in Nogales. Both have a grade-school education.

Eight years after reaching Phoenix, the Felixes opened La Casa de Pablo, the restaurant they had yearned for so long. They were legal residents by then, but none of it came easily.

Their first home was an abandoned one-room house gutted by fire. When she first laid eyes on it, Dolores felt like crying. It was like the hovels that shelter the poorest of the poor in Mexico, the type of house the Felixes assumed they'd left forever when they slipped into Arizona.

Rather than weeping, Dolores wrapped her son in a blanket, set him in an empty box and got to work. The couple cleaned the piles of charred debris, lined the walls with flattened cardboard boxes and moved in.

Undaunted by their dismal surroundings, Pablo quit construction for a higher-paying job at a slaughterhouse. In those days, documents weren't needed for work because employers weren't required to ask job applicants whether they were legally in the country.

A few months later, the growing *family* moved into a three-room house, where they stayed for eight years. Five more *children* were born there. One, Isaias, died in a choking accident at age 2.

Never losing sight of why they came to the United States, the couple forged ahead. When the slaughterhouse laid him off, Felix played his squeeze box and did odd jobs to keep his *family* going.

The couple often loaded the *children* in their truck and drove to affluent neighborhoods to pick through trash. They brought home chairs, hardware, bathroom fixtures, anything they could fix up and sell in their humble neighborhood.

"She and I worked equally hard," Pablo said of his wife of 25 years. "We had the same ambition, the same determination, the same dreams."

"There is always a door to be opened for people who want to accomplish something." [....] (Medrano Leslie, 1995, p. A9)

This excerpted example is not a typical "crime" news story, but it does detail at length the difficulties immigrants face living without documents. While the tone seems compassionate and the subject matter focuses on the family's "struggle," problematic subtext emerges. Chavez (2001) argues that women are depicted in immigration discourse as "insidious invaders" because of their association with reproduction and birth. The depiction signals a concern with immigrants forming families and communities (Chavez, 2001). Pat Buchanan (2002), former presidential candidate for the reform party in 2000, argued in his book *The Death of the West: How Dying Populations and Immigrant Invasions Imperil Our Country and Civilization*, that immigrant women give birth to more children than native White women and would lead to the demise of Western civilization/White people (see chapter 1). President Trump (2018h) seemed to mimic Buchanan's concern with his tweet on October 31, 2018:

So-called "Birthright Citizenship," which costs our Country billions of dollars and is very unfair to our citizens, will be ended one way or the other. It is not covered by the 14th Amendment because of the words "subject to the jurisdiction thereof." Many legal scholars agree.

He later continued his thoughts on Birthright Citizenship with a follow-up tweet less than an hour later:

Harry Reid was right in 1993, before he and the Democrats went insane and started with the Open Borders (which brings massive Crime) "stuff." Don't forget the nasty term Anchor Babies. I will keep our Country safe. This case will be settled by the United States Supreme Court! (Trump, 2018i)

In 1993, then Nevada Democrat Senator Harry Reid argued that "no sane country" would award citizenship to children of undocumented immigrants born in their country, but changed his position six years later and apologized for his earlier argument (Sonmez & Wagner, 2018, para. 17). Like I argued earlier in chapter 3, border militarization policies and racist nativism is a bipartisan effort that both Democrats and Republican symbolically profit and contribute. President Trump's logic in his desire to repeal birthright citizenship is an attempt to racially solve the nativist "enemy within" problem of multiculturalism and immigration that threatens Whiteness of the nation. His comment on "anchor babies" shows his fear of a racialized child, born in the United States, with the legal ability to petition for their parents' citizenship when they turn eighteen years old. While Chavez (2001) focuses on the depiction of women as "insidious invaders," President Trump's focus is on "anchor babies" as "insidious invaders," yet both signal a concern with immigrants establishing and growing families.

This example from the *Arizona Republic* is a heteronormative journalistic sketch of a "struggling" Mexican couple, Pablo and Dolores Felix, with their six mostly nameless children "lured" by "dreams" of the "Promised Land" in Arizona. "And Dolores was pregnant again" reflects this "insidious invasion." "[T]he growing family moved into a three-room house, where they stayed for eight years. Five more children were born there" elaborates on the family's establishment in "their humble neighborhood." This news reporting is sympathetic to the difficulties of this family but still deploys new race neutral racist scripts. This "insidious invaders" narrative capitalizes on descriptions like "hunger pangs," "barely survived," "minimum-wage," and "must struggle a lot" in describing family growth and settlement. The news reports toward the end of the article (not shown above) states that "Because of their [now adult] children, Pablo and Dolores became U.S. citizens, giving up their dream of investing in a ranch in Mexico." This development helps to "depict unauthorized immigrant women as people who wish to conquer the United States [of America] by bearing [US] American citizens" (Cunningham-Parmeter, 2011, p. 1583). It also helps to depict birthright citizenship and immigrant children born in the United States as means to this "invasion." Since immigrants reside and work in the nation, magical thinking permits contagion to spread through the formation of immigrant families and communities, which is seen as a national assault by immigrants that will lead to racial conquest (see chapter 1).

The next most frequent concept is fear (2,700 references) that is composed of a collection of synonyms. See table for full synonym list. Below is an example of fear:

Houston Chronicle: "Immigration chief: Instinct
to survive accounts for masses"

WASHINGTON—Illegal immigrants are coming to the United States in extraordinary numbers not to take undue advantage of a generous social welfare system but "to stay alive," the nation's new immigration chief said Friday. Countless thousands—such as those from El Salvador and Guatemala—are fleeing economic disaster and political unrest and not to obtain health care or welfare benefits, Immigration and Naturalization Service Commissioner Doris Meissner said.

"They're coming to survive," she said.

Meissner, in her first meeting with reporters since assuming her post Oct. 18, mixed a blend of compassion for the struggles of illegal immigrants with a desire for more stringent enforcement of existing immigration laws and development of more effective legal tools for fighting the problem.

The most experienced immigration expert to head the agency in many years, she also attempted to place the current outcry over both legal and illegal immigration in the country—particularly in California—in a historical and cultural context, contending that a harsh economic climate, racial, and ethnic differences and "*fear* of the stranger" attitudes have combined to produce the *anxiety*.

The *uneasiness* has led many state and local politicians, as well some federal officials, to call for tougher laws, beefed-up border patrols to ferret out illegal immigrants and limitations on legal immigration. [...] (Ostrow, 1993, p. A16)

Here the "fear," "anxiety," and "uneasiness" of the nation is contrasted with the "instinct to survive" among the "masses," "countless thousands," and "extraordinary numbers" of border-crossing immigrants "fleeing economic disaster and political unrest." Immigration and Naturalization Service Commissioner Doris Meissner (who served the Clinton Administration from 1993 to 2000) states, "They're coming to survive," which suggests an instinctual reflex for migration. Fear leads to "beefed-up border patrols to ferret out illegal immigrants" that suggests more muscularized enforcement to hunt illegal immigrants. "Beefed-up" has a gendered quality when linked to enforcement that masculinizes its efforts. More on this in the next chapter that reviews the "Battleground" theme in the region scale. "Ferret out" evokes images of using ferrets to hunt animals like rabbits, but in this case the human hunter is border patrol, and the prey are immigrant rabbits.

The next most frequent concept is "catch" (2,247 references) that is composed by a collection of synonyms (see table). I offer two examples of this concept. First, the concept of "catch":

Houston Chronicle: "South Texas prosecuting more illegal immigrants/ Study shows rise of 345% during latest fiscal year in Southern District"

The government often is criticized for failing to prosecute border crossers. Critics have focused especially on the policy under which immigrants from countries other than Mexico are frequently released to enter the United States, a program known as "*catch* and release."

All illegal immigrants captured by the Border Patrol are fingerprinted and photographed, and first-time offenders can be charged with illegal entry, Villarreal said. [....] (Hegstrom, 2005, p. B)

On April 6, 2018, President Trump (2018) issued an official memorandum titled: "Ending 'Catch and Release' at the Border of the United States and Directing Other Enhancements to Immigration Enforcement). "Catch and release" is political rhetoric and a policy directive that constrains forms of parole from detention such as release on recognizance (Macías-Rojas, 2016). Sullivan (2018), Deputy Director of Editorial and Strategic Communications for the ACLU:

> The phrase actually describes allowing people who are seeking asylum to wait for their hearing in the community, rather than in custody. They are not freed, but tethered, always by law, often by more: Sometimes the asylum-seeker must wear an ankle monitor. Sometimes she must pay a bond. Sometimes the tether is administrative: checking in regularly with immigration officials. (para. 3)

President Trump (2018b) tweeted on June 18, 2018 ". . . Any Immigration Bill MUST HAVE full funding for the Wall, end Catch & Release, Visa Lottery and Chain, and go to Merit Based Immigration. Go for it! WIN!." Trump's repeated use of this political rhetoric and the news' responsibility to report on what he communicates pushed the *New York Times* (2018) to issue a statement in regard to reader feedback about the racist connotation of Trump's repeated use of the term saying the NYT reporters would use it "only in reference to the administration's use of the phrase." The short example provided demonstrates why the use of this phrase is so dehumanizing. After immigrants are "captured by Border Patrol" they are "fingerprinted and photographed." This discourse is too similar to sport fishing people or marine researchers who catch, tag, and release fish for tracking purposes typically in conservation efforts.

Beneath is an example of this "catch" concept with the stem word "round up" (124 references).

> *The Albuquerque Journal*: "117 Immigrants Detained in 2 Days: Border agents expect traffic in Bootheel to increase as security in Arizona is beefed up"
>
> More than 100 illegal immigrants have been apprehended in New Mexico's Bootheel in the last 48 hours, and the situation is not going to get any better, U.S. Border Patrol agents said Thursday." Increases in Border Patrol personnel and equipment around southern Arizona are causing a rising number of immigrants to try this area west of Antelope Wells," said John Hackworth, assistant agent in charge at the Border Patrol office in Lordsburg.
>
> Antelope Wells is on the U.S.-Mexico border at the bottom of the desolate, sparsely populated Bootheel.
>
> Hackworth said a group of 107 illegal immigrants, including women and children, had been *rounded up* on Wednesday, while Border Patrol a separate group of 10 was apprehended Thursday morning.

Tracks and aerial surveillance of the larger group showed that about 30 more had fled south, back across the border into Mexico. They escaped when about five agents first took 89 people into custody at 1 a.m. Wednesday.

"They scattered," Hackworth said. "Later on that morning we caught 18 more." (Thompson, 2001, p. A1)

The use of the term "rounded up" to describe law enforcement activity toward immigrants is dehumanizing, especially in the context of the southwest border region. The image of cowboys "rounding up" cattle contribute to the mythology of the U.S. American west and its frontier romanticization of Manifest Destiny mandates: "The two symbolic figures, the hunter and cowboy, made identical appeals to the trait traditionally valued above all others in the United States [of America]: freedom" (Fishwick, 1952, p. 77). Fishwick writes, "Rousseau's 'Natural man,' that romantic symbol of unbridled freedom captivated the eighteenth century, triumphantly entered the American forests as the buckskin-clad hunter, only to emerge on the Great Plains a century later as the American cowboy" (p. 77). In the border region, the use of the term "round up" in the Chandler Arizona immigration case of 1997 that I describe in the Introduction chapter, and the example provided here, demonstrate how metaphors of hunting and herding animals reduce immigrants to prey, beasts of burden, and livestock. In addition, "beefed-up" Border Patrol "tracks" and uses "aerial surveillance" in an attempt to capture people that "scattered," "fled," and "escaped" reinforce that cowboy round-up script. In addition to the cowboy and cattle imagery, time is portrayed as moving faster on the border region with human "traffic" expected to "increase" resulting in "100" apprehensions "in the last 48 hours." This is an example of the theme "active time" that contributes to biomedical pathologies in describing the border region analyzed in chapter 6.

The next frequent concept for the house scale is "threat" (1,576 references) that includes the stem word "threat" (724 references), the stemmed synonyms "danger" (652 references) and additional synonyms found Table X for a total of 1,593 references for this synonym group. Below are two examples:

The Arizona Republic: "MORE PEOPLE, MORE TECHNOLOGY, MORE *DANGER* BORDER PATROL STRUGGLES TO STEM TIDE"

Agents Tom Madrid and Dana Banks start tracking "fresh sign" at about 9 a.m., following footprints into the Perilla Mountains just above the U.S.-Mexican border east of town. They aren't sure who they're after, but they know they aren't far behind. Humping up the steep slopes northbound toward Arizona 80, they find themselves on a trail 100 yards below the crest of the peaks. Their quarry is moving fast, especially for such radical climbs, and Madrid and Banks can't see anyone . . . (Flannery, 2000, p. A15)

These examples show in the headlines that immigration is a "threat" to the nation and as "more people" come across the border, "more danger" results, requiring "more technology" to "stem the tide" of border crossings. The second news article portrays Border Patrol agents as hunters "tracking 'fresh sign'" or "footprints" in the mountainous terrain. "Their quarry is moving fast." Later, in this article [not shown in this example], border patrol agent Augie Clarkson "the youngest agent in Naco [southeaster border of Arizona]" and "son of a Yuma Border Patrol agent" boasts, "I have a fun job . . . I get to hunt humans for a living."

"Spanish" (1,146 references) is the final concept for this theme of "Immigrants as threatening fauna." Just as English is associated with Whiteness and the language of the national house scale, Spanish is associated with Brownness and seen as a threat to Whiteness and its supremacy. Beneath is an example of this concept:

The Albuquerque Journal: "PAYING THE PRICE: STATE
RESIDENTS ABSORB SOME OF ILLEGAL IMMIGRANTS'
COSTS IN RETURN FOR INEXPENSIVE LABOR"

Bob Wright, one of the leaders of New Mexico's small chapter of the Minutemen.

Wright, who lives in Eunice and works the night shift at a butane processing plant in Hobbs, is tired of hearing *Spanish* spoken in schools, at the convenience store and on the streets.

These immigrants living here now, he said, aren't like the immigrants who built the United States. They don't even try to fit in.

"These people are coming here to suck up what they can get, and they don't come here to become Americans," Wright said. "In my opinion, it's a coarsening of the culture. Loud music, I guess they call it norteo. I tell you, something's changed."

Wright doesn't like a portion of his taxes going to schools where *Spanish* is spoken and Cinco de Mayo is celebrated. In a small town where Anglos outnumber Hispanics (citizens and noncitizens alike), Wright feels under siege.

"I think I should be able to walk in my town and understand what's being said," Wright said. "I've watched southeast New Mexico go from being part of New Mexico to being part of Mexico. We're in danger of losing our culture down here." [....] (Linthicum, 2005, p. A1)

This example is an expression of the "culture war" thesis. In 1992, Pat Buchanan in his speech at the Republican National Convention stated, "There is a religious war going on in this country. It is a cultural war, as critical to the kind of nation we shall be as was the Cold War itself, for this war is for the soul of America" (joelabrown, 2017). Later, his culture war thesis was dramatically broadcast in a campaign ad for his Reform Party presidential bid in 2000 titled "meatball ad."

The TV ad begins with a White, middle-aged man sitting down and eating his spaghetti dinner while listening to the radio in his kitchen. He begins to choke to his dog's alarm when a voice on the radio says "have signed an executive order saying that English is no longer American's national language. It's executive order 13136." He picks up the phone and dials 911 for his medical emergency and hears a woman's automated voice say, "Thank you for calling 911. Please listen for your language. For Spanish, press one, for Korean, press two." As the man panics, a man's voiceover asks, "Do you ever miss English? Immigration is out of control. Bush and Gore are writing off English for good. What can you do? Vote for the third party that puts Americans first. Vote for Buchanan for president." While listening to 911, the man collapses on the floor.

The automated 911 voice continues with, "For Swahili, press 12" (Buchanan, 1992). The hidden message is that languages other than English will "choke" the Whiteness of this nation represented by the White man who is eating spaghetti. The Spanish language option is featured first because it is considered the most threatening. In a similar manner, Bob Wright in this example is also like the White man in the "meat ball" campaign ad when he states, "We're in danger of losing our culture." He is accusing immigrants of not desiring to assimilate ("they don't come here to become Americans" and "They don't even try to fit in") and "coarsening" U.S. American culture with "loud music." He is accusing immigrants of coming to the United States to "suck up what they can get" while lamenting that when he walks in town he does not "understand what's being said" so much so that his town looks like "a part of Mexico."

Furthermore, he is also part of the border vigilante Minutemen who tend to believe in the "Reconquista" thesis that Mexico is taking back its former territories from the United States through undocumented Mexican immigration (Chavez, 2013; also see chapter 1). What is important to note is that in this region, "Spanish has been spoken for many more years than any other European language, has never been eliminated from the region, and counts more native speakers than ever before (Santa Ana, 2002, p. 313). In addition to "cultural wars," policy "wars" also affect the discourse of immigration along the border. The next chapter analyzes the larger scale of region and begins with the theme of "battleground."

In conclusion, this chapter offers an empirical analysis of the second larger nested scale of the house. The scale of the house was the only scale analyzed in a bifurcated manner in this study in order to show the social construction of the house scale as a national home/ranch, occupied by citizens and legal residents, protected with fences and walls, and yet possessing a "revolving door" that makes it vulnerable to threatening immigrant workers, families, and children. The border newspaper coverage helps to imagine immigrants as both home intruders and wild, threatening fauna that cause fear and need to be caught because they threaten the home's safety and economic vitality. These border news scripts communicate White, middle-class, hetero-patriarchal ownership about the national house and property under threat of security breaches. Both racist dirt fixations and nested scales work together to help explain how the physical body contributes to the immigration coverage by offering symbolic borders between inside/outside, purity/pollution and health/disease and particularly how the worries over the USA-Mexico border factor into the production of the White body politic that produces racial genealogies, justifications, and nightmares about border crossings at the scale of the house.

The following chapter will detail the next scale: region. The region scale is imagined and reported on in two ways: as a battlefield and as a cataclysmic flood.

REFERENCES

Agnew, J. (1994). The territorial trap: The geographical assumptions of international relations theory. *Review of International Political Economy*, *1*(1), 53–80.

Ahmed, S. (2007). A phenomenology of whiteness. *Feminist Theory*, *8*(2), 149–168.

Alonso, A. M. (1994). The politics of space, time and substance: State formation, nationalism and ethnicity. *Annual Review of Anthropology*, *23*, 379–405.

Anzaldúa, G. (1987). *Borderlands: La frontera* (Vol. 3). San Francisco, CA: Auntie Lute.

Bachrach, S. (2004). In the name of public health-Nazi racial hygiene. *New England Journal of Medicine*, *351*(5), 417–419.

Borden, T. (2000). Illegal crossers jeered at rally: Calif. groups help stage forum in ranch country. *The Arizona Republic*, May 14, 2000, B1.

Buchanan, P. (1992). Pat Buchanan campaign ad—for Spanish Press 1 [video]. *Youtube.com*. Retrieved from https://www.youtube.com/watch?v=4-KkiYcK7IA.

Buchanan, P. (2002). *The Death of the West: How Dying Populations and Immigrant Invasions Imperil Our Country and Civilization*. New York, NY: St. Martin's Press.

Calavita, K. (1992). *Inside the State: The Bracero Program, Immigration, and the I.N.S.* New York, NY: Routledge.

Carroll, S. (2005). Ariz. border "weakest spot." *The Arizona Republic*, March 31, 2005, A1.

Chavez, L. R. (1996). Borders and bridges: Undocumented immigrants from Mexico and the United States. In S. Pedraza, & R. G. Rumbaut (Eds.) *Origins and Destinies: Immigration, Race, and Ethnicity in America* (pp. 250–262). Belmont, CA: Wadsworth.

Chavez, L. R. (2001). *Covering Immigration: Popular Images and the Politics of the Nation*. Berkeley: University of California Press.

Chavez, L. (2013). *The Latino Threat: Constructing Immigrants, Citizens, and the Nation.* Stanford: Stanford University Press.

Cunningham, H. (2004). Nations rebound? Crossing borders in a gated globe. *Identities: Global Studies in Power and Culture, 11*(3), 329–350.

Cunningham-Parmeter, K. (2011). Alien language: Immigration metaphors and the jurisprudence of otherness. *Fordham Law Review, 79*(4), 1545–1598.

Davis, J. H. (2018). Trump calls some unauthorized immigrants "animals" in rant. *The New York Times,* May 16, 2018. Retrieved from https://www.nytimes.com/2 018/05/16/us/politics/trump-undocumented-immigrants-animals.html.

Delson, J. (2006). Border battle is new turf for Costa Mesa mayor. *Los Angeles Times,* March 6, 2006, B5.

Democracy Now. (2018, November 28). How tear gas became a favorite weapon of U.S. Border Patrol, despite being banned in warfare. *www.democracynow. org.* Retrieved from https://www.democracynow.org/2018/11/28/how_tear_gas_be came_a_favorite.

Després, C. (1991). The meaning of home: Literature review and directions for future research and theoretical development. *Journal of Architectural and Planning Research, 8*(2), 96–115. Retrieved from http://www.jstor.org/stable/43029026.

Douglas, M. (1966). *Purity and Danger.* New York: Routledge.

Fishwick, M. W. (1952). The cowboy: America's contribution to the world's mythology. *Western Folklore, 11*(2), 77–92.

Flannery, P. (2000). More people, more technology, more **danger** border patrol struggles to stem tide. *The Arizona Republic,* January 16, 2000, A15.

Fox, L. (2002). The meaning of home: A chimerical concept or a legal challenge? *Journal of Law and Society, 29*(4), 580–610.

Gaouette, N. (2006). Senate toughens border stand, approves miles of new fence." *Los Angeles Times,* May 18, 2006, A1.

García, J. R. (1980). *Operation Wetback: The mass deportation of Mexican undocumented workers in 1954.* Westport, CT: Greenwood Press.

Gonzalez, G. (2016). *Guest Workers or Colonized Labor? Mexican Labor Migration to the United States.* New York, NY: Routledge.

Grandin, G. (2103). History's sinkhole: How did the U.S.-Mexican border become the place where America chokes on itself? *www.thenation.com,* November 11, 2013. Retrieved from https://www.thenation.com/article/historys-sinkhole/.

Hegstrom, E. (2005). South Texas prosecuting more illegal immigrants/Study shows rise of 345% during latest fiscal year in Southern District. *Houston Chronicle,* August 24, 2018, B.

Hurst, J., & Rotella, S. (1994). U.S. weighing controversial border crossing fee, Reno says: Checkpoints: In Beverly Hills speech, she unveils program to close "revolving door for illegal immigrants." *Los Angeles Times,* September 18, 1994, A-3.

Ilias, S., Fennelly, K., & Federico, C. M. (2008). American attitudes toward guest worker policies. *International Migration Review, 42*(4), 741–766.

Jenkins, A. (2018). *www.TIME.com.* Retrieved from http://time.com/5268572/jeff-s essions-illegal-border-separated/.

Joelabrown. (2017). https://voices.uchicago.edu/religionculture/2017/07/11/the-s truggle-is-real-understanding-the-american-culture-war-by-russell-d/.

Kaiser, R. J. (2002). 12 Homeland making and the territorialization of national identity. In D. Conversi (Ed.), *Ethnonationalism in the Contemporary World: Walker Connor and the Study of Nationalism* (pp. 229–247). New York, NY: Routledge.

Kaplan, A. (2003). Homeland insecurities: Reflections on language and space. *Radical History Review, 85,* 82–93.

Kil, S. H., Menjívar, C., & Doty, R. L. (2009). Securing borders: Patriotism, vigilantism and the brutalization of the U.S. American public. In *Immigration, Crime and Justice* (pp. 297–312). Bingley, UK: Emerald Group.

Kohn, M. (2004). *Brave New Neighborhoods: The Privatization of Public Space.* New York, NY: Routledge.

Lazarus, E. (1883). The new colossus. *www.poetryfoundation.org.* Retrieved from https://www.poetryfoundation.org/poems/46550/the-new-colossus.

Lee, E. (2002). The Chinese Exclusion example: Race, immigration, and American gatekeeping, 1882–1924. *Journal of American Ethnic History, 21*(3), 36–62. Retrieved from http://www.jstor.org.libaccess.sjlibrary.org/stable/27502847.

Lee, E. (2003). *At America's Gates: Chinese Immigration during the Exclusion Era, 1882–1943.* Chapel Hill: University of North Carolina Press.

Linthicum, L. (2005). Paying the price: State residents absorb some of illegal immigrants' costs in return for inexpensive labor. *The Albuquerque Journal,* August 28, 2005, A1.

Lucas, T., & Katz, A. (1994). Reframing the debate: The roles of native languages in English-only programs for language minority students. *Tesol Quarterly, 28*(3), 537–561.

Macedo, D. (2000). The colonialism of the English only movement. *Educational Researcher, 29*(3), 15–24.

Macías-Rojas, P. (2016). *From Deportation to Prison: The Politics of Immigration Enforcement in Post-civil Rights America.* New York: NYU Press.

Medrano Leslie, L. (1995). Couple fought way to success, immigrants "must struggle a lot," they say immigration el otro lado—the other side. *The Arizona Republic,* May 7, 1995, A9.

Mohanty, C. T. (2004). *Feminism without Borders: Decolonizing Theory, Practicing Solidarity.* Durham: Duke University Press.

Neiwert, d. (2014). Jim Gilchrist continues denying ties to Shawna Forde as he tries to revive Minutemen. www.splcenter.org, August 05, 2014. Retrieved from https://www.splcenter.org/hatewatch/2014/08/05/jim-gilchrist-continues-denying-ties-shawna-forde-he-tries-revive-minutemen.

New York Times. (2018). Trump says it. Should journalists? On "catch and release." *The New York Times,* July 11, 2018. Retrieved from https://www.nytimes.com/2018/07/11/reader-center/trump-catch-and-release.html.

O'Neill, P. L. (1995). Construction jobs draw host of illegal workers. *The Albuquerque Journal,* September 18, 1995, p. 1.

Ordover, N. (2003). *American Eugenics: Race, Queer Anatomy, and the Science of Nationalism.* Minneapolis: University of Minnesota Press.

Perry, S. (1983). Rhetorical functions of the infestation metaphor in Hitler's rhetoric. *Communication Studies, 34*(4), 229–235.

Prchal, T. (2007). Reimagining the melting pot and the golden door: National identity in gilded age and Progressive Era literature. *Melus, 32*(1), 29–51.

Quinnipiac University National Poll. (2018, July 3). *Harsh Words for U.S. Family Separation Policy, Quinnipiac University National Poll Finds; Voters have Dim View of Trump, Dems on Immigration.* Hamden, CT: Quinnipiac University National Poll. Retrieved from https://poll.qu.edu/images/polling/us/us07032018_utsl28.pdf/.

Ranch Rescue. (2018). About. Retrieved from www.ranchrescue.com.

Rhodan, M. (2018). *www.TIME.com,* June 20, 2018. Retrieved from http://time.com/5314769/family-separation-policy-donald-trump/.

Rodrigúez, N. (1997). The social construction of the U.S.-Mexico border. In J. F. Perea (Ed.), *Immigrants Out! The New Nativism and the Anti-immigrant Impulse in the United States* (pp. 223–243). New York: New York University Press.

Rosenberg, E. (2018). Sessions defends separating immigrant parents and children. *Washington Post.* Retrieved from https://www.washingtonpost.com/news/post-politics/wp/2018/06/05/sessions-defends-separating-immigrant-parents-and-children-weve-got-to-get-this-message-out/?utm_term=.b07986a25b7f.

Said, E. (1993). *Culture and Imperialism.* New York, NY: Vintage Books.

Santa Ana, O. (1999). Like an animal I was treated': Anti-immigrant metaphor in U.S. public discourse. *Discourse & Society, 10*(2), 191–224.

Santa Ana, O. (2002). *Brown Tide Rising: Metaphors of Latinos in Contemporary American Public Discourse.* Austin: University of Texas Press.

Sit, R. (2018). Jeff Sessions faces fresh racism charge after praising "Anglo-American heritage of law enforcement." *Newsweek,* February 12, 2018. Retrieved from https://www.newsweek.com/jeff-sessions-racism-anglo-american-sheriff-803624.

Sonmez, F., & Wagner, J. (2018). Trump lashes out at Paul Ryan over birthright citizenship comments, says he "should be focusing on holding the Majority." *The Washington Post,* October 31, 2018. Retrieved from https://www.washingtonpost.com/politics/trump-presses-on-with-case-to-end-birthright-citizenship-one-way-or-the-other/2018/10/31/bcd69dc2-dd12-11e8-85df-7a6b4d25cfbb_story.html?utm_term=.94d4b99d3665.

Southern Poverty Law Center. (2009a). Arizona nativist found liable in vigilante action. *www.splcenter.org.* Retrieved from https://www.splcenter.org/fighting-hate/intelligence-report/2009/arizona-nativist-found-liable-vigilante-action.

Southern Poverty Law Center. (2018). Leiva v. Ranch Rescue: Case number CC-03-77. *www.splcenter.org.* Retrieved from https://www.splcenter.org/seeking-justice/case-docket/leiva-v-ranch-rescue.

Stiles, M. (2006). 500 protest immigrant "invasion" in Crawford/Minutemen join a Latino group to show disfavor with current policy. *Houston Chronicle,* May 7, 2006, B.

Sullivan, S. (2014). Arizona GOP official resigns after controversial comments. *Washington Post,* September 15, 2014. Retrieved from https://www.washingtonpost.com/news/post-politics/wp/2014/09/15/arizona-gop-official-resigns-after-controversial-comments/?utm_term=.e527614c8d19.

Sullivan, S. (2018). We shouldn't take the bat on "catch and release." *ACLU.org,* July 20, 2018. Retrieved from https://www.aclu.org/blog/immigrants-rights/immigrants-rights-and-detention/we-shouldnt-take-bait-catch-and-release.

Thompson, F. (2001). 117 immigrants detained in 2 days: Border agents expect traffic in Bootheel to increase as security in Arizona is beefed up. *The Albuquerque Journal*, June 8, 2001, A1.

TIME. (2018). Top 10 campaign ads of all time: Willie Horton. *www.TIME.com*. Retrieved from http://content.time.com/time/specials/packages/article/0,28804,18 42516_1842514_1842557,00.html.

Trump, D. J. (2018a, April 6). Presidential memoranda. *www.whitehouse.gov*. Retrieved from https://www.whitehouse.gov/presidential-actions/presidential -memorandum-secretary-state-secretary-defense-attorney-general-secretary-he alth-human-services-secretary-homeland-security.

Trump, D. J. [realDonaldTrump]. (2018b, June 18). It is the Democrats fault for being weak and ineffective with Boarder Security and Crime. Tell them to start thinking about the people devastated by Crime coming from illegal immigration. Change the laws! [Twitter moment]. Retrieved from https://twitter.com/realDonaldTrump/stat us/1008709364939677697?ref_src=twsrc%5Etfw%7Ctwcamp%5Etweetembed% 7Ctwterm%5E1008709364939677697&ref_url=http%3A%2F%2Fdidtrumptweet it.com%2F2018%2F06%2F18%2F.

Trump, D. J. [realDonaldTrump]. (2018c, June 19). Democrats are the problem. They don't care about crime and want illegal immigrants, no matter how bad they may be, to pour into and infest our Country, like MS-13. They can't win on their terrible policies, so they view them as potential voters! [Twitter moment]. Retrieved from https://twitter.com/realdonaldtrump/status/1009071403918864385.

Trump, D. J. (2018d, June 20). Executive orders: Affording Congress an opportunity to address family separation. *www.whitehouse.gov*. Retrieved from https:// www.whitehouse.gov/presidential-actions/affording-congress-opportunity-addres s-family-separation/.

Trump, D. J. [realDonaldTrump]. (2018e, June 24). We cannot allow all of these people to invade our Country. When somebody comes in, we must immediately, with no Judges or Court Cases, bring them back from where they came. Our system is a mockery to good immigration policy and Law and Order. Most children come without parents . . . [Twitter moment]. Retrieved from https://twitter.com/reald onaldtrump/status/1010900865602019329?lang=en.

Trump, D. J. [realDonaldTrump]. (2018f, July 5). . . . Country being forced to endure a long and costly trial. Tell the people "OUT," and they must leave, just as they would if they were standing on your front lawn. Hiring thousands of "judges" does not work and is not acceptable—only Country in the World that does this! [Twitter moment]. Retrieved from https://twitter.com/realdonaldtrump/status/1014875 575557804034?lang=en.

Trump, D. J. [realDonaldTrump]. (2018g, July 29). Please understand, there are consequences when people cross our Border illegally, whether they have children or not - and many are just using children for their own sinister purposes. Congress must act on fixing the DUMBEST & WORST immigration laws anywhere in the world! Vote "R" [Twitter moment]. Retrieved from https://twitter .com/realDonaldTrump/status/1023538164298858497?ref_src=twsrc%5Etfw%7C twcamp%5Etweetembed%7Ctwterm%5E1023538164298858497&ref_url=https% 3A%2F%2Fwww.yahoo.com%2Fnews%2F.

Trump, D. J. [realDonaldTrump]. (2018h, October 31). So-called Birthright Citizenship, which costs our Country billions of dollars and is very unfair to our citizens, will be ended one way or the other. It is not covered by the 14th Amendment because of the words "subject to the jurisdiction thereof." Many legal scholars agree . . . [Twitter moment]. Retrieved from https://twitter.com/realDonaldTrump/status/1057624553478897665?ref_src=twsrc%5Etfw%7Ctwcamp%5Etweetembed%7Ctwterm%5E1057624553478897665&ref_url=https%3A%2F%2Fwww.washingtonpost.com%2Fpolitics%2Ftrump-presses-on-with-case-to-end-birthright-citizenship-one-way-or-the-other%2F2018%2F10%2F31%2Fbcd69dc2-dd12-11e8-85df-7a6b4d25cfbb_story.html.

Trump, D. J. [realDonaldTrump]. (2018i, October 31). . . . Harry Reid was right in 1993, before he and the Democrats went insane and started with the Open Borders (which brings massive Crime) "stuff." Don't forget the nasty term Anchor Babies. I will keep our Country safe. This case will be settled by the United States Supreme Court! [Twitter moment]. Retrieved from https://twitter.com/realDonaldTrump/status/1057637708296794114?ref_src=twsrc%5Etfw%7Ctwcamp%5Etweetembed%7Ctwterm%5E1057637708296794114&ref_url=https%3A%2F%2Fwww.washingtonpost.com%2Fpolitics%2Ftrump-presses-on-with-case-to-end-birthright-citizenship-one-way-or-the-other%2F2018%2F10%2F31%2Fbcd69dc2-dd12-11e8-85df-7a6b4d25cfbb_story.html.

Trump, D. J. (2018j). Donald Trump denies being a racist after recent crude remark. *BBC.com*. Retrieved from https://www.bbc.com/news/world-us-canada-42685356.

Wagner, D., & Flannery, P. (2000). Questions Trump answers in war on drugs: Lots of cash, little to show for all of it. *The Arizona Republic*, January 16, 2000, A14.

Watters, C. (2006). Lawmakers sift through 21 surviving referendums. *The Arizona Republic*, May 22, 2006, B1.

West, C. (1988). Marxist theory and the specificity of Afro-American oppression. In C. Nelson & L. Grossberg (Eds.), *Marxism and the Interpretation of Culture* (pp. 17–33). Urbana: University of Illinois Press.

Willett, C. (2001). *The Soul of Justice: Social Bonds and Racial Hubris*. Ithaca: Cornell University Press.

Young, I. M. (2005). House and home: Feminist variations on a theme. In S. Hardy & C. Wiedmer (Eds.), *Motherhood and Space*. New York: Palgrave Macmillan.

Chapter 5

A Battlefield and a Cataclysmic Flood (Region Scale)

In her book, *Playing in the Dark: Whiteness and the Literary Imagination*, Toni Morrison (1992) writes:

> Race has become metaphorical—a way of referring to and disguising forces, events, classes, and expressions of social decay and economic division far more threatening to the body politic than biological "race" ever was. Expensively kept, economically unsound, a spurious and useless political asset in election campaigns, racism is as healthy today as it was during the Enlightenment. It seems that it has a utility far beyond economy, beyond the sequestering of classes from one another, and has assumed a metaphorical life so completely embedded in daily discourse that it is perhaps more necessary and more on display than ever before. (p. 63)

Morrison argues that notions of individualism, freedom, masculinity, and innocence among U.S. American classics by White authors such as Herman Melville, Ernest Hemingway, and Edgar Allen Poe rely on the reflexive construction of Blackness as inherently unfree. These authors used Blackness to project a terror and negative desire without having to acknowledge these racialized feelings as their own. Her work thus helps to shift the "critical gaze from the racial object to the racial subject; from the described and imagined to the describers and imaginers; from the serving to the served" (p. 90).

The "war on the border," "war on terror," and "war on drugs" that affect the border region are racialized policies disguised as race neutral necessities in fighting undocumented immigration, terrorism, and drug crimes. Much like the literacy criticism that Morrison (1992) applies to classic White men authors, there is a racialized construction that occurs on the border region where these "wars" rely on the reflexive construction of the "Brownness"

107

of border crossings that in turn create the "Whiteness" of the nation without having to acknowledge racist beliefs in the superiority of Whiteness to Brownness. The racism of these "wars" is embedded in news discourse about the border.

Moreover, the racism of these "wars" reflects in the rising count of human beings that have perished in the border region. U.S. American Border Patrol tracks border sector deaths by fiscal year beginning in 1998 and ending in its most recent publication of 2017. In total, Border Patrol (2017) has counted 7,216 deaths on the border based on human remains the agency has discovered and counted. However, academics, government agencies, and news organizations have criticized the Border Patrol for undercounting in these deaths. The General Accounting Office (2006) notes that the Border Patrol method of tracking deaths in the border region was inconsistent across Border Sectors. Hinkes (2008) argues that there needs to be better cooperation between forensics scientists, investigative agencies, and border nations in

Table 5.1   Racist Dirt Fixations at the Regional Scale

Tier 1 Theory	Racist Dirt Fixations	
Tier 2 4 Scales	Region	
Tier 3 Themes	"Battleground"	"cataclysmic flood"
Tier 4 Concepts	War (4,037 references) [includes war (981), attack (830), fight (783), battle (359), struggle (323), combat (219), confront (196), invade (166), clash (78), overcome (66), taking over [exact phrase] (15), conquer (14), onslaught (7)]	"flow" (652 references)
	Smuggle (4,043 references) [includes smuggle (3,050) and trafficking (984)]	"river" (646 references),
	Protect (2,975 references) [includes protect (1,021), guard (966), defend (540), save (448)]	"waves" (379 references)
	Foreign (2,384 references) [includes foreign (1,492), alien (770), strange (122)]	"overwhelm" (220 references)
	Arrest (2,357 references)	"flood" (213 references).
	Military (2,273 references) [includes military (794), troop (491), army (305), soldier (278), marine (221), air force (71), navy (63), militia (50)]	
	Kill (1,676 references) [kill (1,103), murder (433), homicide (140)]	
	Courts (1,632 references)	
	Terrorism (1,356 references).	

order to improve the accuracy of the count. Eschbach, Hagan, and Rodriguez (2003) reveal there are an "uncounted number of additional persons whose bodies have yet to be—and perhaps may never be—discovered" (p. 47). CNN's Bob Ortega (2018) reported:

> Over the 16 fiscal years ended last September [2002–2017], CNN has identified at least 564 deaths of people crossing illegally in the border region, above and beyond the Border Patrol's tally of 5,984.

Those uncounted deaths were identified through a review of federal, state, and local records and databases, and interviews with medical examiners, pathologists, sheriffs, and justices of the peace along the border. It is by no means a complete count, and there are strong indications that the actual toll could be thousands higher.

This chapter offers an empirical analysis of the third nested scale: region. The border newspaper coverage ascribes imaginings to immigrants that renders them as less-than-human abstractions by portraying them as enemies in a battle as well as a cataclysmic flood. First, in the "Battlefield" theme, border newspapers help to portray immigrants as an invading army that naturalize and justify the deaths in this region as collateral damage. Second, in the "Flood" theme, these newspapers associate immigration with menacing waters that suggest the drowning of the nation, either by natural forces or by means of a biblical flood.

BATTLEGROUND

Recall in chapter 2 that I used two frameworks together to make sense of the militarization of the border and the human rights crisis of immigrant deaths that occur in the region. First, Mbembe's (2003) concept of Necropolitics refer to the process of colonization that allows the colonizer to decide who will live and who will die. I extend Mbembe's analysis of Necropolitics to not only encompass the state's right to kill as punishment or in war, but to also includes the right to expose people to death. In regard to the USA-Mexico border, the policy strategy of "prevention through deterrence" and the use of the desert as a border-crossing deterrent is an exercise of state control over immigrant mortality. Second, I use the concept of Necropolitics with brutalization theory to help explain why border policies have a negative, wide-ranging effect on the general public. Brutalization theory explains how the public imitates the state as it metes out punishments on criminals, in that the public morally identifies with the state as it punishes (Bowers & Pierce, 1980). Thus, the state conveys a brutal moral lesson to its citizenry that deadly violence is an acceptable solution for people who break the law. The Posse Comitatus Statute was altered in 1982 to allow civilian law enforcement agents to deputize members of the military to help control civilian populations (Dunn, 1996).

Thus the "war on drugs," the "war on terror," and the "war on the border," all these discursive "wars" influence the public in a negative, racialized way to seek the "enemies" of these wars and mete out "justice" to them. However, these wars also reflect a type of moral disgust in relation to nativist anxiety that lead to magical thinking about geographic contagion in the border region in that immigrants are seen as enemy invaders intent on taking over the nation (see chapter 1).

The "war" concept (4,037 references) leads this region scale with the stemmed word "war" (981) and the additional stemmed synonyms of "attack" (830), "fight" (788), "battle" (363), and more (see Table 5.1 for all stemmed words that make-up this concept). I include the concept "military" (2,273 references) here with "war" concept for efficiency purposes, even though the "military" concept is less frequent than the "war" concept (see Table 5.1). Underneath is an example of the "war" and "military" concept:

> *The Houston Chronicle*: "Border Shooting Spurs New *Military* Training/Officials Defend Use of *Marines* in Drug *War*"

EL PASO—In a California forest near the Mexican border in 1991, a poacher saw a greenish glint in the darkness. Assuming he was looking into an animal's eyes, the poacher fired his rifle, wounding a camouflaged U.S. *Marine* wearing night-vision optical gear. In Northern California four years later, a carload of target shooters rolled to a stop on a desolate forest road. A passenger got out and fired randomly into the woods, striking a well-hidden U.S. *Army soldier* who was stationed there to monitor illegal drug activity.

Although *military* rules of engagement allow fired-upon *troops* to shoot civilians in self-defense, these *soldiers* held their fire after deciding that they were attacked unintentionally.

But in May, on the stark desert terrain near Redford, Texas, a *Marine* who felt threatened by a goat herder, who had fired two shots from a .22-caliber rifle, returned the fire with his M-16. The 18-year-old civilian was killed, and new questions were raised about the wisdom of using *battle*-ready *troops* in the border drug *war*.

Military officials adamantly defend the legal authority of the *troops* in Texas to answer a perceived threat. But they also call the California *troops'* decision not to shoot back an example of quick thinking, proper training and restraint. They also acknowledge that new training has been mandated since the Redford shooting to clarify that deadly force isn't always warranted.

"The last thing we want to do is have the American people afraid of us," said *Air Force* Col. Henry Hungerbeeler, chief of staff of Joint Task Force-6, an El Paso-based command that has coordinated 3,300 *military* counterdrug missions since its inception in 1989.

The shooting of Esequiel Hernandez in Redford has prompted a Presidio County grand jury probe and a *military* investigation—unprecedented in the history of the U.S. *armed forces'* role in the *war* on drugs. *Military* officials say it is the ninth incident in which gunfire has erupted during JTF-6 missions. [. . . .] (Gonzalez, 1997, p. 1)

Timothy Dunn, one of the first theorist of border militarization, writes, "The Southwest border is perhaps the key locus of militarization of law enforcement in the United States, for it is also the site of the longest-running manifestation of such efforts . . . [since 1991] and the home of the deepest institutional ties between the military and police bodies" (Dunn, 2001, p. 7). Dunn (1996) applies the military doctrine of low-intensity conflict (LIC) used to control target civilian populations in developing countries (particularly Central America) to quell uprising and revolutions to the border region. LIC possesses three key qualities: "(1) an emphasis on the internal defense of a nation, (2) an emphasis on controlling targeted civilian populations rather than territory, and (3) the assumption by the military of police-like and other unconventional, typically nonmilitary roles, along with the adoption by the police of military characteristics (Dunn, 1996, p. 21). JTF-6 represents this integration of police and military LIC doctrine on the border. "Since its inception in 1989, the joint task force has completed more than 5,800 counter-drug missions in direct support of more than 430 different local, state and federal law enforcement agencies and counter-drug task forces" (U.S. Northern Command, 2004).

JTF-6 (now called JTF-North) is one of the longest-lasting joint task forces in U.S. American military history and is the "principal coordinating body for collaborative drug enforcement efforts in the Southwest border region" (Dunn, 2001, p. 10). The newspaper article example opens with two incidents where camouflaged or hidden military personnel were shot by unknowing civilians where "military rules of engagement allow fired-upon troops to shoot civilians in self-defense," however only "restraint" prevented the injury or death of these civilians whose deaths would have been justifiable otherwise. But that was not the case for Esequiel Hernández, Jr. In 1997, in an example of how brutalizing Necropolitics not only apply to undocumented immigrants but to racialized U.S. American citizens as well, Marines with Joint Task Force 6 stalked and killed 18-year-old Esequiel Hernández, Jr. who had been herding his family's goats near the border. The Marines did not provide immediate aid thinking he was a drug runner and the teenager bled out on the hill overlooking his home. No one was convicted of his murder (see chapter 2).

The next most frequent concept is "smuggle" (4,034 references) and includes the stemmed word "smuggle" (3,050 references) and also includes the synonym "trafficking" (984 references). Below is an example of "smuggle" concept:

> *The Houston Chronicle*: "Rider tells a stark story of fatal trip/Witness
> says Williams ignored immigrants' cries from inside trailer"

> After ignoring the screams and banging that came from his trailer for hours as he drove toward Houston, Tyrone Williams finally pulled off the highway, opened the trailer doors and got a look at his human cargo, his traveling companion testified Wednesday.
> Quickly unhitching his truck and muttering to himself as he drove away, he told his wife on the phone, "The people are dead," Fatima Holloway said.
> "He said, 'They're dead. They're dead,'" she told jurors.
> Taking the witness stand on the seventh day of Williams' trial, Holloway gave a stark account of the botched *smuggling* attempt that led to the deaths of 19 illegal immigrants in May 2003.
> During four hours of testimony, her story sometimes differed sharply from the accounts that Williams gave authorities after driving to Houston and checking himself into a hospital.
> Holloway, of Cleveland, Ohio, said she heard the screams and pounding during the journey and yelled at Williams to let the riders out of his sealed trailer.
> "He didn't respond to it," she said.
> Prosecutors are seeking the death penalty, contending that Williams, a legal Jamaican immigrant from Schenectady, N.Y., knew his passengers were enduring lethal conditions but did nothing to save them.
> Defense attorneys acknowledge that Williams *smuggled* illegal immigrants, but says he is not responsible for the deaths. (Lezon, 2005, p. B)

This is one of the more horrific examples of human smuggling in the border region that resulted in the death of nineteen people by dehydration, overheating, and suffocation. One of the victims was a five-year-old boy. The brutality of this incident was detailed in the U.S. American Court of Appeals for the Fifth Circuit in a 2010 ruling when describing what authorities found in Williams' trailer:

> There were several dead bodies on the ground by the trailer doors. Bodies, both dead and living, were stacked in a pile in the trailer. Some of the aliens were standing behind the pile. The aliens were stripped down to their underwear and were sweating. They had clawed at the foam on the inside of the trailer, and the trailer smelled of vomit, urine, feces, and blood. (Hawkins, 2016, para. 17)

In May 13, 2003, Williams, a dairy trucker, agreed to smuggle 74 people for 120 miles for $7,500 in southeast Texas. The plan changed, and the smugglers ordered him to drive an additional 200 miles. William never turned on the refrigeration in his trailer for the trip and temperatures rose to 173 degrees inside. In 2011, he was sentenced to nearly thirty-four years in prison without parole (Hawkins, 2016).

While this example is sympathetic to the horrible plight these immigrants endured in that trailer, the use of the term "human cargo" exemplifies another manner of dehumanization that applies to immigrants. Santa Ana (2002) notes that immigrants are seen as a commodity or resource in public debates. Immigrants are also treated in discourse like an "object" or "material" "whose distinctive characteristic was in their value to the nation as cheap labor" (O'Brian, 2003, p.39). "Human cargo" is an example of how immigrants are treated as a thing or commodity.

The next most frequent concept is "protect" (2,975 references) and includes the stemmed word "protect" (2,975 references) and the additional stemmed synonyms (see Table 5.1). Below is an example of the "protect" concept.

The Arizona Republic: "CALIF.'S LESSON: REFORMS
DON'T STOP ILLEGAL IMMIGRATION"

Known as *Protect* Arizona Now, the measure requires public employees to check citizenship when individuals register to vote or apply for non-federally mandated public benefits.

Like California's *Save* Our State measure, it has gained widespread support. Sixty-six percent of 600 registered voters surveyed earlier this month said they supported the measure, 15 percent said they opposed it and 19 percent said they didn't have an opinion, according to The Arizona Republic Poll.

"When voters speak, politicians listen," said Randy Pullen, the chairman of the Yes on Proposition 200 Committee. "This is the first step toward an immigration reform."

Earl de Berge, a Phoenix pollster who has conducted surveys on Proposition 200, said the initiative is designed to encourage the most conservative voters in Arizona to turn out at the polls, thus pressuring local and federal lawmakers to discuss the illegal immigration problem.

Regardless of the outcome, the vote sends a message. It triggers a debate that could, as Proposition 187 did, set the stage for congressional action on immigration. [. . . .] (*The Arizona Republic*, 2004, p. A1)

In 2004, Arizonans approved Proposition 200 called the Arizona Taxpayer and Citizen Protection Act, also known as "Protect Arizona Now" (PAN), which requires individuals to show proof of citizenship to vote or receive certain public benefits. Inspired by California's Prop 187's "Save our State" or "S.O.S" (sinking ship distress call) initiative, PAN's chairman of the national advisory board Virginia Abernethy, then professor emeritus at Vanderbilt University School of Medicine, promoted White supremacy and racial "separation" (Wells, 2001, para. 3). Much like Prop 187 "sent a message" to both the federal government and undocumented immigration that California voters were frustrating with immigration in 1994 (Calavita, 1996), ten years later, Prop 200 again "sends a message" to undocumented immigrants, voters, and the nation that Arizona's resources need to be "saved" and "protected" from undocumented immigration. President Trump also attempted to revive these types of nativist fears by insinuating that undocumented immigrants participate in voter fraud (Huseman, 2018), but the commission he appointed to investigate the matter found no widespread evidence of such (Rosenberg, 2018).

The next frequent concept for the "battlefield" region scale is "foreign" (2,384 references) and includes the stemmed word "foreign" (1,492 references) as well as the synonyms "alien" (770 references) and "stranger" (122 references) for a total of 2,395 references for this synonym group. Below is an example of this concept.

The Arizona Republic: "HULL CALLS FOR MEXICAN JOB
PROGRAM IMMIGRANTS COULD TAKE SHUNNED WORK"

Gov. Jane Hull on Friday called for a program to let Mexicans take jobs Arizonans shun as part of campaign to stop immigrants from illegally streaming across the state's southeastern border. At a luncheon attended by officials from Agua Prieta, Sonora, and Douglas, Hull heard some grim accounts of the havoc being caused from Douglas to Naco by immigrants.

"We're being invaded," said resident Larry Vance Jr., who complained of trash, health and crime problems associated with *aliens*.

"Most of them are economic refugees. Some of them are criminals. . . . This problem has caused everyone around here to arm themselves."

Residents and authorities agree the influx stems from beefed-up border blockades in California, Texas, and Nogales—measures that have closed traditional routes and forced immigrants into southeastern Arizona.

Hull told Douglas leaders she is going to the nation's capital Monday and hopes to meet with key congressional leaders and Attorney General Janet Reno. The agenda is simple, she added: "To see if we can loosen up those Washington purse strings" for more Border Patrol agents and equipment.

Hull expressed amazement when she learned that the Immigration and Naturalization Service has no aircraft based in the Douglas-Naco border area.

"We have a war in Kosovo, yet we can't get three helicopters in Douglas, and that offends me," she said.

Hull went to Douglas in a bid to reassure residents who have become harried by the immigration mess. Noting that an estimated 49,000 immigrants are entering Arizona each month, she said, "I know it's stretching you as completely as you can be stretched." [. . . .] (Wagner, 1999, p. B2)

The racist dirt fixations that have been analyzed in a symbolic way in regard to the four scales (body, house, region, and nation), manifest in a literal way with the "trash" and "mess" association with immigrants in this example along with "health and crime problems." Immigrants are portrayed as a social pathology and "havoc." "We're being invaded .... This problem has caused everyone around here to arm themselves." "Beefed-up border blockades" describe the results of the "prevention through deterrence" strategy in the Arizona region. Popular culture and images of health tend to associate beef with muscle and masculinity (Stibbe, 2004). In addition, after "September 11, 2001, the Bush administration and the nation embarked on a strange and fated project of 'manning up'" (Mann, 2008, p. 179) that involved preemptive wars in his global "war on terror." This "war on terror's manning-up" also affected the "war on the border's beefing-up" with the same association of muscle to masculinity. In addition, Dyer (1997) examines the "White man's muscles" in colonial settings among popular films like Tarzan and Rambo and finds that the White "hero is up against foreignness, its treacherous terrain and inhabitants, animal and human" (p.156). Governor Jane Hull's "amazement" that her call for "muscle" with "three helicopters in Douglas" is thwarted despite the nation's "war in Kosovo" at that time, "offends" her. In addition, Hull proposes a program where "Mexicans take jobs Arizonans shun" at the same time hearing residents of Southeast Arizona call immigration a foreign "invasion." Cacho (2012) notes that this argument that immigrants do the jobs citizens shun attempts to put value on undocumented immigrant work but also constructs these jobs as a privilege and naturalizes the logic that these jobs should be exploitative with low pay and those that hold them, citizen or not, should feel "lucky" to have them (p. 19). The U.S. American middle-class consumer "assumes the position of [USA's] valued population" within this argument (Cacho, 2013, p. 19) and the "invasion" metaphor helps to put more value in middle-class purchasing power of undocumented people's labor.

The next leading region concept for the "battlefield" theme is "arrest" (2,357 references).

The Los Angeles Times: "Formal Deportation Is
Much Less Common Than Expulsion"

Deportation is the enforcement activity most closely associated with the U.S. Immigration and Naturalization Service.

But deportation—usually after a final order by an immigration judge—is far from the most frequently used method.

The vast majority of people expelled by the INS do not go through formal proceedings. Most never have their day in court. There simply wouldn't be enough agents, immigration judges or detention spaces. During the 1996 fiscal year, the INS recorded a near-record 1.6 million *arrests* of suspected illegal immigrants, the great bulk of them from Mexico. That huge volume makes the INS the nation's most prolific arresting agency.

Of those, however, only 68,657 were formally deported. Officials say that about an equal number of illegal immigrants were expelled from the United States interior after agreeing to leave without formal orders of deportation.

But the vast majority of expulsions—more than 1.5 million—involved illegal immigrants arrested by Border Patrol agents in the U.S.–Mexico border area and quickly returned to Mexico. All were considered "voluntary returns"—that is, those who left signed forms agreeing to be sent home without hearings. Once back, many just turned around in Tijuana or other points and attempted to cross again—the oft-lamented "revolving door" that has long characterized the Southwest border. (McDonnell, 1997, p. A-14)

This narrative is framed though the "war" paradigm and reflects frustrations that "1.6 million" arrests do not go to court and deportations but instead lead to "voluntary returns" only for many immigrants to try the "revolving door" of the USA-Mexico border. Again, the invocation of "revolving door" as a crime script suggests that immigrants of color are here to rape or pillage rather than work and live in the United States. This presents an interesting juxtaposition to "beefed-up." When President Trump declares that immigrants are rapists, and crime scripts like "revolving door" are used that suggest people of color rape White women (much like the President Bush, Sr.'s Willie Horton campaign ad, see chapter 3) and calls to "beef-up" the border are answered, the femininization of Whiteness of the nation is contrasted by the masculinization of border militarization. The Whiteness of the nation is feminized in gendered scripts as vulnerable and in need of protection (see chapter 3). The feminine body tends to be "otherized" as "open" and "leaky" with too many orifices (De Ras & Grace, 1997, p. 10), much like the border. While the militarization of the border is masculinized and "beefed-up" as seen in the many prior examples in this study. Additionally, since the masculinized body tends to be seen as "whole" and "closed" (p. 10), calls to "beef-up" the border are masculinized attempts to close the border.

The next frequent concept for the "battlefield" region scale is "kill" (1,676 references) and includes the stem word "kill" (1,103 references) and also stemmed synonyms "murder" (433 references) and "homicide" (140 references). Beneath is an example of this concept.

The Arizona Republic: "*MURDERS* GO UNSOLVED
AS SMUGGLING GROWS: PHOENIX *HOMICIDES*
SETTING RECORD PACE THIS YEAR"

Two out of three *killers* are getting away with murder in Phoenix this year as the city's homicide tally climbs toward a record. Through October, 216 people were *killed* in Phoenix, more than in all of last year. At the current pace, Phoenix will pass the record 241 *homicides* in 1994.

Beleaguered *homicide* detectives say they are so overwhelmed by bodies that, in some cases, they can do little more than just document the *murder* scene and move on to the next one.

As a result, the city's clearance rate has dropped to an unprecedented 31 percent. The average clearance rate last year was 58 percent for cities with populations greater than 250,000. In Phoenix last year, 48 percent of *murders* were solved. (*The Arizona Republic*, 2003, p. A1)

The mass casualties of the "war on drugs," "war on terror," and "war on the border" are not citizens but immigrants. This example shows that they do not just perish in the desert, but because they are driven underground by border militarization policies, that this violence continues to affect them long after they cross the border (Kil & Menjivar, 2006) as a result of the growth in the smuggling industry. Fulginiti (2008) elaborates in detail:

1998–1999, the number of deaths among border crossers was 28. That number increased dramatically in 1999–2000 to 106 and has exceeded 200 in each of the past 2 years. In the past, many immigrant deaths occurred as a result of dehydration and exposure. More recently, a new trend has emerged, that is, death of border crossers at the hands of the persons ("*coyotes*" or "*polleros*") hired to lead them across the border to safety. In some cases, the smugglers attempt to extort additional money from the families by holding the victims hostage once they have crossed the border into the United States. If the families fail to pay, the hostage is killed. Rival gangs are also murdering one another over their human cargo. (p. 41)

The use of the Spanish terms *coyotes* or *polleros* are examples of Mock or Cowboy Spanish (Hill, 2009) and will be discussed in the next chapter.

The next example of the "battlefield" region is the concept "courts" (1,632 references).

The Albuquerque Journal: "*Court* Overload; Illegal immigrants crush *courts* in an already overburdened judicial system. It's reached a crisis point. So say judges, prosecutors, defense attorneys, and the U.S. marshals' service. Immigration cases are overwhelming the federal *court* system—with no end in sight."

LAS CRUCES—A stream of men and women file into federal court, the clinking of their leg shackles punctuating the hum of activity from lawyers and interpreters.

More than twenty detainees, every one of them Spanish speakers and most facing various illegal immigration charges, fill the seats in the jury box and spill into other *courtroom* seats under the watchful eye of guards.

"You caught us on a slow day," one defense lawyer remarks.

Illegal immigrants are not causing a major amount of the state's crime problems, according to law-enforcement officials and figures from jails and prisons.

What illegal crossers are doing, however, is pushing the entire New Mexico federal *court* system near a breaking point.

The sheer volume of immigration cases filed in federal *courts* is crushing. And thousands of federal prisoners are being housed in county lockups—on Uncle Sam's dime—while they await the outcome of their cases. [. . . .] (Jones, 2005, p. A1)

The alarmist title of this example declares "Illegal immigrants crush *courts* . . . . It's reached a crisis point . . . with no end in sight." "A stream of men and women" with "leg shackles" speaking "Spanish" "spill" into "other courtroom seats." A defense attorney remarks that this is a "slow day," despite the watery rhetoric of flooding throughout in this example. The region scale offers the theme of "cataclysmic flood" later in this chapter. However, immigrants, as "multitudes and masses" (Chavez, 2013, p. 69), are depicted as "pushing the entire New Mexico federal **court** system near a breaking point." "[S]heer volume" is "crushing." Macías-Rojas (2017) notes that historically, Border Patrol treated border crossing as a civil offense rather an as a criminal one. However, "[o]ver the past decade, criminal prosecution rate for immigration has tripled" and while policy analyst points to this rise to DHS's "consequence-driven" enforcement strategy that punishes immigration violations, Macías-Rojas argues it stemmed from a lack of bed space in immigrant detentions/prison system. "The need to free up detention beds on the border, in turn, lead to a greater reliance on federal prosecution for immigration offenses" (p. 90). These federal courts like the one in this example prosecute more low-level immigration cases than drug crimes, mostly undocumented border crossings and those that attempt to reenter after deportation. These hearings are usually "en masse" (p. 92), which explain the "stream of men and women [that] file into federal court" in this example.

The final concept of the "battlefield" theme of the region scale is "terrorism" (1,356 references). Beneath is an example of this concept.

The Arizona Republic: "HOMELAND SECURITY TAKES OVER
AT BORDERS: FACES IMPOSSIBLE JOB, EXPERTS SAY"

The Department of Homeland Security will take over a daunting task Saturday: guarding America's borders against *terrorism*. Despite the reorganization, which eliminates the beleaguered Immigration and Naturalization Service, the new agency likely will face an impossible challenge guarding 6,000 miles of border with Mexico and Canada, experts say.

"There is literally nothing to stop a *terrorist* from coming across our border," said Sen. Jon Kyl, R-Ariz., chairman of the Senate's terrorism subcommittee. "It is unpatrolled for many miles, with only limited surveillance."

The government cracked down after investigators discovered that the 19 *terrorists* responsible for the Sept. 11 attacks entered the country using temporary visas. Some experts worry that without legal avenues, potential *terrorists* may try to enter through Mexico or Canada, a fear echoed in Arizona border communities.

Walter Kolbe, who owns a bed and breakfast in Hereford near the U.S.–Mexican border, knows these fears firsthand. He found a small notebook in a weather-beaten backpack on his property earlier this month that fueled fears about *terrorists* crossing into Arizona.

Kolbe and his wife called the FBI after thumbing through the diary, which appeared to be written in Arabic.

"Our eyes were popping out of our heads," said Kolbe, 67, who is the older brother of U.S. Rep. Jim Kolbe, R-Ariz.

The diary contained writings in Farsi. A few messages written in Spanish and English, seemed to be saying farewell, Kolbe said.

"The problem was, we couldn't tell if it was totally innocent, like people saying 'Goodbye, good luck with working in the United States, or goodbye, good luck on your suicide mission,' " Kolbe said. "It absolutely raised the hair on my back." [. . . .] (Carroll, 2003, p. A1)

It is very important to note, that despite the intense scrutiny post 9/11 on the USA-Mexico border for terrorist infiltration of the nation, there is no evidence to support that terrorists have crossed into the nation by way of this region since the terrorist attacks. The only confirmed reported terrorist border crossing was pre-9/11 and occurred at the USA-Canada border. The "Millennium Bomber" Ahmed Ressam who planned an Al-Queda attack on the Los Angeles International Airport in 1999, crossed the U.-Canada border by ferry with a fraudulent Canadian passport (Salter & Piché, 2011). The "hair-raising," "eye popping" panic produced in this example over finding a journal with some writing in Farsi near the border shows the construction of fear that supports the defensive posturing on the border in this region facing the "impossible job" of security.

The second and final section of the region scale offers analysis on the "cataclysmic flood" theme in the next section.

CATACLYSMIC FLOOD

Lakoff and Johnson (2008) analyze the role of metaphor as a fundamental mechanism of the mind. They argue that metaphors structure basic understandings of human experiences and shape our perceptions and action without an awareness of metaphoric power both linguistically and cognitively. For example, they analyze container metaphors for land areas that both possess a bounded quality and also relate to size. "When you get into the tub, you get into water. Both the tub and water are viewed as containers, both of different sorts. The tub is a CONTAINER OBJECT, while the water is a CONTAINER SUBJECT" (p. 30, original emphasis). When container metaphors are applied to immigration debates, for example in Britain, it can express a concern with a build-up of pressure within or outside a container (Charteris-Black, 2006). The container metaphor is persuasive in British political discourse because it implies that controlling immigration through the security of borders (spatially based concept) will curb the rate of demographic change in society (time-based concept). It is also alarmist rhetoric that express fears about penetration of a container.

Water as a metaphor is powerful because of its universality. All humans experience water-related weather and humans live on a planet mostly covered by water. Experiences with water-related weather constitute a core component of this embodied knowledge. For example, great floods have devastated societies and civilizations throughout history. Floods help to explain stories of origin like the biblical floods that purportedly forced Noah to build his arc. In addition, people observe seasonally how rivers and tides affect society when they become rapid, rise, or overflow. Thus it is not surprising that water metaphors drive immigrant debates and discourse (Cunningham-Parmeter, 2011; O'Brien, 2003; Santa Ana, 2002).

Santa Ana (2002) noted in his study of immigration debates in California that "flowing water" is widely used in immigration debates and this study does not depart from that reality. This section departs from the prior analysis in this study by just offering headlines that include frequent concepts. I chose to do this because these watery themes and images have already appeared many times in other examples provided in this book, the imagery does not need much context to make its point, and I want to show how water images help headlines become more alarmist and suggestive in order to capture reader attention. Beneath is an example of "flow" (652 references) the most frequent concept of "cataclysmic flood" them of this region scale, which includes the stemmed word "flow" (652 references) and followed by stemmed synonyms "waves" (379 references), "overwhelm" (220 references), and "flood" (213 references). While "river" was the second most frequent concept (646 references), it did not appear in any border newspaper headline and was omitted here from the thematic analysis. While the concept of "cataclysmic flood," is less frequent than concepts that make up the battlefield theme, or the house and body scale, the power of water helps to communicate existential issues about undocumented immigration in a succinct and alarmist manner. Beneath are examples of headlines with water imagery:

The Albuquerque Journal: "UNENDING HUMAN TIDE *FLOWS* NORTH" (Contreras, 2000, p. A1)

The Arizona Republic: "CHANDLER'S TIDAL *WAVE* OF ILLEGALS: YEAR AFTER ROUNDUP THEY'RE STILL COMING" (Magruder, 1998, p. B1)

The *Albuquerque Journal*: "DRUG-SMUGGLING SURGE *OVERWHELMS* BORDER" (Romo, 1996, p. A1)

The *Albuquerque Journal*: "'*FLOOD*' OF ILLEGALS WASHES INTO N.M." (Gonzalez, 1995, p. A1)

These headlines instill a sense of cataclysmic destruction much like the watery, global catastrophes portrayed in popular films such as *San Andreas* (2015) and *The Day After Tomorrow* (2003). But why is water so closely associated with immigration? I think there is a religious influence for using this type of water imagery.

The flood myth is one of the most popular, global myths. In fact, the flood myth might be one of the most studied stories in human history. "No other myth or folktale or legend has been subjected to anything like the intensive scrutiny that has been lavished on the story of a cataclysmic deluge" (Dundes, 1988, p. 1). And while many cultures and societies have flood myths, the Judeo-Christian story of the flood in the Genesis chapter of the Bible's Old Testament bears a great influence on U.S. American culture. The basic structure of this flood myth contains five elements:

(1) Humans live in fundamental opposition to the laws of God or nature and ignore warnings of potential catastrophe;
(2) Select individuals listen to warnings and take action to survive;
(3) The storm sweeps across the land, destroying both the physical and social structures of the human kind;
(4) Social order is reorganized in line with the laws of God/nature; and
(5) The Earth is purified. (Salvador & Norton, 2011, p. 50)

Nativist water imagery may signal a symbolic warning that White dominance in the nation will inevitably perish. If we apply this myth's basic structure to the contemporary border region and the shifting demographic changes in the nation, we can start to see how water imagery can be religious imagery coupled with a racialized nightmare of the end of the world:

1) the nation is ignoring warnings of the dangers of undocumented immigration;
2) select individuals like White supremacists and border vigilantes listen to the warnings and take action to survive like "hunting" immigrants and agitating for more law enforcement policies on the border (like President Trump);
3) undocumented immigration continues to increase (because of neoliberal policies and increased militarization on the border) and is forecasted to help change the racial demographic from a mostly White to mostly

people of color nation by the year 2045 social and racial order is reorganized along more multiracial, non-White lines; and

4) the nation is "purified" of White supremacy. (Frey, 2018, para. 4)

In addition, Santa Ana (2002) notes that the "dangerous water" nativist discourse transforms "aggregates of individuals into an undifferentiated mass
quantity . . . . as this mass moves from one contained space to another, some
sort of kinetic energy is released . . . . such movements are inherently powerful, and if not controlled, they are dangerous" (p. 76). Ono and Sloop (2002)
argue that "in colonialist discourse, the metaphor of water is used to lump
people together, to suggest their unified agenda, and to reduce them to objects
that lack any significant variations, feelings, or emotions, save for physically
predictable ones" (p.55). Santa Ana (2002) also notes the "dangerous water"
threat is more cultural/racial than economic. Instead of reducing immigrants
to animals, the water imagery reduces immigrants to nameless and faceless
molecules that make up a "Brown flood." If likening immigrants to animals
is an abstraction, then further reducing them to molecules that make up water
takes that abstraction and reduces individuals to a scale beyond what the
naked eye can detect. But the molecules together, *en masse*, can be a force of
nature and destruction.

Thus, these headlines that communicate "unending human tide flows
north," "tidal wave of illegals surge," "surge overwhelms," and "'flood' of
illegals washes," represent "the storm [that] sweeps across the land, destroying" the White dominance of the current racial structure of the nation through
a "Cataclysmic Flood." The invocation of the flood myth in these headlines
warn of the end of White dominance in both demography and political power,
by a force of nature in undocumented immigration that will change the social
and racial order of the nation.

Ironically, the work of Leslie Marmon Silko, a native American novelist,
prophesized such a revolution in her novel *The Almanac of the Dead* (1991)
that is set in the border region of Tucson, Arizona. Her novel mirrors the
flood myth that I argue is used in immigration discourse. She envisions in her
novel a revolution, a coalition of indigenous peoples that also include people
of color, descendants of slaves, marginalized political groups, unhoused
people, and prisoners, who gain strength from their association and move
from the margins to the center in order to rise up against White supremacy
and capitalism as a new people's army of the dispossessed. Her novel would
predict the Mayan Zapatista uprising against the Mexican Government in
1994 (Silko, 1996).

In conclusion, the scale of the region occupies two themes: the "Battleground" and "Cataclysmic Flood." In the Battleground theme, the "war on
drugs," the "war on terror," the "war on the border" influence the public in

a negative, racialized way to see immigrants as "enemies." However, these wars also reflect a type of moral disgust in relation to nativist anxiety about "dirty crossings" that lead to magical thinking about geographic contagion in the border region in that "foreign" immigrants are seen as intent on taking over the nation. The military that supports law enforcement efforts in the border region are there to "protect" against those that "smuggle" drugs and "human cargo" into the nation as well as preventing threats of "terrorism." However, the mass casualties of these rhetorical policy wars are not citizens but immigrants killed in the desert as well as who are driven underground by border militarization policies long after they cross the border (Kil & Menjivar, 2006). This militarized border region is a necropolitical deathscape that place immigrants crossing the border in constant contact with the possibility of death that they become a type of "living dead" (Mbembe, 2003, p. 179), even after successfully crossing the border. The millions of "arrests" in the region justify the "beefing-up" of militarized enforcement linking meat, to muscle, to masculinity, which contrasts the vulnerability of the body in the first scale where the body is feminized with nurturing resources that immigrants pillage.

In contrast, the "Cataclysmic Flood" theme includes concepts such as "flow," "waves," and "overwhelm" to describe immigration hydrokinetically. If likening immigrants to animals is a racialized abstraction, then further reducing them to molecules that makeup water takes that abstraction and reduces individuals to a scale beyond what the naked eye can detect. But the molecules together, *en masse*, can be a force of great natural destruction. It is this natural destructive force that resonates with biblical story of the Great Flood. Similar to the "changing face" concept of the body scale where the race of the nation's face was changing from White to Brown, the biblical flood imagery seems to warn about the end of White dominance in the nation that will drown in a "Brown flood."

The next chapter analyzes the last scale: the nation.

REFERENCES

The Arizona Republic. (2003). Murders go unsolved as smuggling grows: Phoenix homicides setting record pace this year. *The Arizona Republic*, November 9, 2003, A1.

The Arizona Republic. (2004). Calif.'s lesson: Reforms don't stop illegal immigration. *The Arizona Republic*, September 26, 2004, A1.

Bowers, W. J., & Pierce, G. (1980). Deterrence or brutalization? *Crime and Delinquency, 26*(4), 453–84.

Calavita, K. (1996). The new politics of immigration: "Balanced-budget conservatism" and the symbolism of Proposition 187. *Social Problems, 43*(3), 284–305.

Carroll, S. (2003). Homeland security takes over at borders: Faces impossible job, experts say. *The Arizona Republic*, February 27, 2003, A1.

Charteris-Black, J. (2006). Britain as a container: Immigration metaphors in the 2005 election campaign. *Discourse & Society, 17*(5), 563–581.

Chavez, L. (2013). *The Latino Threat: Constructing Immigrants, Citizens, and the Nation.* Stanford: Stanford University Press.

Contreras, G. (2000). Unending human tide flows north. *The Albuquerque Journal,* May 21, 2000, A1.

Cunningham-Parmeter, K. (2011). Alien language: Immigration metaphors and the jurisprudence of otherness. *Fordham Law Review, 79*(4), 1544–1598.

De Ras, M. E. P., & Grace, V. (Eds.). (1997). *Bodily Boundaries, Sexualised Genders & Medical Discourses.* Palmerston North: Dunmore Press.

Dundes, A. (Ed.). (1988). *The Flood Myth.* Berkeley: University of California Press.

Dunn, T. J. (1996). *The Militarization of the U.S.-Mexico Border, 1978–1992: Low Intensity Conflict Doctrine Comes Home.* Austin: University of Texas Press.

Dunn, T. J. (2001). Border militarization via drug and immigration enforcement: Human rights implications. *Social Justice, 28*(2, 84), 7–30.

Dyer, R. (1997). *White: Essays on Race and Culture.* Abingdon, Oxen: Routledge.

Eschbach, K., Hagan, J., & Rodríguez, N. (2003). Deaths during undocumented migration: Trends and policy implications in the new era of homeland security. *In Defense of the Alien, 26,* 37–52. Retrieved from https://www.jstor.org/stable/23142811?seq=1#page_scan_tab_contents.

Frey, W. H. (2018). The U.S. will become "minority white" in 2045, Census projects: Youthful minorities are the engine of future growth. *www.brookings.edu,* March 14, 2018. Retrieved from https://www.brookings.edu/blog/the-avenue/2018/03/14/the-us-will-become-minority-white-in-2045-census-projects/.

Fulginiti, L. (2008). Fatal footsteps: Murder of undocumented border crossers in Maricopa County, Arizona. *Journal of Forensic Sciences, 53*(1), 41–45.

General Accounting Office. (2006). *Illegal Immigration: Border-crossing Deaths have Doubled Since 1995; Border Patrol's Efforts to Prevent Deaths have not been Fully Evaluated. GAO-06-770.* Washington, DC: General Accounting Office.

Gonzalez, J. W. (1997). Border shooting spurs new military training/Officials defend use of Marines in drug war. *Houston Chronicle*, July 13, 1997, 1.

Gonzalez, R. C. (1995). "Flood" of illegals washes into N.M. *The Albuquerque Journal*, February 19, 1995, A1.

Hawkins, D. (2016). San Antonio truck deaths recall horror of 19 who died in 2003 Texas smuggling case. *The Washington Post*, July 24, 2017. Retrieved from https://www.washingtonpost.com/news/morning-mix/wp/2017/07/24/san-antonio-truck-deaths-recall-horror-of-19-who-died-in-2003-tex-smuggling-case/?utm_term=.212e0a396d45.

Hill, J. H. (2009). *The Everyday Language of White Racism.* New York, NY: John Wiley & Sons.

Hinkes, M. J. (2008). Migrant deaths along the California–Mexico border: An anthropological perspective. *Journal of Forensic Sciences, 53*(1), 16–20.

Huseman, J. (2018). How the case for voter fraud was tested—and utterly failed. *Pro Publica*, June 19, 2018. Retrieved from https://www.propublica.org/article/kris-kobach-voter-fraud-kansas-trial.

Jones, J. (2005). Court overload; Illegal immigrants crush courts in an already over-burdened judicial system. *The Albuquerque Journal*, November 5, 2005, A1.

Kil, S. H., & Menjívar, C. (2006). "The 'War on the border': The criminalization of immigrants and militarization of the USA-Mexico border." In R. Martinez, Jr. & A. Valenzuela, Jr. (Eds.), *Immigration and Crime: Race, Ethnicity, and Violence* (pp. 164–188). New York: New York University Press.

Lakoff, G., & Johnson, M. (2008). *Metaphors We Live By*. Chicago: University of Chicago Press.

Lezon, D. (2005). Rider tells a stark story of fatal trip / Witness says Williams ignored immigrants' cries from inside trailer. *The Houston Chronicle*, March 17, 2005, B.

Macías-Rojas, P. (2016). *From Deportation to Prison: The Politics of Immigration Enforcement in Post-civil Rights America*. New York: New York University Press.

Magruder, J. (1998). Chandler's tidal wave of illegals: Year after roundup they're still coming. *The Arizona Republic*, July 26, 1998, B1.

Mann, B. (2008). Manhood, sexuality, and nation in post-9/11 United States. In B. Sutton, S. Morgen, & J. Novkov (Eds.), *Security Disarmed: Critical Perspectives on Gender, Race and Militarization* (pp. 179–197). New Brunswick: Rutgers University Press.

Mbembe, J. (2003). Necropolitics. *Public Culture*, 15(1), 11–40.

McDonnell, P. J. (1997). Formal deportation is much less common than expulsion. *The Los Angeles Times*, June 23, 1997, A-14.

Morrison, T. (1992). *Playing in the Dark: Whiteness and the Literary Imagination*. New York, NY: Vintage.

O'Brian, G. V. (2003). Conquering hordes, and waste materials: Metaphors of immigrants and the early immigration restriction debate in the United States. *Metaphor and Symbol*, 18(1), 33–47.

Ono, K. A., & Sloop, J. M. (2002). *Shifting Borders: Rhetoric, Immigration, and California's Proposition 187*. Philadelphia: Temple University Press.

Ortega, B. (2018). Border Patrol failed to count hundreds of migrant deaths on US soil. www.cnn.com, May 15, 2018. Retrieved from https://www.cnn.com/2018/05/14/us/border-patrol-migrant-death-count-invs/index.html.

Romo, R. (1996). Drug-smuggling surge overwhelms border. *The Albuquerque Journal*, July 18, 1996, A1.

Rosenberg, E. (2018). "The most bizarre thing I've ever been a part of": Trump panel found no widespread voter fraud, ex-member says. *The Washington Post*, August 3, 2018. Retrieved from https://www.washingtonpost.com/news/politics/wp/2018/08/03/the-most-bizarre-thing-ive-ever-been-a-part-of-trump-panel-found-no-voter-fraud-ex-member-says/?utm_term=.6a807c311c99.

Salter, M. B., & Piché, G. (2011). The securitization of the U.S.–Canada border in American political discourse. *Canadian Journal of Political Science/Revue Canadienne de Science Politique*, 44(4), 929–951.

Salvador, M., & Norton, T. (2011). The flood myth in the age of global climate change. *Environmental Communication, 5*(1), 45–61.

Santa Ana, O. (2002). *Brown Tide Rising: Metaphors of Latinos in Contemporary American Public Discourse.* Austin: University of Texas Press.

Silko, L. M. (1991). *Almanac of the Dead: A Novel.* New York, NY: Simon & Schuster.

Silko, L. M. (1996). An expression of profound gratitude to the Maya Zapatistas, January 1, 1994. In L. M. Silko, (Ed.), *Yellow Woman and a Beauty of the Spirit: Essays on Native American Life Today* (pp. 152–154). New York, NY: Touchstone.

Stibbe, A. (2004). Health and the social construction of masculinity in Men's Health magazine. *Men and Masculinities, 7*(1), 31–51.

U.S. Customs and Border Protection. (2017). U.S. Border Patrol fiscal year Southwest BORDER SECTOR DEATHS (FY 1998–FY 2017). *www.cbp.gov.* Retrieved from https://www.cbp.gov/document/stats/us-border-patrol-fiscal-year-southwest-border-sector-deaths-fy-1998-fy-2017.

U.S. Northern Command. (2004). Joint Task Force Six gets new name, new mission. *www.northcom.mil*, November 5, 2004. Retrieved from http://www.northcom.mil/Newsroom/Article/563131/joint-task-force-six-getsnew-name-new-mission/.

Wagner, D. (1999). Hull calls for Mexican job program immigrants could take shunned work. *The Arizona Republic*, May 8, 1999, B2.

Wells, B. (2004). Migrant foe tied to racism. *East Valley Tribune*, August 16, 2004. Retrieved from http://www.eastvalleytribune.com/news/article_bb6cb865-a006-5636-915d-89e501942701.html.

Chapter 6

Border Symptoms and Border Treatments

A Disease Body Politic (Nation Scale)

In October 2018, President Trump escalated his racist, nativist stance on the USA-Mexico border shortly before midterm elections. Under his administration, "Operation Faithful Patriot" was launched by the Pentagon and sent c. 5,200 troops to the border in an effort to stop a migrant caravan seeking asylum moving north through Mexico toward the United States (Clark, 2018). This is in addition to "Operation Guardian Support" authorized earlier in the year that provided 2,000 troops to stop an earlier, different migrant caravan seeking asylum. "In years past, advocacy groups have organized caravans through Mexico both as a form of protection for migrants, particularly those traveling from Central America, and as a demonstration highlighting the lack of institutional safeguards that defines migration through the region" (Devereaux, 2018, para 6). President Trump (2018a) tweeted on October 29, 2018, and stated:

> Many Gang Members and some very bad people are mixed into the Caravan heading to our Southern Border. Please go back, you will not be admitted into the United States unless you go through the legal process. This is an invasion of our Country and our Military is waiting for you.

President Trump, in an attempt to further stoke fear and panic, commented on claims that people in the migrant caravan threw rocks at the Mexico-Guatemala Border and threw sticks at Mexican police during a standoff where one migrant was killed (O'Rourke, 2018, para 6). Trump (2018b) stated, "We're not going to put up with that. If they want to throw rocks at our military, our military fights back. We're going to consider—and I told them, consider it a rifle" (para 82). This logic is eerily similar to the situation in New Orleans, shortly after Hurricane Katrina made landfall on August 28,

2005, when FEMA failed to help the victims who did not or could not evacu-
ate the region and law enforcement were given orders to "shoot looters"
when a state of emergency was declared and national guard troops brought
to the region (*The Times-Picayune*, 2010, para 1). In that case, Governor
Blanco referred to the mostly Black and frequently poor victims who were
seeking survival supplies as "hoodlums," and in this case, mostly Brown
and poor migrants seeking political asylum by caravan are viewed as foreign
"invaders," and their attempts to protect their goal of seeking humanitarian
protection are deemed a shoot-able offense where a rock thrown is equal to
rifle shot.

These "operations" at the border reflect the image of a nation state at war
over its boundaries. This image parallels popularized, scientific understandings of the immune system, where "the body [is a] nation state at war over its
external borders, containing internal surveillance systems to monitor foreign
intruders" (Martin, 1990, p. 410) and the job of the immune system is to
maintain the boundary between self and other, where the other is "foreign
and hostile" (Martin, 1992, p. 126). Donna Haraway (1999) writes that "the
immune system is a plan for meaningful action to construct and maintain the
boundaries for what may count as self and other in the crucial realms of the
normal and pathological" (p. 204).

This chapter elaborates on the nation scale with a specific focus on the
medicalized discourse informed by a popularized, modern, and scientific
understanding of disease and the immune system that reflects concerns about
the White body politic and "dirt." The news media's construction of this
"diseased body politic" communicates Whiteness and nativism about the
border through discursive "border symptoms" and "border operations" that
represent the intersection of immunology discourse, the racial construction
of the body politic, and anxiety about postmodern economic transformation
and its impact on borders. Here I detail four themes: "growing number,"
"active time," "congested space," and "operations." The first three themes
represent a pattern in the discourse of "border symptoms" of the body politic. This is the subtlest form of New Race Neutral Racism that plays upon
distorted notions of quantity, time, and space in order to communicate a
racialized need for a "sealed" border. These distortions complement popularized notions of cancer and knowledge of the immune system that also
reflect late-capitalist hallmarks of "technological innovation, specificity, and
rapid, flexible change" (Martin, 1992, p. 123) that emerge in border news
discourse. In response to these "symptoms," the state deploys "operations"
in order to criminally treat and control the border. These "operations" reflect
the rhetorical crossroads of the medical, military, and law enforcement field
in communicating racist, nativist ideologies. "Border symptoms" and "border operations" help to criminalizes immigrant border crossers as surplus

populations, which make them more vulnerable to economic exploitation because of their "dirty" status as violators of the boundary between self and other, in which the imagined militaristic, immune system of the body politic needs to maintain the boundary between self and the "foreign and hostile" other (table 6.1).

In chapter 3, I analyzed the "vulnerable" body politic in border news discourse and offered analysis about how the body is imagined as a nation. The body politic at the scale of the physical body demonstrates a racial, spatial, and geographic metaphor grounded in embodied understandings of the human body based on simplistic notions of "aches," "functions," and "parts." This more literal understanding of the human body was most evident in the "body parts" theme in chapter 3 where the "face" of the nation was racially changing from White to Brown and suggested disfigurement or disability. "Hand" and "arm" represented law enforcement and the protection of Whiteness against the racialized geographic contagion in the form of an "invasion." As the lowest point in the body scale image, "foot" represents how immigrants have to cross the dangerous border and also reflects their poverty. While "face," "hand," "arm," and "foot" did not deviate from Rasmussen and Brown's understanding of the body politic (rooted in the idea that the king's

Table 6.1   Racist Dirt Fixations at the Nation Scale

Tier 1 Theory	Racist Dirt Fixations		
Tier 2 4 Scales	Nation		
Tier 3 Themes	Border symptom: "growing number"	Border symptom: "active time"	Border symptom: "congested space"
Tier 4 Concepts	"million" (3,394 references)	"act" (2,255 references) [includes "act" (826 references), "action"(779 references), "active" (650 references]	"Group" (3,374 references)
	"numbers" (2,734 references)		"push" (774 references)
	"increase" (2,324 references)		"gang" (743 references)
	"much" (1,832 references)	"effort" (1,689 references) "continual" (1,222 references)	"traffic" (626 references)
	"billion" (876 references)	"often" (1,117 references)	"load" (334 references)
	"additional" (857 references)	"wait" (1,019 references)	"tight" (302 references)
	"thousand" (772 references)	"emergency" (839 references)	
	"hundred" (656 references)		

body is literally his kingdom, where the head represents the king, the arms and hands are his royal military, and the feet represent the peasants in the kingdom), "heart" did deviate from this older, more medieval understanding of the body politic.

Rasmussen and Brown (2005) argue that the spiritual "heart" of the king's body politic is the priesthood; however, the "heart" concept did not demonstrate this and instead shows a medicalized understanding of the body politic that is much more modern. In particular, this imagines immigrants as a type of blood clot or virus/bacteria that travels via veins and arteries to the "heart" of the United States. This example shows how popularized, current knowledge of medicine seeps into cognitive frames of the body politic while making racialized judgments of immigrants and their role in the nation, for which this chapter expands with the nation scale. Scientific, popularized knowledge of the immune system parallels the criminalizing, policing efforts at the border that imagines the nation as a body in need of defense. Instead of the policing "arm" or "hand" found at the body scale, the "immune system" polices at the nation scale.

Emily Martin (1994) researches the intersection of gendered scientific discourse, social construction of the body, and economic systems and transformations. Martin (1992) argues that there are two body systems: the Fordist body and the late-capitalism body. The former is driven by imagery of "reproductive biology, [where] bodies are organized around principles of centralized control and factory-based production" (p. 121). For example:

> Men continuously produce wonderfully astonishing quantities of highly valued sperm, women produce eggs and babies (though neither efficiently) and, when they are not doing this this, either produce scrap (menstruation) or undergo a complete breakdown of central control (menopause). The models that confer order are hierarchical pyramids with the brain firmly located at the top and the other organs ranged below. The body's products all flow out over the edge of the body, through one orifice or another, into the outside world. Steady, regular output is prized above all, preferably over the entire life span, as exemplified by the production of sperm. (Martin, 1992, pp. 121–122, citing Martin, 1987, 1991)

The body of late capitalism contains two contradictory and coexisting body formations: "a body organized as a global system with no internal boundaries and characterized by rapid flexible response, and a body organized around nationhood, warfare, gender, race, and class" (Martin, 1992, p. 129).

The late-capitalism body is also informed by more advanced knowledge of the immune system, which possess hallmarks of "technological innovation, specificity, and rapid, flexible change" (p. 123) that also describe global capitalism and its dramatic restructuring of the economic system motivated by profitmaking. Thus, society internalizes changes in scientific knowledge to create a new type of worker whose body reflects major economic models and changes over time. Martin suggests that there is now a transition:

> from bodies suited for and conceived in the terms of the era of Fordist mass production to bodies suited for and conceived in the terms of the era of flexible accumulation. We are seeing not the end of the body, but rather the end of one kind of body and the beginning of another kind of body. (p. 121)

She furthers argues that when Fordist factory was the operating economic model, Henry Ford sent investigators into workers' homes to evaluate their private lives and police "thrifty and hygienic" habits in order to be eligible for a higher wage (Martin, 1992, p. 122, citing Gelderman, 1981). Today, new knowledge about HIV and the immune system may contribute to heterosexual, patriarchal, controlling scripts where scientific language of immunity suggests not just a weakening body, but a "loss of heterosexual potency," and that the "body as a centralized nation state had lost its virility" (p. 131). Hence, the science of immunology offers a system of "purity and danger," where the job of the immune system is to maintain the boundary between self and other, where the other is "foreign and hostile" (p. 126). Here the self becomes more heteronormative and patriarchal in light of economic restructuring that erodes the welfare state and increasingly criminalizes "superfluous" or surplus populations, while propping the heteronormative family as a necessary pillar of society (Martin, 1992).

A similar phenomenon takes place at the border where knowledge about cancer and the immune system help to influence public discourse about immigration and the nation. General Barry McCaffrey, President Clinton's drug czar (1996–2001), began his tenure backing away from military concepts like the "War on Drugs" and instead treating drug abuse issues like a type of social cancer. He states that using the cancer analogy "is far more adaptive and useful as a model to a way of thinking and talking about the problem . . . . None of those associated military concepts are useful to us talking and thinking about this problem, but cancer probably is" (Wren, 1996). General McCaffrey thus advocates antidrug efforts that focus on treatment and education as opposed to stopping drug traffic at the USA-Mexico border (*The Los Angeles Times*, 1996).

However, the irony of General McCaffrey's statement is that the medical industry uses the war analogy with cancer. The "war on cancer" began under former President Nixon when he created the National Cancer Institute in 1971. Despite the irony of using a war metaphor about a health issue, war imagery pervades the health-care industry's discourse and the media that reports on this "war" (Harrington, 2012). Williams Camus (2009) analyzes cancer metaphors in popular scientific articles in the British press and finds the leading conceptual metaphor "Cancer is War" expressed within this thematic formulation:

> After the cancer's *invasion* of the body, the immune system *launches* an *offensive* to *beat* the disease. The *army of killer T cells* and *stealth viruses fight* the tumor cells. However, this is not enough to *wipe out* or *eradicate* the *invader* completely, especially if it has spread throughout the body becoming *lethal*. Thus, a bigger *arsenal of weapons*, consisting of *magic bullets* and *blunt instruments*, *target the enemy*. If the cancer is still *resistant* to the *cancer-fighting tools*, other *weapons* are injected to *attack* the disease or to boost the body's own *defences*. This attack may eventually lead to *defeating* the disease, although it also involves serious side effects as healthy cells are also *destroyed* by the *weapons*. (p. 475, original emphasis)

In addition to the war metaphor, cancer patients also use imagery of natural disasters (Domino, Affonso, & Hannah, 1991; Harrington, 2012), or personifications (Harrington, 2012) like "foreign intruder" (Domino, Affonso, & Hannah, 1991, p. 1), as well as animal qualities (Harrington, 2012).

> Susan Sontag (1978) also noted the intersection of cancer and warfare imagery:To describe a phenomenon as a cancer is an incitement to violence. The use of cancer in political discourse encourages fatalism and justifies "severe" measures—as well as strongly reinforcing the widespread notion that the disease is necessarily fatal. The concept of disease is never innocent. But it could be argued that the cancer metaphors are in themselves implicitly genocidal. (p. 84)

She notes that the Nazis also used cancer imagery when describing the "Jewish Problem" in the 1930s which encouraged not only cutting out the "cancer" but also the healthy tissue surrounding it.

GROWING NUMBER

One of the more salient characteristics of cancer is that it is seen as a growth (Laranjeira, 2013; Sontag, 1978). In this first most frequent border symptom theme of "growing number," there are biomedical suggestions of unregulated growth. For example, the concept "more" is in 8,358 references in the data while "less" is at 934 references, making the concept of "more" ubiquitous in the data and present in many of the examples in the analysis chapters of this book, in stark contrast to "less." The three concepts that lead the theme of "growing number" are "million" (3,394 references) and "numbers" (2,734 references). Following is an example that contains both concepts:

The Los Angeles Times: "The Nation, *Number* of Illegal
Migrants Growing, INS reports 7 *million* undocumented
immigrants in 2000, with 30% in California"

The *number* of undocumented immigrants in the United States reached 7 *million*
in 2000 and the net growth of the population could be as much as half a *million*
new arrivals a year, the Immigration and Naturalization Service reported Friday.

With 2.2 *million* undocumented residents, California had the largest *number*
of any state, about 30% of the total population.

Texas, where the *number* of undocumented immigrants passed 1 *million* for
the first time, had the second-largest figure. But some of the most rapid growth
took place in states such as Georgia, Iowa, and South Carolina, which had relatively few undocumented immigrants before 1990.

The figures marked an upward revision from a previous INS estimate of 5.8
million undocumented immigrants in January 2000. Many other authorities—
including the Census Bureau—regarded that *number* as too low. Some experts
believe the actual figure exceeds 10 *million*.

Mexico has long been the leading source of undocumented immigrants,
but the new INS estimates showed that the Mexican share of the population
increased from about 58% in 1990 to 69% in 2000. The *number* of undocumented Mexicans increased from about 2 *million* in 1990 to 4.8 *million* in 2000.

The decade saw economic travails in Mexico, the implementation of the
North American Free Trade Agreement, and the spread of Mexican migration
beyond traditional destinations such as California and Texas to states in the
South, Midwest and Northeast.[. . . .] (Alonso-Zaldivar, 2003, p. A-14)

While the use of the concept "number" and "million" seems frequent and
straightforward in this example, the idea that the "spread of Mexican migration beyond traditional destinations" is repeated with "some of the most rapid
growth" taking "place in states such as Georgia, Iowa and South Carolina,
which had relatively few undocumented immigrants before 1990." Sontag
(1978) argues that cancer is seen as invasive growth, able to colonize from
"the original tumor to far sites in the body, first setting up tiny outposts
('micrometastases')" . . . . Rarely are the body's defenses vigorous enough to
obliterate a tumor that has established its own blood supply and consists of
billions of destructive cells" (p. 64). Additionally, the ambiguity of an exact
number of undocumented immigrants represented by the Census Bureau
critique of INS estimates of "5.8 *million* undocumented immigrants in January 2000" as "too low" with "some experts" placing the "actual figure" in
excess of "10 *million*" contributes to the anxiety of the unknown and perhaps
unknowable, given that these immigrants are undocumented. Thus, the use
of concepts "numbers" and "million" suggest an "invasive colonization"
and "micrometastases" of undocumented immigration that could be fatal for
Whiteness and the nation.

The next most frequent concepts are "increase" (2,324 references) and "much" (1,832 references). Following is an example of both these concepts:

The Houston Chronicle: Judges Come Off Bench to Seek
Help, Congress Urged to Provide More Jurists, Funding

WASHINGTON—Federal courts in Texas and other Southwestern border states have become overburdened by a dramatic *increase* in illegal-immigration and drug-related prosecutions in recent years, judges from the region told Congress on Thursday. The seven jurists, in a rare personal lobbying effort by sitting judges, urged federal lawmakers to add judgeships and *increase* funding for the courts to lighten the workload.

The judicial docket is especially large in southern and western Texas, where too few judges are being called upon to handle too many criminal cases, said Carolyn Dineen King, chief judge of the New Orleans-based 5th U.S. Circuit Court of Appeals.

"We have to get some help," said King, who led the delegation of judges from five courts in Texas, New Mexico, Arizona and California. "Someone has to speak. Someone has to say this isn't working."

King said judges and court employees have been working longer hours to handle the explosion in prosecutions. Civil attorneys and their clients, meanwhile, have been waiting *much* longer than usual to have their lawsuits heard by judges who are constitutionally bound to see that criminal defendants get a speedy trial, she said.

King, who oversees the administration of federal courts in Texas, Louisiana, and Mississippi, said she has had to shuffle judges in the three states to ensure that criminal defendants have not languished in jail due to the massive backlog or been set free too early.

She said she too often has had to send jurists with a relatively light workload to southern and western Texas to help judges there handle cases.

"We're managing to tough it out," she said. But this temporary fix will soon fail unless Congress adds more judges and provides more funding for courts, King told lawmakers. [. . . .] (Lash, 2000, p. A8)

Recall that Williams Camus' (2009) conceptual metaphor "Cancer is War" begins with the thematic formulation, "After the cancer's *invasion* of the body, the immune system *launches* an *offensive* to *beat* the disease. The *army of killer T cells* and *stealth viruses fight* the tumour cells" (p. 475; original emphasis). In a similar manner, this example shows that "[j]udges come off bench to seek help" to "add judgeships and **increase** funding for the courts" because judges in the border states are "overburdened by a dramatic **increase** in illegal-immigration and drug-related prosecutions" and the "explosion in prosecutions." "King, who oversees the administration of federal courts in Texas, Louisiana and Mississippi, said," "We're managing to tough it out," by the "shuffle [of] judges in the three states" to deal with the "massive backlog," but it is a "temporary fix [and] will soon fail" unless Congress hears their pleas for more judges in this region. Like the immune system, these jurists battle the "cancer" of undocumented immigration and its growth with a call for help with "more jurists, funding" because the present offensive "isn't working," thus "more" is needed.

The next most frequent concepts are "billion" (876 references) and "additional" (857 references). Following is an example that includes both concepts:

The Albuquerque Journal: "Ridge Juggles Needs at Borders"

[. . . .] Tougher inspections at U.S. borders since Sept. 11 have led to long delays at some crossings, including El Paso, which in turn has led to an overload of traffic at the Santa Teresa port of entry in New Mexico.

Ridge said the administration is considering issuing "smart cards" to people who frequently cross U.S. borders for business reasons. Checkpoints could be established away from borders to alleviate congestion at the actual crossings, he said.

"As we take a look at a smart border arrangement with our friends in Mexico, we will be looking at different kinds of technology that we can apply to people who traverse the border on a regular basis, and cargo," Ridge said. "The challenge . . . is to try to identify no-risk traffic, or low-risk traffic."

The Bush administration might support footing the bill for technology improvements on Mexico's side of the border, Ridge said. The enhancements would be made in consultation and full collaboration with the Mexican government, he added.

Ridge said he "would certainly be prepared to recommend that we accept, at least in some of these initial stages, a significant part or perhaps all of the cost. We've got to keep an open mind because it will benefit both countries."

In his 2003 budget proposal, President Bush requested $11 *billion* for border security, an increase of $2.2 *billion* over current-year spending. The Bush proposal calls for a $619 million increase in the U.S. Customs Service budget.

Much of the money would be used to hire an *additional* 800 new inspectors and agents to carry out new security initiatives, according to the White House. [. . . .] (Coleman, 2002, p. A1)

Williams Camus' (2009) "Cancer is War" thematic formulation continues with ". . . a bigger *arsenal of weapons*, consisting of *magic bullets* and *blunt instruments*, [that] *target the enemy*" (p. 475; original emphasis). In a similar manner, "smart border" technology in this example is like "magic bullets." Ackleson (2003) argues that "smart borders" are the preferred policy solution of the United States for screening for terrorist via air and land borders, while allowing the globalized flow of capital and labor that involves complicated advances in surveillance and security technologies. Post 9/11, there is a renewed effort on the border to advance three types of technologies at the points of entry: "surveillance, biometrics, and information technology . . . . While a 'Smart Border' infrastructure has enormous rhetorical and symbolic appeal, none of the three technologies offers a complete, or in some cases, even feasible solution given the reasonable demands of a globalized and open society" (Ackleson, 2003, pp. 69–70). In this sense, these magic, "smart" bullets do not work. In addition, Heyman (2008) argues that the border wall is not just physical but virtual as well. The virtual wall uses advanced computer and surveillance technology like ground-level radar and computerized detection systems as well as "the massing of police forces, including military and intelligence agencies, in the border region, which presents a web of obstacles to northward movement of illegalized people and goods, obstacles that usually are overcome, but at great risk and cost" (p. 305).

These "smart border" initiatives both virtual and physical as well as the border policy in general amount to symbolic political acts (Heyman, 2008, citing Calavita, 1990, 1994). Heyman further argues:

> Symbolic politics involves adopting policy measures that give the appearance, in this case, of law enforcement, but are not carried out in meaningful ways. Or, if they are carried out, it is in a place and manner, as on the border, that does not actually injure powerful interests, such as employers who hire undocumented workers. Indeed, the virtual wall, taken as an entirety, produces the appearance rather than the reality of law enforcement.
>
> Such symbolic politics satisfy the military-industrial and bureaucratic interests—after all, billions of dollars are spent on them. They placate the anti-immigrants—we are doing more and more at the border. They address some of the contradictory needs of the globalizers—satisfying the way of the economic integration of Mexico into the North American system . . . . Symbolic politics even satisfies the American public in important cultural ways. Outside is clearly separated from inside, legal from illegal. The troubling American addictions to drugs and inexpensive services can be put out of mind—no need for excessive self-honesty here—by displacing them onto the magnificent symbol of a threatened and then defended border. (pp. 321–322)

Thus, if "smart borders" are *magic bullets* that do not really work, then erecting border walls are the *blunt instruments* that are part of the bigger arsenal of weapons used, not to stop undocumented immigration, but to symbolically appear like the border enforcement spectacle is working. In this example, "President Bush requested $11 *billion* for border security, an increase of $2.2 *billion* over current-year spending," while huge sums of money also help to contribute to the symbolic impressiveness of this border and "an *additional* 800 new inspectors and agents to carry out new security initiatives" help contributes to the border arsenal that targets the "enemy" border crosser. Hence, the border is a racial divide that is "[e]xpensively kept, economically unsound, a spurious and useless political asset" (Morrison, 1992, p. 63).

The next most frequent concepts are "thousand" (772 references) and "hundred" (656 references). Beneath is an example that include both concepts:

> *The Los Angeles Times*: "An Immigrant Underground: In San Diego,
> the storm drain system is being used to smuggle illegal crossers,
> confronting the Border Patrol with a unique challenge"

Armando Reyes climbed over the border fence and prepared for the dash into San Diego. But his smuggler instead led him and four other migrants through a patch of reeds to a stinky drainage pipe, and ordered them inside.

The black sludge reached Reyes' chin as he crawled through the shoulder-width tube. Rats scurried by. Terrified of losing his way in the darkness, Reyes reached for the illegal immigrant in front of him and clutched his sneaker.

The stocky 28-year-old from Oaxaca had followed the smuggler into a vast labyrinth of drainage pipes under Otay Mesa, a booming commercial area of San Diego 15 miles southeast of downtown.

The 23-mile network leads to about 500 manholes scattered across about three square miles. From those openings into the bowels of the city, mud-covered migrants crawl out into streets, busy intersections and parking lots, creating a dizzying guessing game for U.S. Border Patrol agents.

"They're popping up all over the place," said Joe Perez, the agent in charge of the area. The migrant traffic below truck-clogged streets and new office parks underscores the persistence and desperation of people faced with crossing one of the most heavily fortified sections of the border.

Illegal crossings will soon get even tougher. President Bush is sending 6,000 National Guard troops to the border, Congress is mulling its own enforcement plans and starting next month, this busy frontier across from Tijuana will be monitored by remote surveillance cameras.

So the underground beckons.

The tunnels channel rainwater out of flood-prone areas, but when the waters aren't running, the waves of migrants flow, a phenomenon that has bedeviled agents for years and recently spiked as aboveground routes have become more heavily patrolled.

The cat-and-mouse game took an ironic turn last month when migrants even surfaced outside the offices of the U.S. Border Tunnel Task Force. Those manhole covers—one in a secured parking lot—were welded shut after that, one of them also topped with three 35-pound bags of rocks and gravel.

But six more manholes, all potential escape hatches, lie within a block of the federal facility.

"They're all interlinked, so you never know where they'll come up," said David Badger, a Border Patrol supervisor.

Other border cities have wrestled with similar situations, most notably Nogales, Arizona, which is linked underground to Nogales, Mexico, by two large storm-drain tunnels patrolled regularly by heavily armed agents.

Unlike Nogales, the drainage system under Otay Mesa doesn't extend into Mexico. But most of the tunnel outlets are just a quick run from the border. Illegal immigrants typically traverse the pipes, many of which are 2 to 3 feet in diameter, at night, sometimes crawling for hours. Vehicles waiting on deserted streets then whisk them to stash houses.

Border Patrol agents have arrested *hundreds* of migrants exiting storm drains in the last year but don't know how many get through. Some estimate that *thousands* make it. (Marosi, 2006, p. A1)

While the use of the concepts "thousand" and "hundred" are used once, this example is notable for the interesting parallels to the cult sci-fi film *C.H.U.D* (1984) also known as Cannibalistic Humanoid Underground Dweller. Movie posters for *C.H.U.D.* show an inhumane creature coming from a city manhole at night with the tagline "They're not staying down *there*, anymore!" [original emphasis]. Immigrants are dehumanized in this example with the headline: "An Immigrant Underground." Immigrants are further dehumanized with descriptions like "stinky drainage pipe," "black sludge . . . [up to the] chin," "Rats scurried by," and "500 manholes . . . . into the bowels of the city." These descriptions associate immigrants with dirt, excrement, and orifices. Disgust and abjection results from boundary violations that lead to fantasies of geographic contagion based on racialized fears that the other is taking over (see chapter 1). The hard to detect, sneaky nature of border crossers reflects in the discourse like, "[immigrants are] popping up all over the place," "cat-and-mouse game," and "[manholes are] all interlinked, so you never know where they'll [immigrants] come up." Cancer cells also hide, avoiding detection (Reynolds, 1998). In addition, "crawl" is used three times in this truncated example that associates immigrants with an animal or sub-human state. Cancer (crab) cells "crawl and migrate" (Williams Camus, 2009, p. 480). This example also overlaps with the "congested space" theme later in this chapter that helps to cause alarm over the tight, spatial nature associated with undocumented immigration.

The next two themes of the Border Symptoms are "active time" and "congested space." These themes reflect the general trend of postmodern, late capitalism in the acceleration in time and the shrinking of space through the process of globalization. This time-space compression intersects with popularized, scientific knowledge about cancer in the construction of the "diseased body politic."

ACTIVE TIME

In this time of postmodern late capitalism, the speeding up of time in life occurs with the shrinking of space (erosion of spatial barriers) aided by technological innovations that help to construct a "global village" characterized by flexible accumulation. David Harvey (1999) calls this "time-space compression." For the purpose of analyzing this "active time" theme, the focus here is more on the temporal dimension in the border news discourse. Space will be analyzed in the next theme "congested space." According to Harvey (1990):

> Time is a vital magnitude under capitalism because social labor time is the measure of value and surplus labor time lies at the origin of profit. Furthermore, the turnover time of capital is significant because the speed-up (in production, in marketing, in capital turnover) is powerful competitive means for individual capitalist to augment profits. In times of economic crisis and of particularly intense competition, capitalist with a faster turnover time survive better than their rivals, with the result that social time horizons typically shorten, intensity of work and living tends to pick up and the pace of change accelerates. (p. 425)

Thus, the world seems to be shrinking and time is flying, and this intensified "compression" affects the organization of labor and social practices fundamental to capitalist production.

Cancer also possesses elements of both time and space. Sontag (1978) argues that cancer is thought to possess stages that end in death:

> Metaphorically, cancer is not so much a disease of time as a disease or pathology of space. Its principle metaphors refer to topography (cancer "spreads" or "proliferates" or is "diffused"; tumors are surgically "excised"), and its most dreaded consequence, short of death, is the mutilation or amputation of part of the body. (pp. 14–15)

However, cancer's main symptoms are seen as invisible "until the last stage, when it is too late. The disease, often discovered by chance or through a routine medical checkup, can be far advanced without exhibiting any appreciable symptoms" (p. 12). Since Sontag's work on cancer as a metaphor over thirty years ago, advances in scientific research on cancer help make metaphoric constructions of cancer less prolific in popular media than in Sontag's time, with more "one-off images" used to convey cancer meanings like "snowball effect" or "chain reaction" (Hanne & Hawken, 2007, p. 97). Military images are still frequently used like "bomb in the nucleus" or cancer is still seen as a criminal gang "lurking, quiescent and ready to spring" (p. 97). However, there is a common theme of time that relates to these contemporary cancer images that make the disease seem fast, active, and quick, contrary to Sontag's findings decades ago that cancer was more about space than time.

There is a social construction of the acceleration of time in the border region that contrasts the reality of this region that is more rural than urban, more slow than fast. The concept "act" (2,253 references) leads this theme. Beneath is a concept of "act":

The Houston Chronicle: "20 Suspected Illegal Immigrants Found in Truck"

LOS ANGELES—Twenty suspected illegal immigrants were found crammed inside the sweltering camper compartment of a pickup truck on a freeway Monday.

Seven were taken to the hospital. The discovery came amid a hot spell, with temperatures already into the 80s at midmorning.

"They were suffering from dehydration, shortness of breath and chest pains," Fire Department spokesman Jim Wells said. "Their illness did not appear life-threatening."

California Highway Patrol officers stopped the pickup on a Harbor Freeway exit south of downtown, tipped off by a motorist who noticed people in the back of the pickup waving, possibly asking for help, CHP Officer Alex Delgadillo said.

"He called us and he stayed on the phone with us until we were finally able to catch up with the truck," Delgadillo said. "They were in very cramped spaces, in need of medical attention."

Immigration investigators planned to interview the driver and passengers.

Delgadillo said one of the passengers indicated the group came Sunday night from Mexicali, a Mexican border city about 90 miles east of San Diego. Immigration agent Robert Goetsch said, however, the group was believed to have been smuggled through Arizona.

"It's the **active** place right now," Goetsch said. "This is a very season for being smuggled in because it's before the hot weather and after the holidays." [. . . .] (Wides, 2004, p. A)

In this example, immigrants "crammed inside the sweltering camper" "were in very cramped spaces." Again, these reflect the "congested space" theme in the next section. However, the "congested space" theme in this example helps to bolster the "active time" theme when Agent Goetsch described the situation as an "active place" and "active season." First, this example shows how militarized border policies intentionally created Arizona as an "active" border crossing place in a necropolitical manner (see chapter 2). Necropolitics (Mbembe, 2003) encompasses the state's right to kill through the border policy strategy of "prevention through deterrence," where the state intentionally pushed border crossers away from safer, urban crossing points such as San Diego and El Paso and into the harsh and deadly desert of Arizona. The use of the desert as a border-crossing deterrent is an exercise of state control over immigrant mortality. Second, time in this place fluctuates in activity like a "season," which helps reduce immigrants to migrating herds that are subject to changes in weather and light patterns from the earth's changing position to the sun, with the ideal time to cross the border "before the hot weather and after the holidays." This again relates to the "immigrants as threatening fauna" theme (see chapter 4) given that immigrants are treated like seasonally controlled, migrating animals, willing to risk their lives "cramped" in cars and trucks crossing the border.

The next most frequent concepts are "effort" (1,689 references) "continual" (1,222 references). Following is an example that contains both concepts:

The Arizona Republic: "2,100 DANGEROUS ILLEGAL IMMIGRANTS CAUGHT IN NATIONWIDE CRACKDOWN"

Federal immigration officials on Wednesday said they had arrested more than 2,100 undocumented immigrants, including 49 in Arizona, as part of a nationwide crackdown on illegal immigration.

The action, called Operation Return to Sender, was aimed at taking dangerous criminal undocumented immigrants, including gang members and child molesters, off the streets, Immigration and Customs Enforcement officials said.

The agency also wanted to send a message that the government is beginning to aggressively enforce immigration laws not just at the borders but elsewhere in the country, they said. [. . . .]

In Arizona, agents arrested thirty-eight undocumented immigrants who had re-entered or stayed in the United States after deportation, said Patricia Schmidt, ICE assistant special agent in charge of investigations.

The other eleven included six sexual predators convicted of child pornography and other sex offenses involving minors, she said, as well as a member of the Mexican Brown Pride gang, and four undocumented immigrants convicted of drug charges and other deportable crimes.

Schmidt said the agency plans to **continue** hunting undocumented immigrants who commit crimes, even small infractions, as part of an **effort** to deter illegal immigration, and relieve pressure at the border so immigration officials can concentrate on preventing terrorism and improving national security.

The blitz began May 26. ICE agents arrested 2,179 undocumented immigrants.

About half have criminal records, Julie Myers, assistant secretary for U.S. Immigration and Customs Enforcement, said in a statement. Some 367 were members or associates of violent gangs, she said. (Gonzalez, 2006, p. B8)

The last section of this chapter analyzes the significance of these "operations" at the border like "Operation Return to Sender" example here and describes how these "operations" occupy the rhetorical intersections of crime, medicine, and warfare, given that all these industries use this term to describe their "operations." In this example, immigrants are animals that the Immigration Customs Enforcement "hunts" in order to "relieve pressure at the border so immigration officials can concentrate on preventing terrorism and improving national security." In addition, the use of "return to sender" suggests that immigrants are not residents of the national house, they are undeliverable mail that needs to return to their sending countries. In addition, Williams Camus (2009) writes "If the cancer is still *resistant* to the *cancer-fighting tools*, other *weapons* are injected to *attack* the disease or to boost the body's own *defences*" (p. 475; original emphasis). Here, "Operation Return to Sender, was aimed at taking dangerous criminal undocumented immigrants, including gang members and child molesters, off the streets" in order "to send a message that the government is beginning to aggressively enforce immigration laws not just at the borders but elsewhere in the country." So the use of "Operation Return to Sender" is another *weapon* injected to *attack* the disease of undocumented gangs and child predators, and in order to boost the body politics' *defenses*, an aggressive enforcement of the interior of the nation is declared. Analysis of the concept "gang" reflects the theme "congested space" and will be analyzed in the following section.

The next most frequent concepts are "often" (1,117 references) and "wait" (1,019 references)

The Los Angeles Times: "Fight for Human Freight: Gangs of kidnappers are stealing immigrants from smugglers after they've made it to the U.S. through the latest backdoor—Arizona."

[. . . .]"Phoenix is [the] epicenter of illegal smuggling of people and contraband," said Kyle Barnette, special agent in charge of the immigration and customs enforcement bureau in Phoenix. "And now these bandits are stealing each other's loads."

The victims are *often* sexually assaulted, pistol-whipped or tortured until their relatives come up with the ransom, about $1,800 for Mexicans and as high as $10,000 for South Americans. Kidnappers figure those who travel farther are more desperate and worth more money to *waiting* families. Federal agents say immigrants, including children, are *often* raped while kidnappers are on the phone with their family demanding money. Many children travel alone to meet their parents.

"They let the family hear what is going on; they let them listen while they rape their mother or daughter," said Armando Garcia who heads the human smuggling division of the Phoenix immigration office. "It's a whole new breed."

In a recent case, kidnappers threatened to hack off the arm of a 9-year-old girl and send it to the family if they didn't pay up. Authorities tracked the calls and raided the house where they found the girl cowering in a bathroom about to be raped. Another woman was sexually assaulted so *often* she screamed whenever a man came near.

"They realize there are hardships along the way," said customs agent Angel Rascon. "But they don't expect to be raped, extorted and kidnapped."

The attacks have become ever more brazen.

The Interstate 10 shooting happened outside Casa Grande, near Phoenix. Kidnappers *waited* along the road for a van of illegal immigrants that informants said would be heading north. They spotted the vehicle, ran it off the road and forced the passengers into another van at gunpoint.

The smugglers, incensed over losing their cargo, called their boss in Phoenix, who dispatched a team armed with Chinese SKS assault rifles to find the kidnappers. When they saw the van on the highway, the smugglers opened fire, killing four people inside. [. . . .] (Kelly, 2003, p. A1)

The work of Susan Coutin (2000) on "legal nonexistence" helps to understand this dangerous and extreme situation described in this example that is direct result of the militarized border policy (Kil & Menjívar, 2006). "Legal nonexistence" describes the situation of undocumented immigrants as being physically present and socially active in civil society but lacking legal recognition (Coutin, 2000). It is also a state of subjugation that results in vulnerability to deportation, confined to low-wage jobs, and denied basic human rights, such as access to decent housing, education, and health care (Menjívar & Kil, 2002). Placing undocumented people outside the legal order into a realm of lawlessness supports extreme actions and exempts authorities from obligations to them and, thus, the rights of those who are legally nonexistent are ambiguous (Coutin, 2000). This example shows the extreme vulnerability of undocumented immigrants who occupy this "legal nonexistence" as well as complimenting the more extreme notion of Necropolitics (Mbembe, 2003) where the state's right to kill—via exposure to death and deadly situations, for the most part—plays out in a growing and dangerous organized human smuggling operations at the border.

In this example, sexual assault and rape happen "often" for border crossers where kidnappers and families are constantly "waiting" to complete the smuggling exchange. Immigrants legal nonexistence reduce them to "freight" and "cargo" smuggled through the nation's "backdoor." Necropolitics in the border region is a state exercise in "control over mortality and to define life as the deployment and manifestation of power" (Mbembe, 2003, p. 12). Brutalizing immigration border policies control immigrants' lives, making them both more vulnerable and more exploitable to both legal *and* illegal industries, where rising human smuggling networks are a "whole new breed" that would threaten to dismember the arm of a "9-year-old girl and send it to the family if they didn't pay up."

The next and final concept of the "active time" theme is "emergency" (839 references). Following is an example of this concept:

The Los Angeles Times: Q&A/STATE OF *EMERGENCY*—A
Drastic Step Against Illegal Immigration

Full text: The governors of New Mexico and Arizona recently declared a "state of *emergency*" over what they characterized as a growing wave of illegal immigration, drawing national attention to frustrations that have reached a boiling point in those border states.

New Mexico Governor Bill Richardson and Arizona Governor Janet Napolitano accuse the federal government of negligence and inattention in dealing with illegal immigration-related problems gripping counties that border the Mexican states of Sonora and Chihuahua.

Question: What does it mean to declare a "state of *emergency?*"

Answer: A state of *emergency* means something so serious has happened that government must step in to send money or resources to the affected area. *Emergency* declarations are usually made by states in response to natural disasters such as fires or floods, and are often accompanied by requests for federal disaster relief. [. . . .]

Q: What do the *emergency* declarations bring to each state?

A: Money. In the case of New Mexico, it made $750,000 in state *emergency* funding immediately available to the counties of Dona Ana, Luna, Grant and Hidalgo—among the nation's busiest gateways for illegal immigration. Richardson also pledged an additional $1 million from a separate *emergency* pool.

In Arizona, the declaration freed $1.5 million from the governor's $4-million *emergency* fund for use in Cochise, Pima, Santa Cruz, and Yuma counties.

In addition to allowing the governors to quickly tap *emergency* funds, the declarations empower them to marshal equipment, personnel, and other resources.

Q: Is either state seeking federal aid?

A: No. There is no expectation that a state's *emergency* will trigger matching federal dollars, though spokespeople for Richardson and Napolitano say they hope their declarations spur the federal government to better control the border.

Q: Under what authority did the governors make these *emergency* declarations?

A: Laws in New Mexico and Arizona grant the governors broad powers to declare *emergencies* and direct resources toward man-made or natural disasters that threaten physical or economic harm. In both states, officials say there is an urgent need to combat the violence, drug trafficking, and destruction of property associated with illegal immigration.

A spokesman for Richardson said the governor decided on the spot to make the *emergency* declaration after a helicopter and ground tour of a border area near Columbus, N.M. [. . . .] (Alvarez, 2005, p. B2)

This example relates to the "cataclysmic flood" theme in the prior chapter in that immigration in the border region is declared an "emergency" by New Mexico Governor Bill Richardson (2003–2011) and Arizona Governor Janet Napolitano (2003–2009) where such "declarations are usually made by states in response to natural disasters." In addition to border vigilante groups (see Introduction chapter), politicians also capitalize on the intersections of emergencies and border crossings. For example, Patrick J. Buchanan's (2006) book, *State of Emergency: The Third World Invasion and Conquest of America*, renders an apocalyptic analysis of undocumented immigration making parallels to the fall of Rome. He makes the case that the real "emergency" is the declining birth rates of White babies and the loss of White national identity to immigrant newcomers who do not want to assimilate but maintain loyalties to their home countries in an act of "invasion," not migration. Buchanan's book is a form of magical thinking, an emotional reaction to boundary violations that lead to feelings of racial disgust and abjection, which are the foundation for fantasies of geographic contagion in the form of invasions (see chapter 1). And in his book, he cites these declarations of states of emergencies by both border governors in this example to make the case that the "emergency" is not just in the border region, but the "state of emergency is a national one. [United States of] America is being invaded, and if this is not stopped, it will be the end of the United States [of America]" (Buchanan, 2006, p. 7). Thus, the "state of emergency" warns of the end of White dominance in both demography and political power, by a force of nature in undocumented immigration that will change the social and racial order of the nation (see chapter 5). President Trump, in recycling both border vigilante and neoconservative political rhetoric, declared a "national emergency" on February 15, 2019 and stated, "we are declaring it for virtual invasion purposes—drugs, traffickers, and gangs" (Paschal, 2019, para 32).

CONGESTED SPACE

Harvey (1999) continues in his analysis of "space time compression" and argues the "elimination of spatial barriers and the struggle to 'annihilate space by time' is essential to the whole dynamic of capital accumulation" (p. 425):

> The foreboding generated out of the sense of social space imploding in upon us . . . translates into a crisis of identify. Who are we and what space/place do we belong? Am I a citizen of the world, the nation, the locality? . . . [T]he diminution of spatial barriers has provoked an increasing sense of nationalism and localism, and excessive geopolitical rivalries and tensions, precisely because of the reduction in the power of spatial barriers to separate and defend against others. (p. 427)
> Superior command over space becomes an even more important weapon in class struggle. It becomes one of the means to enforce speed-up and the redefinition of skills on recalcitrant work forces. (p. 106)

The "congested space" theme also indicates a socially constructed pathology. Cancer is seen as something that hides avoiding detection (Reynolds, 1998). Cancer cells are "crawling and migrating" animals given that etymologically the term "cancer" (crab) is itself an animal metaphor. Therefore, the spread of the cancer is metaphorically expressed in terms of a crawling, crab-like movement or migration (Williams Camus, 2009, p. 480).

The anxiety of space imploding on itself in the border region and the pathology of a cancer in the body politic that hides detection translates into a crisis of Whiteness where freedom is associated with having space and being settled in that space and racial subjugation or lack of freedom is associated with migrating, "congested space." "Time-Space compression always exacts its toll on our capacity to grapple with the realities unfolding around us. Under stress, for example, it becomes harder and harder to react accurately to events" (Harvey, 1989, p. 306). Hence, even the border region is a mostly rural place that is not highly populated, the border news coverage reflects a foreboding of space in regard to immigration, that focuses on immigrants in a tightly confined or grouped phenomenon.

The "group" concept leads this "congested space" theme with 3,379 references. In the following I offer an example of this concept:

The Albuquerque Journal: "AGENTS STOP 2 RIGS HAULING
IMMIGRANTS, AROUND NEW MEXICO"

LAS CRUCES—Border Patrol agents in the El Paso area halted two drivers hauling *groups* of undocumented immigrants in the backs of tractor-trailer rigs over the weekend. Border Patrol agents and El Paso County sheriff's deputies found 68 immigrants "stacked like cord wood" in the cargo trailer of a rig stopped late Friday night as it headed eastbound on Interstate 10, spokesman Doug Mosier said. One other immigrant was found in the truck's sleeper compartment. [. . . .] (*The Albuquerque Journal*, 1999, p. D3)

In this example, "*groups* of undocumented immigrants" are "stacked like cord wood," an analogy that compares immigrants to a natural resource like wood, cut in uniform lengths, and stacked in large volume for the purpose of firewood. Santa Ana (2002) notes that immigrants are seen as a commodity or resource in public debates so referring to them as cord wood reflects that dehumanization. In addition, Bonilla-Silva (2003) contends that nation of immigrants ideal of the "melting pot" really only applied to White immigrants, and that immigrants of color "could not melt into the pot. They could be used as wood to produce the fire for the pot, but they could not be used as material to be melted into the pot."

The next most frequent concept is "push" (774 references).

The Arizona Republic: "INS TARGETS SMUGGLERS AGENTS
TO FOCUS ON AIRPORTS AND SAFE HOUSES"

U.S. Immigration Commissioner Doris Meissner this morning will announce a new enforcement *push* to destroy the networks immigrant smugglers use to move human cargo—airports and safe houses. The effort, dubbed Operation Denial, will pull U.S. Immigration and Naturalization Service agents from other duties in Phoenix and other offices in Tucson, Las Vegas, and Reno. It will assign them round the clock at Sky Harbor International Airport, Las Vegas' McCarran Airport, and the main land routes in between.

They hope to choke a distribution system in which smugglers use Phoenix addresses as safe houses and commercial flights as large-scale "mules" to move illegal immigrants from city to city.

"Phoenix has emerged as a real focus point of the violence and victimization associated with smuggling," Meissner said in an interview with The Arizona Republic on Tuesday. "We have become more and more aware of the depth and sophistication of smuggling in Phoenix." (Borden, 2000, p. A1)

In this example, time and space work together to make Phoenix the "focus" of a "round the clock" enforcement "push." Again, immigrants are reduced to "cargo" and "Operation Denial" reflects another "operation" (see last section in this chapter) that intends to "choke" smuggling networks. Airplanes and safe houses are "large scale 'mules'" in immigrant smuggling. Mules refer to human carriers who traffic prohibited drugs. Here mules are not human but airplanes and houses that are typically markers for middle-class wealth, misused by border crossers for smuggling purposes. Airplanes in particular "annihilate space by time" by making the travel of long distances much faster than car or train. The reconfiguring of airplanes [human carrier] as mules for immigrants [prohibited drugs] shows the anxiety of the diminution of spatial barriers that "move illegal immigrants from city to city" like "Tucson, Las Vegas and Reno." Houses are not homes or havens (see chapter 4) but "safe houses" or "mules" that move immigrants who in themselves are like unlawful drugs. Here both the airplane and house become like human bodies that act like drug couriers. Immigrants here are reduced to illegal drugs that the nation wants to addictively consume in large quantity, which results in "violence and victimization associated with smuggling." The "depth and sophistication of smuggling" calls for a more superior command over space under flexible conditions of accumulation (Harvey, 1999, pp. 106–107). The "new enforcement *push*" of Operation Denial is a speed up and redefinition of skills focused at "airports and safe houses" used to move the addictive "human cargo."

The next leading concepts are "gang" (743 references) and "traffic" (626 references). Beneath is an example of both concepts:

The Houston Chronicle: "A Shootout Last Week Underscores
the Dangers of 'Drop Houses' as Tougher Border Enforcement
Raises the Stakes for Smugglers: Deadly Way Stations"

Mar. 20—On the journey into the United States, a stay in one of Houston's "drop houses" often is the last stop illegal immigrants make before their lives begin in this city.

It's a dehumanizing experience. Immigrants—treated as cargo—are known as pollo, or chickens. They're often held at gunpoint and forced to subsist for days or weeks in stifling and filthy conditions before their smuggling debts are paid.

These houses are all over Houston, say federal authorities, who find at least one a week. A shootout last week in southwest Houston underscored how problematic these illegal transfer sites have become as rival smuggling *gangs* target them to kidnap illegal immigrants to collect fees.

"It's similar to narcotics *traffickers* and groups that do rips of drug shipments," said Assistant U.S. Attorney Edward Gallagher. "In Houston, it's still not on par with the violence in Phoenix and Los Angeles—where smugglers are shooting each other in the middle of *traffic*—but we did have a shooting last week at 9 o'clock in the morning."

At least one suspected smuggler was shot by rival *gang* members who kicked in a door at 9011 Sandpiper on Tuesday morning, authorities said. It looked like a scene from an action movie to neighbors such as 89-year-old James DeMoss, who watched as police and immigration officials surrounded the drop house.

"I heard seven shots, total," he said. "It was like the Wild West."[. . . .] (Crowe, 2006)

Again, Whiteness and freedom are associated with having space and being settled in that space like in a home or house. However, immigrants and smugglers misuse homes as a "drop houses" that are "[d]eadly way stations" located "all over Houston." In this example, "rival smuggling *gangs*" and "rival *gang* members" are "similar to narcotics traffickers and groups that do rips of drug shipments." While in Phoenix and Los Angeles, "smugglers are shooting each other in the middle of *traffic*," Houston "did have a shooting last week at 9 o'clock in the morning" that "looked like a scene from an action movie" where "police and immigration officials surrounded the drop house" and "seven shots, total" made the location like the "Wild West." The Wild West here is "the fashioning of some localized aesthetic image, [and] allows the construction of some limited and limiting sense of identity in the midst of a collage of imploding spatialities" (Harvey, 1989, pp. 303–304). Smugglers commit Wild West shootouts over immigrants as "cargo" in this border region that represents a "collapse of spatial barriers" (Harvey, 1999, p. 229). While this news example expresses in an unusual way some racial knowledge of the "dehumanizing experience" of immigrants "treated as cargo," the article nevertheless refers to immigrants as animals with the Spanish word for chicken (*pollo*). In summarizing the work of Marco Kunz, who had mined the laudable newspaper reporting of legendary Tijuana newspaperman J. Jesús Blancornelas, Spener (2014) traces the origin of the word *pollo* in this region:

Mexican customs agents in Tijuana in 1963 found some chickens under the hood of a smuggler's car, where they had been *chamuscados* (scorched) by the heat of the motor. A couple of years later, a long-bed pickup truck passed through the same checkpoint on the way into the United States. On the U.S. side, an agent inspected the vehicle and discovered *un doble fondo*, a hidden compartment under the bed of the truck. Ten Mexican men were crammed into the space. The Immigration and Naturalization Service called journalists from both sides of the border, who photographed the frustrated migrants packed into the hidden compartment. Someone who had seen the burnt chickens on the Mexican side two years earlier exclaimed, "They look like those chickens!" Supposedly indocumentados have been referred to as pollos ever since, and the people who guide and transport them as polleros. (p. 85)

Smugglers are also called "coyotes," which is a Spanish word appropriated from the Nahuatl people. Jane Hill (2007) refers to this as "cowboy" Spanish, a register of loan words from the Spanish language associated with the "technology of managing range cattle from horseback" (p.274). "Cowboy" Spanish overlaps with her critique of "mock Spanish" a form of covert racism used among educated, middle- and upper-class Whites who do not speak Spanish well but use Spanish words or phrases to be humorous ("hasta la vista, baby") or show regional authenticity much to the chagrin of native Spanish speakers (Hill, 2009). In this example, the use of the word *pollo* demonstrates a journalistic attempt for regional authenticity in the Houston area but still communicates the racist notion that immigrants are animals (see chapter 4).

The final two most-frequent concepts of "congested space" theme are "load" (334 references) and "tight" (302 references). Following is an example that contains both concepts:

The Albuquerque Journal: "IMMIGRANT SMUGGLERS THRIVING;
Larger *loads* mean more profits and a rise in traffic-related deaths"

EL PASO—Need a good deal on a truck, minivan, even a tractor-trailer? You might try a lot in El Paso where the seized vehicles of immigrant smugglers are put up for auction. At any time, 30 percent to 40 percent of the roughly 350 vehicles in the lot run by Lone Star Auctioneers Inc. are vans, pickups, or commercial trucks, facility manager Joe Solis said.

Smugglers increasingly have turned to large vehicles, especially the trailers of 18-wheelers, to transport immigrants, Border Patrol agents say.

Smuggling used to be a small-scale affair. Illegal immigrants simply bought cars and drove across the border.

But in the past four years, as federal agents *tightened* their grip on the Mexican border, immigrant smuggling has thrived.

In the process, passenger safety is sacrificed as immigrants are crammed into vans and the crawl spaces of tractor-trailers.

"It's a trend organizations are using because they can move bigger *loads*," said Celio Parra, agent-in-charge of the El Paso Border Patrol sector's anti-smuggling unit. "It means more money." [. . . .] (Romo, 2000, p. A1)

Table 6.2 Border Treatments: "O"

Tier 1 Theory	Racist Dirt Fixations
Tier 2 4 Scales	Nation
Tier 3 Theme	Operations
Tier 4 Concept	"operation" (2175 references)
Tier 5 All 66 operations mentioned in the data listed by frequency and in alphabetical order	Operation Gatekeeper [155 references] Operation Hold the Line [77 references] Operation Rio Grande [64 references] Operation Blockade [25 references] (later referred to as Operation Hold the Line) Operation ICE Storm [25 references] Operation Safeguard [22 references] Operation Jobs [17 references] Operation Alliance [8 references] Operation Hardline [7 references] Operation Lively Green [7 references] Operation Second Hand [7 references] Operation Wetback [7 references] Operation Hard Hat [6 references] Operation White Shark [6 references] Operation Distant Shores [5 references] Operation Community Shield [5 references] Operation Crossroads [5 references] Operation Predator [4 references] Operation Return to Sender [4 references] Operation Dignity [3 references] (boycott by Mexican border residents) Operation Forerunner [3 references] Operation Hard Line [3 references] Operation Highpoint [3 references] Operation Lifesaver [3 references] Operation Pedro Pan [3 references] (brought 14,000 Cuban children) Operation Restoration [3 references] Operation Skywatch [3 references] Operation Stone Garden [3 references] Operation Summerheat [3 references] Operation Tarmac [3 references] Operation Casablanca [2 references] Operation Denial [2 references] Operation Desert Risk [2 references] Operation Dixie Junction [2 references] Operation Great Basin [2 references] Operation Last Call [2 references] Operation Linebacker [2 references]

(continued)

Table 6.2   Border Treatments: "O" *(continued)*

Operation Night Rider [2 references]
Operation Streamline II [2 references]
Operation Train Stop [2 references]
Operation White Fields [2 references]
Operation Against Smugglers Initiative on Safety and Security [1 reference]
Operation Backfill [1 reference]
Operation Bait Box [1 reference]
Operation Black Jack [1 reference]
Operation Brass Ring [1 reference]
Operation Cornerstone [1 reference]
Operation Dark Shadows [1 reference]
Operation Del Rio [1 reference]
Operation Distant Shore [1 reference]
Operation Eagle Eye [1 reference]
Operation Eastern Star [1 reference]
Operation Firestorm [1 reference]
Operation Global Reach [1 reference]
Operation Green Quest [1 reference]
Operation Guatemala Express [1 reference]
Operation July Jobs [1 reference]
Operation Jump Start [1 reference]
Operation Mirror [1 reference]
Operation Paul Revere (Glenn Spencer border vigilante) [1 reference]
Operation Restore [1 reference]
Operation Rollback [1 reference]
Operation Secure Mexico [1 reference]
Operation Sovereignty (Minuteman Project) [1 reference]
Operation Sudden Stop [1 reference]
Operation Vanguard [1 reference]

"Larger *loads* mean more profits" in the headline emphasize immigrants as a type of commodity so much so that "30 percent to 40 percent of the roughly 350 vehicles in the lot run by Lone Star Auctioneers Inc. are vans, pickups or commercial trucks" that are "seized vehicles of immigrant smugglers." Demand for "18-wheelers" reflect the larger scale of the human smuggling industry where immigrants are "crammed into vans and the crawl spaces of tractor-trailers" where "bigger *loads*" mean "more money." Human smuggling is "thriving" which have led to a "rise in traffic-related deaths." As "federal agents *tightened* their grip on the Mexican border," human smugglers squeeze immigrants into smaller spaces where "passenger safety is sacrificed." Lack of space means a lack of freedom that reflects in the political and economic subjugation for undocumented immigrants in this example. In contrast, passenger safety is associated with proper sitting space in a vehicle.

The association with immigrant to "congested spaces" in the border region helps in the reflexive construction of Whiteness as more open, free, and safer space even as passengers in a car or vehicle and immigrants are simply crammed "loads" due to "tightened" enforcement efforts.

In sum, the three themes emerge "growing number," "active time," and "congested space" in border newspapers that represent "border symptoms" reflect the intersection of biomedicalized discourse about cancer, the racial construction of the body politic and its pathology, and postmodern economic transformations involving space-time compression. The next and last section details the response to these "border symptoms," where the state deploys "operations" in order to criminally treat and control the border.

OPERATIONS

In response to the border "symptoms" previously described in this chapter, the state deploys "operations" in order to control the border. These "operations" reflect the rhetorical convergence of the medical, military, and law enforcement field in communicating racist, nativist ideologies, given that all these industries use "operations." Anzaldua (1987) writes that the U.S-Mexico "border es *una herida abierta* [is an open wound] where the Third World grates against the first and bleeds" (p. 25; see chapter 3). Her analogy of the border as type of bodily damage has far-reaching consequences given that "time-space compression" reflects the fast mobilization of capital and labor that encourages the collapse of spatial barriers that challenge nation states and their borders. For example, the concept of "operation" had 2,181 references in the border newspapers. Among those, sixty-six "operations" were named in the data (see table X). It is beyond the scope of the study to provide the details for each of these operations, but I include them *en masse* to illustrate the urge for "operations" to solve the immigration border "open wound" issue in a medicalized/ militarized/criminalized way. Not all of these operations take place in the border region during the data's time period, and some of these are not official state operations but involve vigilantes or their opponents, but most of these operations occurred during the period under study (table 6.2).

I close this chapter with one more example from the Chandler incident (also known officially as Operation Restoration) that also shows the damage of these types of "operations" can have in this region. Recall from the introduction chapter that Chandler incident was popularly called a "raid," "sweep," and "roundup," that insinuated that the targets of this "operation" were criminals, dirt, and animals, respectively. Following is an example of "Operation Restoration" (3 references). The example below contains two of those references:

The Houston Chronicle: "Illegal-Immigrant Sweep Backfires on Suburb"

[. . . .] In few places are the contradictions of rapid urban growth—and the role of immigrants, legal and illegal, in that growth—as stark as they are in Chandler, the second-fastest growing city in the United States.

Chandler's operation may have provoked the strongest outcry because the local authorities failed to take into account that its immigrants live side by side with a large, well-established Mexican-American community. Latinos make up about 15 percent of the population. Officially dubbed *Operation Restoration*, Chandler's initiative against illegal immigrants has provoked an aftermath similar in tone and duration to the police abuse controversies that have absorbed other U.S. cities.

Operation Restoration began on July 27, 1997. What happened over the next five days has been dissected in two investigations released so far, first by the Arizona attorney general's office and then by the city itself.

Both inquiries agree that the joint operation was a dramatic event that saw two dozen police officers and five Border Patrol agents fan out across downtown, sometimes chasing suspected illegal immigrants from work sites, and then filling up buses with detained people.

In all, the police held and eventually deported 432 illegal immigrants, all but three of them from Mexico.

As the police questioned people leaving markets patronized by Latinos, they invariably encountered U.S. citizens. Venecia Robles Zavala, a resident of nearby Mesa, said she was stopped outside a grocery store as she was leaving with her children.

She was disciplining her son, in Spanish, when an officer stopped her and asked for her papers.

"What papers?" Zavala responded in English. "Newspapers?"

"No," the officer said. "Immigration papers."

Thirty tense minutes later, she found a copy of her birth certificate in her car and the officer let her go.

Another U.S. citizen, Catalina Veloz, charged that officers placed her in handcuffs and released her only when she started to curse at them in English.

Four months after the operation, Arizona Attorney General Grant Hill released the results of his inquiry. The Chandler police, the report concluded, had stopped residents and had entered the homes of suspected illegal immigrants without warrants "for no other reason than their skin color or Mexican appearance or the use of the Spanish language."

What's more, city officials had failed to request formal permission from the U.S. attorney general to pursue such an action, as required by a 1996 federal law. (Tobar, 1998, p. A2)

In continuing and finishing the thematic formulation of "cancer is war" and applying it to the border news coverage, Williams Camus (2009) writes:

If the cancer is still *resistant* to the *cancer-fighting tools*, other *weapons* are injected to *attack* the disease or to boost the body's own *defences*. This attack may

eventually lead to *defeating* the disease although it also involves serious side effects
as healthy cells are also *destroyed* by the *weapons*. (p. 475; original emphasis)

Here as in other places in this book, I have argued that the necropolitical
deathscape is not contained at the border but affects people far away from
the border as well. Specifically, those that racially look like undocumented
border crossers are also harmed in the policing and enforcement of citizen/
undocumented dichotomy. This also parallels the image of the immune system where the body as a nation state is not only at war over boundaries but
also "containing internal surveillance systems to monitor foreign intruders"
(Martin, 1990, p. 410).

The Chandler example in the introduction chapter was a city/suburb example, while the attempts to formalize apartheid with SB1070 in Arizona is a
state example. Both these examples are an attempt to "defeat" undocumented
immigration as if it were a cancerous disease "although it also involves
serious side effects as healthy cells [citizens and legal residents] are also
destroyed by the *weapons*." The Chandler incident demonstrates how these
"operations" destroy more than their "target," with diminished rights for legal
residents and citizens of Brown color in particular.

In conclusion, the scale of the nation and the image of the body politic
demonstrate "border symptoms" with "growing number," "active time,"
"congested space" themes analyzed in the data. These social constructions of
disorder reflect the intersection of popularized, scientific understandings of
the immune system and cancer, social construction of the body politic, and
economic systems and transformations of late capitalism. While the "growing number" theme offers biomedical suggestions of unregulated growth that
reflect both an increase of spending and numbers in the region, the "active
time" and "congested space" themes reflect elements of "time space compression" (Harvey, 1999), where late capitalism makes the world seem like
it is shrinking due to technological advances in transportation and telecom-
munication as well as makes time seem like it is faster because of intensified
"compression" that affects the organization of labor and social practices
fundamental to capitalist production. "Operations" then become the "border
treatment" to these "border symptoms." However, these "operations" come
at great costs: the cost of militarizing a border for symbolic politics, the cost
of human rights crisis in the border deaths, and the cost of diminished civil
rights for citizens and legal residents in the border region and beyond.

REFERENCES

Ackleson, J. (2003). Securing through technology? "Smart borders" after September
11th. *Knowledge, Technology & Policy, 16*(1), 56–74.

The Albuquerque Journal. (1999). Agents stop 2 rigs hauling immigrants, around New Mexico. *The Albuquerque Journal*, March 9, 1999, D3.

Alonso-Zaldivar, R. 2003. The nation, number of illegal migrants growing, INS reports 7 million undocumented immigrants in 2000, with 30% in California. *The Los Angeles Times*, February 1, 2003, A-14.

Alvarez, F. (2005). Q&A / state of emergency: A drastic step against illegal immigration. *The Los Angeles Times*, September 14, 2005, B2.

Anzaldúa, G. (1987). *Borderlands: La frontera* (Vol. 3). San Francisco, CA: Auntie Lute.

Bonilla-Silva, E. (2003). Me, my race & I: Slideshow transcripts. *www.pbs.org*. Retrieved from https://www.pbs.org/race/005_MeMyRaceAndI/005_01-transcripts-04.htm.

Borden, T. (2000). INS targets smugglers agents to focus on airports and safe houses. *The Arizona Republic*, August 9, 2000, A1.

Buchanan, P. J. (2006). *State of Emergency: The Third World Invasion and Conquest of America*. New York, NY: St. Martin's Press.

Clark, D. (2018). Pentagon sending 5,200 troops to the border in "Operation Faithful Patriot" amid Trump condemnation of migrant caravan. *www.nbcnews.com*, October 29, 2018. Retrieved from https://www.nbcnews.com/politics/white-house/pentagon-send-5-200-troops-u-s-mexico-border-operation-n925866.

Coleman, M. (2002). Ridge juggles needs at borders. *The Albuquerque Journal*, March 1, 2002, A1.

Coutin, S. B. (2000). *Legalizing Moves: Salvadoran Immigrants' Struggle for U.S. Residency*. Ann Arbor: University of Michigan Press.

Devereaux, R. (2018). The military's justification for sending thousands of troops to the border is the opposite of the truth. *www.theintercept.com*, October 31, 2018. Retrieved from https://theintercept.com/2018/10/31/operation-faithful-patriot-border-troops-bad-intel/.

Domino, G., Affonso, D. A., and Hannah, M. T. (1992). Assessing the imagery of cancer: The cancer metaphors test. *Journal of Psychosocial Oncology*, 9(4), 103–121.

Gonzalez, D. (2006). 2,100 dangerous illegal immigrants caught in nationwide crackdown. *The Arizona Republic*, June 15, 2006, B8.

Hanne, M., & Hawken, S. J. (2007). Metaphors for illness in contemporary media. *Medical Humanities*, 33(2), 93–99.

Haraway, D. (1999). The biopolitics of postmodern bodies: Determinations of self in immune system discourse. In J. Price & M Shildrick (Eds.), *Feminist Theory and the Body: A Reader* (pp. 203–214). New York, NY: Routledge.

Harrington, K. J. (2012). The use of metaphor in discourse about cancer: A review of the literature. *Clinical Journal of Oncology Nursing*, 16(4), 408–412.

Harvey, D. (1989). *The Condition of Postmodernity: An Enquiry into the Origins of Cultural Change*. Malden, MA: Blackwell.

Harvey, D. (1990). Between space and time: Reflections on the geographical imagination. *Annals of the Association of American Geographers*, 80(3), 418–434.

Harvey, D. (1999). Time–space compression and the postmodern condition. In Waters, M. (Ed.), *Modernity: Critical Concepts* (pp. 98–118). New York: Taylor & Francis.

Heyman, J. M. (2008). Constructing a virtual wall: Race and citizenship in US–Mexico border policing. *Journal of the Southwest, 50*(3), 305–333.

Hill, J. H. (2007). Mock Spanish: A site for the indexical reproduction of racism in American English. In J. F. Healey & E. O'Brien (Eds.), *Race, Ethnicity, and Gender: Selected Readings* (pp. 270–284). Thousand Oaks, CA: Sage.

Hill, J. H. (2009). *The Everyday Language of White Racism*. New York, NY: John Wiley & Sons.

Kelly, D. (2003). Fight for human freight: Gangs of kidnappers are stealing immigrants from smugglers after they've made it to the U.S. through the latest backdoor—Arizona. *The Los Angeles Times*, December 14, 2003, A1.

Kil, S. H., & Menjívar, C. (2006). "The 'War on the border': The criminalization of immigrants and militarization of the USA-Mexico border." In R. Martinez, Jr. & A. Valenzuela, Jr. (Eds.), *Immigration and Crime: Race, Ethnicity, and Violence* (pp. 164–188). New York: New York University Press.

Laranjeira, C. (2013). The role of narrative and metaphor in the cancer life story: A theoretical analysis. *Medicine, Health Care and Philosophy, 16*(3), 469–481.

Lash, S. (2000). Judges come off bench to seek help, Congress urged to provide more jurists, funding. *The Houston Chronicle*, May 12, 2000, A8.

Marosi, R. (2006). An immigrant underground: In San Diego, the storm drain system is being used to smuggle illegal crossers, confronting the Border Patrol with a unique challenge. *The Los Angeles Times*, May 25, 2006, A1.

Martin, E. (1990). Toward an anthropology of immunology: The body as nation state. *Medical Anthropology Quarterly, 4*(4), 410–426.

Martin, E. (1992). The end of the body? *American Ethnologist, 19*(1), 121–140.

Martin, E. (1994). *Flexible Bodies: Tracking Immunity in American Culture from the Days of Polio to the Age of AIDS*. Boston, MA: Beacon Press.

Mbembe, J. (2003). Necropolitics. *Public Culture, 15*(1), 11–40.

Menjívar, C., & Kil, S. (2002). Exclusionary language in official discourse on immigrant-related issues. *Social Justice, 29*(1–2), 160–176.

Morrison, T. (1992). *Playing in the dark: Whiteness and the Literary Imagination*. New York: Vintage.

O'Rourke, C. (2018). Viral image supposedly depicting caravan members as rock-throwers dates back years. *www.politifact.com*, November 5, 2018. Retrieved from https://www.politifact.com/facebook-fact-checks/statements/2018/nov/05/blog-posting/viral-image-supposedly-depicting-caravan-members-r/.

Rasmussen, C., & Brown, M. (2005). The body politic as spatial metaphor. *Citizenship Studies, 9*(5), 469–484.

Reynolds, T. (1998). Researchers slowly unveil where cancer cells hide. *Journal of the National Cancer Institute, 90*(22), 1690–1691.

Romo, R. (2000). Immigrant smugglers thriving: Larger loads mean more profits and a rise in traffic-related deaths. *The Albuquerque Journal*, February 20, 2000, A1.

Santa Ana, O. (2002). *Brown Tide Rising: Metaphors of Latinos in Contemporary American Public Discourse*. Austin: University of Texas Press.

Sontag, S. (1978). *Illness as Metaphor*. New York: Farrar. Strauss and Giroux.

Spener, D. (2014). The lexicon of clandestine migration on the Mexico-US border. *Aztlán: A Journal of Chicano Studies, 39*(1), 71–104.

Tobar, H. (1998). Illegal-immigrant sweep backfires on suburb. *The Houston Chronicle*, December 29, 1998, A2.

Trump, D. J. [realDonaldTrump]. (2018a, October 29). Many Gang Members and some very bad people are mixed into the Caravan heading to our Southern Border. Please go back, you will not be admitted into the United States unless you go through the legal process. This is an invasion of our Country and our Military is waiting for you! [Twitter moment]. Retrieved from https://twitter.com/realDonald Trump/status/1056919064906469376.

Trump, D. J. (2018b). Remarks by President Trump on the illegal immigration crisis and border security. *www.whitehouse.gov*, November 1, 2018. Retrieved from https://www.whitehouse.gov/briefings-statements/remarks-president-trump-ill egal-immigration-crisis-border-security/.

Wides, L. (2004). 20 suspected illegal immigrants found in truck. *The Houston Chronicle*, March 9, 2004, A.

Williams Camus, J. T. (2009). Metaphors of cancer in scientific popularization articles in the British press. *Discourse Studies*, *11*(4), 465–495.

Wren, C. (1996). New drug czar is seeking ways to bolster his hand. *New York Times*, March 17, 1996. Retrieved from https://www.nytimes.com/1996/03/17/us/new-drug-czar-is-seeking-ways-to-bolster-his-hand.html.

Chapter 7

The Unbearable Whiteness of Seeing

Recommendations for Resisting Everyday New(s) Racism

In Houston, Texas, in late October 2018, on the midterm election campaign trail, President Trump boldly proclaimed that he was a "nationalist." He explained to the crowd:

> You know what a globalist is? A globalist is a person that wants the globe to do well, frankly, not caring about our country so much [. . .] And you know what, we can't have that. . . . You know, they have a word. It [sic] sort of became old-fashioned. It's called a nationalist [. . .] And I say, "Really, we're not supposed to use that word?" You know what I am? I'm a nationalist. . . . Use that word. (Samuels, 2018, para 3–6)

A few days later, President Trump (2018) also tweeted on October 31, 2018:

> Our military is being mobilized at the Southern Border. Many more troops coming. We will NOT let these Caravans, which are also made up of some very bad thugs and gang members, into the U.S. [of America]. Our Border is sacred, must come in legally. TURN AROUND!

Later that same day, President Trump (2018) tweeted a campaign ad that blamed Democrats for allowing into the country immigrants who then killed cops or attempted murder. The ad also showed Brown people tearing down a chain link fence, which alluded to the expected arrival of the migrant caravan to the nation's southern border. Versions of this ad later aired on NBC, Facebook, and FOX, however, due to its growing controversy, NBC, Facebook, and FOX eventually stopped running the ad. Interestingly, CNN never aired the ad after initially calling it "racist" (Grynbaum & Chokshi, 2018, para 3).

159

Three weeks later, President Trump said, "If they [military troops deployed at the border] have to, they're going to use lethal force. I've—I've given the OK. If they have to. I hope they don't have to" (Axelrod, 2018). A White House memo later clarified that "lethal force" is limited to the protection of federal agents (Domonoske & Gonzales, 2018). President Trump is also seeking to change the asylum application process and limit the ability to apply only at official ports of entry in an attempt to bar undocumented border crossers from seeking asylum (Jordan, 2018), particularly those from the migrant caravan. The Trump administration tear-gassed immigrants from the caravan that had reached the Tijuana border and were protesting their legal right to apply for asylum—various media outlets circulated vivid images of women and small children in diapers scattering in all directions surrounded by this chemical weapon that has been banned in warfare since 1993 (Horton, 2018).

Thus, President Trump declares himself a "nationalist," describes the border as "sacred," and in need of military protection against a migrant caravan seeking asylum, runs a racist campaign ad with unsupported political finger-pointing that perpetuates racial myths about immigrant criminality, and authorizes the use of "lethal force" for troops stationed at the border. It seems that President Trump's racist nativism is on full display, so much so that the news industry that typically embraces race neutrality in its coverage made an unprecedented move to self-censure and not air (or no longer air) his campaign ad due to its overt racism.

This concluding chapter begins with a summary of the key findings of the study by highlighting the meanings of Whiteness and the nation in news discourse about the border. In addition, I provide an overview about news media tenets, like objectivity and neutrality, and describe their contribution to the New Race Neutral Racism. Furthermore, the vertical restructuring of the media market over the past 30 years helps to illuminate the journalistic failings in covering the border as a human rights crisis. I conclude with some recommendations.

SUMMARY OF KEY POINTS OF THE STUDY: WHITENESS AND A DISEASED BODY POLITIC

The scholar-activist impetus for this study was to counter the "postracial" characterization of the nation that seemed to treat racism as an historical artifact. This study instead adopts a NRNR framework to show that racist nativism is thriving particularly in the border region. The election of President Barack Obama (2009–2017) seemed to signal that racism was over; after all, a non-White, biracial (Black/White) person could had attained the highest office as the first Black U.S. American president. However, one of the arguments of this book is that when it comes to the nation's southern border and issues of immigration, bipartisan efforts have contributed to racist border militarization and criminalization policies that harm and kill immigrants and negatively affect them long after they have crossed the border. Militarized border policies sharply escalated with President Clinton's "prevention through deterrence" policy that helped to treat economic refugees of neoliberal trade policies into imagined criminals' intent on disorder and chaos, which inspire armed citizens to become border vigilantes and militias. Furthermore, the "war on the border" rhetoric and posture brutalizes the public in general and motivates the fringe parts of society to bear arms and head for the border to "help" the federal government defend its borders. The Minuteman Project, a hodgepodge of various border vigilante groups, converged in Arizona under the Bush, Jr.'s administration in 2005 and it now seems like there is renewed motivation under President Trump's administration for vigilantes to organize on the border to defend against what President Trump calls an "invasion" by immigrants (O'Rourke, 2018).

The Racist Dirt Fixations theoretical model is a novel interdisciplinary framework that merges Mary Douglas' (1966) embodied notion of "purity and danger" and fixations on transgression of symbolic "dirt," with Cornell West's (1988) racist genealogies that draw from scientific, religious, and psychosexual preoccupations. This model helps to explain how systems of "purity and danger" function among these racial preoccupations, creating categories of health/illness, sacred/profane, pure/impure that intersect with issues of class, gender, sexuality, and ableism. In addition, the geographic scales of body, house, region, and nation amplify the explanatory power of racist dirt fixations by providing cognitive scaffolding for these fixations. What makes this model effective in explaining racism in public discourse also helps to hide that very same racist discourse. That is the power of NRNR—that deeply racist thinking and rhetoric can thrive alongside values of race neutrality. More importantly, the racist dirt fixations model not only illuminates how immigrants are criminalized as agents of harm in imaginative ways in the border news discourse but also shows how threats to Whiteness are expressed as a "diseased body politic" that further justify these brutalizing immigration policies. The rhetorical "wars" that apply to the border rely on a reflexive, racialized construction of the "Brownness" of border crossers that in turn reveal the "Whiteness" of the nation without having to acknowledge any racist beliefs in the "purity" or supremacy of Whiteness.

In this study, President's Trump's direct accusation that immigrants are "rapists" also reflects the "vulnerable body" scale. At the scale of the body, border crossings threaten the Whiteness of the national body through suggestions of (a) rape and (b) disfigurement. Border news discourse genders and feminizes the nation with nurturing resources and services under threat from perceived immigrant criminality. Record-breaking immigrant deaths in the region are not framed as a human rights crisis and nor as a direct result of militarized border policies, but instead immigrants are blamed for their plight and reduced to their dead bodies in the border news discourse.

The discourse about the "face" of the nation naturalizes Whiteness as the default national race and the "change" as a distinctly racial one that also taps into ableist feelings of disfigurement and disability. The imagery of a racially changed face expresses the anxiety of Whiteness, its challenged supremacy, and its tenuous future. Current census data project that Whites will become the racial minority in 2045 (U.S. Census Bureau, 2018).

The next larger scale is the house. Border news coverage constructs immigrants as home intruders, both human and animal. Whiteness at this scale reflexively signifies (a) a law-abiding, rightful owner of property, and (b) a human being. After the 9/11 terror attacks of 2001, the Department of Homeland Security's (DHS) use of "homeland" reflects the myth of the United States as a primordial "home" in need of aggressive territorialization and suggests an ethnoracial assertion of belonging. President Trump's claim that he is a "nationalist" and that the "border is sacred" complements this study's analysis of an aggressive reterritorialization of Whiteness reflected in the discourse about militarized border policies. In particular, the concept of home projected onto this border region is symbolized in owning, residing, and protecting a "ranch" and expresses a settler, pioneer image that depends on the material and discursive ownership and exploitation of the colonized land and people of the Western frontier, a reflection of Manifest Destiny. Meanwhile, border news coverage constructs the border as a "revolving door" to the United States, a highly racialized crime image that harkens to President Bush, Sr.'s Willie Horton campaign ad that again invokes the crime of rape but also suggests a security threat to the citizens that reside in the national house, linking border crossers to terrorism. White citizens reside in this imagined national house as property owners and rightful occupiers, simultaneously mystifying the layered history of imperialism and colonialism in this region and justifying the right to defend the home as property.

However, White citizens are not merely imagined as property owners of the national house. As Cheryl Harris (1993) argues, Whiteness and property have legally and historically evolved to share a common principle in the right to exclude racial "others" so much so that Whiteness is a form of property that (a) racializes privilege economically for Whites (and those who can "pass" for White) as well as (b) legitimates a White legal identity associated with citizenship rights and national identity.

President Trump's (2018f) tweet about immigrants—"Tell the people 'Out,' and they must leave, just as they would if they were standing on your front lawn"—reflects this "Whiteness as property" concept but with a middle-class, suburban reference to a house's "front lawn." President Trump's tweet and Whiteness at this house scale also evoke elements of the legal concept of Castle Doctrine:

> Those who are unlawfully attacked in their homes have no duty to retreat, because their homes offer them the safety and security that retreat is intended to provide. They may lawfully stand ground instead and use deadly force if necessary to prevent imminent death or great bodily injury, or the commission of a forcible felony. (Carpenter, 2002, pp. 656–657)

Lave (2012) notes that the Castle Doctrine fosters racism and incentivizes murder, given that more Black than White people are killed with the "stand your ground" claim. Most notably, Florida has been the setting for egregious cases of "stand your ground." For example in 2013, the court instructed jurors in George Zimmerman's murder trial of Trayvon Martin, a 17-year-old Black child, about that state's "stand your ground" doctrine.

In 2012, George Zimmerman was a resident and neighborhood watch volunteer in a gated community where Trayvon Martin had been visiting family. One night, Zimmerman claimed he shot Martin in "self-defense" even though Martin was unarmed and Zimmerman chased him down. The jury found Zimmerman not guilty of all charges (Lave, 2012). Even though Zimmerman is mixed race (Brown/White), his German surname and status as a resident of a gated community most likely provided him a racial pass to the "Whiteness as property" privilege before the law. For example, police initially refused to arrest Zimmerman, citing that they found no evidence to contradict Zimmerman's self-defense claim, in addition to making investigative missteps which then led to protests, marches, and rallies across the nation. Due to the tireless work of grassroots activists and social justice organizers nationwide, police eventually arrested Zimmerman six weeks after he murdered Martin (Lave, 2012).

Additionally, at the house scale, border news coverage constructs Brown immigrants as wild animals, which reflexively construct Whiteness as fully human and burdened with the task of animal management. President Trump espoused this very same racist view rather transparently when he said that immigrants "aren't people, these are animals, and we're taking them out of the country at a level and at a rate that's never happened before" (Davis, 2018, para. 4). In this study, U.S. American jobs and resources "lure" immigrant workers into the nation much like the smell of food might lure wild animals to a home. "Catch and release" policies and immigrant "round ups" reflect animal management imagery. By establishing and growing communities, Brown immigrant families and children symbolize an invasive, reproductive threat to the Whiteness of the national house (Chavez, 2008). Thus, the desire to repeal birthright citizenship as a constitutional amendment—explicitly in order to prevent what anti-immigrant groups and conservative politicians pejoratively call "anchor babies" (Chavez, 2008)—seems to be President Trump's attempt to racially solve the nativist "enemy within" problem of multicultural immigration that threatens the supremacy of Whiteness in the nation.

The next larger scale of the region occupies two themes: "Battleground" and "Cataclysmic Flood." Whiteness at this scale suggests (a) a masculinized, militarized front under siege, and (b) a settled region threatened by a Brown deluge. The former reflects a win/lose narrative typical of warfare and the latter reflects a survive/die narrative of the flood myth, though these narratives overlap and are not mutually exclusive to their respective themes. However, both narratives reflect zero-sum logics that recklessly fuel a racial animus toward immigrant border crossers. In the Battleground theme, the "war on drugs," the "war on terror," and the "war on the border" influence the public to see immigrants as "enemies."

These wars, however, also reflect a type of embodied disgust in relation to nativist anxiety about "dirty crossings" that lead to magical thinking about geographic contagion in the border region in that "foreign" immigrants are seen as intent on taking over the nation. The military that supports law enforcement efforts in the border region are there to "protect" against those that "smuggle" drugs and "human cargo" into the nation as well as preventing threats of "terrorism." However, the mass casualties of these rhetorical policy wars are not citizens, but immigrants killed in the desert as well as those who are driven underground by border militarization policies (Kil & Menjívar, 2006). This militarized border region is a necropolitical deathscape that place immigrants crossing the border in constant contact with the possibility of their own death that they become a type of "living dead" (Mbembe, 2001, p. 179). The millions of "arrests" in the region justify the "beefing-up" of militarized enforcement that links meat to muscle to masculinity, which contrasts the vulnerability of the body in the first scale where the body is feminized with nurturing resources that immigrants pillage.

On a more abstract level, the "Cataclysmic Flood" theme includes concepts like "flow," "waves," and "overwhelm" to describe immigration hydrokinetically, which then constructs Whiteness as a settled region with calmer, milder weather at risk of a "Brown tide rising" (Santa Ana, 2002). Like the house scale, Whiteness is associated with settlement and civilization and Brownness is associated with nature, but in this case not threatening fauna but foreboding regional weather. If likening immigrants to animals is a racialized abstraction, then further reducing them to water takes that abstraction to a molecular scale. But the molecules together *en masse* can be a force of great natural destruction. It is this natural destructive force that resonates with the biblical story of the Great Flood. Similar to the "changing face" concept of the body scale where the race of the nation's face was changing from White to Brown, the water imagery seems to warn about the end of White dominance in the nation.

Finally, the scale of the nation complements the foundational body scale, but in a more contemporary and scientific way. Whiteness at this scale reflects a body politic fighting the disease of cancer/immigration in two ways: (a) with an imagined militaristic, immune system, and (b) with hi-tech, aggressive "operations." This "diseased body politic" communicates Whiteness and nativism about the border through discursive "border symptoms" and "border operations" that represent the intersection of immunology discourse, the racial construction of the body politic, and anxiety about postmodern economic transformation and its impact on national borders. Border news discourse construct border enforcement efforts like a human body's immune system that polices in a warlike manner the boundary between self/other, citizen/border crosser. "Growing number," "active time," and "congested space" represent a pattern in the discourse of "border symptoms" of the body politic. Undocumented immigrants are seen "invading" far into the nation much like cancer can grow in number and spread in the human body. Time is seen as busy and active to the point where some border states have declared a "state of emergency" to deal with immigration as if it were a natural disaster. However, this "state of emergency" also symbolically represents a racial alarm about the imminent end of White national dominance due to undocumented immigration.

The "congested space" theme reflects the anxiety of space collapsing in the border region due to globalization that resonates with the pathology of a cancer that has not been detected. Brownness is associated with cramped, unfree spaces particularly in transport vehicles as well as in homes "abused" as temporary "drop houses." In contrast, Whiteness is associated with spatial freedom and having a settled, proper home space. Thus, the acceleration of time diminishes spatial barriers like the border, which challenges the monopoly of Whiteness with the USA, given the imagined growth of Brown border crossers. In response to these "symptoms," the state deploys "operations," which is the rhetorical crossroad of the medical, military, and law enforcement field in communicating racist, nativist ideologies in order to criminally treat and control the border. The national immune system is not only at war over boundaries but uses an internal surveillance system in its search for cancer/immigrants, where the "side effects" of the treatment is that healthy cells (citizens and legal residents) are also destroyed by the weapons. These "operations" destroy far more than their "target," with diminished rights for legal residents and citizens who are Brown. "Border symptoms" and "border operations"

criminalizes immigrant border crossers as surplus populations of late capitalism, which make them more vulnerable to economic exploitation because of
their "dirty" status as violators of the territorial boundary, in which the imagined militaristic, immune system of the body politic needs to maintain the
boundary between self (Whiteness) and the "other" (Brownness).

OBJECTIVITY AND NEW(S) RACISM

One of the key reasons why Whiteness will continue in significance is
because race neutrality allows deeply racist ideas to flourish covertly. The
race neutral values typically embraced by the mainstream news media industry insidiously advance Whiteness and White supremacy. In this section, I
analyze the notion of news media objectivity and neutrality to show how
these values distort reality.

First, it is helpful to discuss the news media philosophy of objectivity
to get a sense of its public responsibility and political purpose. Objectivity
emerged as a prevailing professional ethic sometime between the 1890s and
the 1920s (Porwancher, 2011). "Defending 'objectivity' is made difficult by
its slippery nature; since it is often defined in negatives—a lack of bias, a lack
of party affiliation, a lack of sensationalism" (Mindich, 2000, p. 6). However,
metaphors that journalists use to describe their intentions continue to support
notions of objectivity. The news industry frequently uses four metaphors:
window, mirror, net, and seesaw: "A window to the world," "a mirror to
life," a fishing "net" where "journalists see themselves as fishers. They start
off with nothing but a news net, cast it out, and haul back the news of the
day" (Mindich, 2000, p. 6). And the seesaw metaphor offers the notion of
"'balanced' and 'fair' coverage that has long been a standard in journalism
(p. 7). Even though objectivity has been dropped from the Society of Professional Journalists' Code of Ethics in 1996 because of journalists' skepticism
of its achievability (p. 5), and mainstream journalists and news editors have
adopted the fairness principle because "fairness comes closer as a measure
because editors and readers can sense it" (Doyle & Getler, 2004, p. 45, citing
Getler), the beliefs of objectivity remain in journalistic practices.

For example, the practice of objectivity remains a tenet in journalism
textbooks, and it can be broken down to five essential components. The first
of these components is detachment, "to make sure the facts are doing the
talking, not the reporter's own preconceived notions." The ethic of nonpar-
tisanship is the second; reporters must offer "both sides" of each story. The
third is a style of writing called the inverted pyramid, which gives readers
the most important fact in the lead paragraph. Native empiricism, or reliance on "facts" to "report accurately the truth or reality of the event," is

the fourth quality. The fifth and final component is balance, the impossible yet all-important goal that leads to 'undistorted reporting'" (Mindich, 2000, p. 8). These components still make up the core of journalistic ethics that resemble objectivity and neutrality. Typically, journalists take objectivity to mean that the news story is free of their opinion or feelings and contains facts written by an impartial and independent observer (Weber, 2016, citing Mencher, 2011).

However, regardless of whether the U.S. American standard of journalism follows objectivity or that of fairness, the result is still similar in that the "reality" the news media reports upon results in a distorted, "framed" manner. Since news is a social institution, it imparts a public character to daily occurrences, and it is an ally to legitimated institutions like centralized sources, politicians, and bureaucrats, then news is inherently ideological and limits access to ideas through institutional and organizational framing (Tuchman, 1978). Thus, the news industry including all reporters, editors, and managers organize the social world according to their own subjectivity which can contain/minimize or trump/overemphasize events depending upon the social make-up of the news institution (Gitlin, 1980).

Media scholars are critical of the objectivity norm because it can undermine the best interest of its audience. Reporters consider objectivity a useful professional norm because it gives the appearance of fairness by providing a balance in news stories. Since reporters often lack the time and/or scientific expertise to adjudicate facts in complicated policy or political disputes, they use the objectivity norm as a fair approach to cover competing claims (Tuchman, 1978). In an attempt to avoid bias, media scholars note that journalists tell stories with both sides of a dispute equally, without consideration for the truth or empirical evidence (Boykoff, 2007; Dunaway, Davis, Padgett, & Scholl, 2015, citing Entman, 1989). Objectivity and balance concepts then lead journalists to information biases (Boykoff & Boykoff, 2004a).

One area in which journalists are criticized for following this practice is in reporting about climate change, where stories include quotes from environmental scientists on equal footing with quotes from fringe climate change deniers (Boykoff & Boykoff, 2004a, 2004b; Corbett & Durfee, 2004; Dunaway et al., 2015). By quoting both sides of the debate, journalists misrepresent the scientific consensus on the topic that global warming is human-made, real, and dangerous. The public is detached from the realities of global warming and the news media industry help in that detachment through distorted reporting. This type of framing distorts information that will have deleterious effects on the planet. And the same phenomenon is true when it comes to the coverage of race. However, the problem is further exacerbated by neoliberal transformations in the media landscape that have created an oligarchy that impacts news output in a racialized way.

WHITE SUPREMACY AND MEDIA REPORTING:
A VERTICAL INTEGRATION APPROACH

If liberalism is a political philosophy, then neoliberalism "is a transnational political project aiming to remake the nexus of market, state, and citizenship from above" (Wacquant, 2010, p. 213). Omi and Winant (2014) argue that the race neutrality of liberalism "underwrites the neoliberal accumulation project" (p. 15) and neither would be politically possible without the other. Furthermore, liberalism's focus on individual rights through ownership of property, minimal government interference, and faith in free market efficiency opened the door for neoliberalism to protect financial capital (Khiabany, 2017).

Racism drives neoliberalism. Hohle (2015) contends that U.S. American neoliberalism is a political project designed to create the economic conditions for the capital accumulation and the upward redistribution of resources based on meritocracy. He further argues that neoliberalism is a direct legacy of postwar Jim Crow racism, where the southern White segregationists and business class worked together to prevent the racial integration of Blacks that gained the support of White, middle-class Southerners. Today, the neoliberal state protects White, elite privileges to capital and "is not about free markets" (Hohle, 2015, p. 141).

Moreover, Giroux (2003) argues that "under neoliberalism all levels of government have been hollowed out and largely reduced either to their policing functions or to maintaining the privileges of the rich and the interests of corporate power—both of which are largely White" (p. 197). Wacquant (2012) agrees and articulates three aspects of neoliberalism: (a) it is a political project of state-crafting that puts liberal notions of individual responsibility at the service of commodification; (b) it is a "Centaur-state" that practices laissez-faire at the top and punitive paternalism at the bottom, and (c) it relies on the growth and "glorification" of the prison industrial complex (p. 66). Mohanty (2013) clarifies that "while neoliberal states facilitate mobility and cosmopolitanism (travel across borders) for some economically privileged communities, it is at the expense of the criminalization and incarceration (the holding in place) of impoverished communities" (p. 970).

The "neo" of neoliberalism is the state's *re-regulation* rather than deregulation of markets based on commodification (economic), in addition to the attack on the welfare state (social), the rise of the prison industrial complex (penal), and a narrow focus individual responsibility (cultural; Waquant, 2012). In particular, the "neo" of neoliberalism re-regulates "an economic system of corporations. Individuals are refigured as corporations or entrepreneurs and corporations are treated as individuals. Rights are refigured as corporate rights, freedoms as corporate freedoms and even apparatuses of security are aimed at corporations ('corporate welfare')" (Hardin, 2014, p. 215). For example, *Citizens United v. Federal Election Commission (2010)* holds that corporations possess the same First Amendment right like a human person and can use money as a form of speech, which are "the sorts of shifts involved in making economic currency into political currency, people into property, and property into people [which] are nothing less than the logical structure of tyranny" (Kuhner, 2010, p. 467).

In addition, I would also emphasize that the "neo" in neoliberalism is the state's re-regulation in privileging and advancing Whiteness as property covertly through race neutral policies. Goldberg (2009) argues that racial neoliberalism is a response to the "impending impotence of Whiteness" (p. 337) that seeks to privatize property by privatizing race to better protect those racial exclusions in the private sphere that is beyond state intervention. Similarly, Winant (2004) sees neoliberalism as an example of a "White racial project," a new politicization of Whiteness covertly articulated and organized in the post-civil rights age. Lipsitz (1998) describes how neoliberal social policies and racial animus creates a "possessive investment in Whiteness" that impact housing, education, access to wealth accumulation, employment by advantaging Whiteness. "Whiteness has a cash value . . . [and] is, however, a social fact, an identity created and continued with all-too-real consequences for the distribution of wealth, prestige, and opportunity" (Lipsitz, 1998, vii). In addition to its cash value, Lipsitz (1998) agrees with Harris (1992) that Whiteness is like property "but it is also a means of accumulating property and keeping it from others" (viii). Thus, Lipsitz echoes Harris' (1992) exclusion principle where the "whiteness has been characterized, not by an inherent unifying characteristic, but by the exclusion of others deemed to be 'not white'" (p. 1736).

Today, this right to exclude inherent in Whiteness as property underwrites the neoliberal project of vertical integration of the media industry that puts media ownership in the hands of very few White elites that racially affect the media output. However, this has not historically always been the case (Horwitz, 2005; Wilson, 2000). The Supreme Court's 5-4 ruling in *Adarand Constructors, Inc. v. Peña (1995)* challenged Affirmative Action in federal agency contracts that incentivized the hiring of minority subcontractors and reversed the gains of *Metro Broadcasting* by arguing that racial classifications must be analyzed under a "strict scrutiny" principle. Justice O'Conner wrote the majority opinion for *Adarand* and argued that all racial classifications endorse race-based reasoning that contradicts the Equal Protection clause based on the understanding that the state treats people as individuals and not as racial groups (Horwitz, 2005), thereby using race neutral, individualism in her "strict scrutiny" standard. The hollowing out of Equal Opportunity in *Adarand* and subsequent legal cases where the FCC's diversity rubric met with "a distinct lack of judicial sympathy" (Horwitz, 2005, p. 195) helped to promote White corporate power through re-regulatory changes that promote vertical integration.

In addition, neoliberalism promotes a binary of White=Private versus Black=Public, where Whites withdrew their support for public welfare when Whites began associating welfare with Blacks, in favor of the growth of private entities (associated with Whites), like the prison and nonprofit industrial complexes (Hohle, 2015). Another neoliberal White=Private example is the 1996 Telecommunications Act that sharply re-regulated the media industry. U.S. American corporations were allowed to "acquire new properties, enter joint ventures, and otherwise pursue the globe as one giant market for media, information and entertainment" (Gray, 2000, p. 121). "So profound and far reaching was the 1996 Telecommunications Act that no aspect of American (and to a lesser extent global) telecommunications was left unaffected" (p. 121). By 1999, fewer than ten multinational media conglomerates—Time/Warner, Disney, Rupert Murdoch's Newscorp, Viacom, Sony, Seagram, AT&T/Liberty Media, Bertelsmann, and GE—dominated most of the U.S. American media landscape (Wellstone, 1999).

Under the Bush, Jr. Administration, governmental policies effectively re-regulated the media market to create five global media conglomerates: Time Warner, Disney, Murdoch's News Corporation, Viacom, and Bertelsmann, with each company possessing diverse media holdings from newspapers to movie studios (Bagdikian, 2014). In 2018, AT&T bought Time Warner for 85 billion dollars (James, 2018). Herman and McChesney (1997) argue that this increasing transnational corporate control affects content within nations with a focus on stock markets, business, and celebrity over social inequality and problems. "Concentrated ownership in the communications media yields diminished editorial voice, the decline of journalistic values, diminution of the press's watchdog function, and reduction in the diversity of ideas, and, as a consequence, thwarts democratic deliberation" (Horwitz, 2005, p. 186). The state's promotion of vertical integration has moved the industry into a contemporary oligarchy (McLintock, 2004).

Thus, this vertical integration of the media industry reflects a possessive investment in Whiteness as property for the few White global elites that further excludes minorities from ownership opportunities in the market. So while the neoliberal state re-regulates society at the top so that corporations have a First Amendment Right to consolidate media ownership, the media output affects society at the bottom given the lack of diversity and lack of substantive affirmative action gains in the industry in general but also in the newsroom in particular.

Today, mostly White male decision-makers are still the gatekeepers of the newsroom (American Society of Newsroom Editors, 2017), problems persist with minority retention (*Columbia Journalism Review*, 2016) as well as the class divide between journalists and the general public (Cunningham, 2004). Minority journalists feel that having minority executives would improve race depictions and increase minority journalists (Rivas-Rodriguez, Subervi-Velez, Bramlett-Solomon, & Heider, 2004). At the intersection of race and gender, it gets bleaker. Between "2009 and 2015, the number of black women in newsrooms dropped from 1,181 to 730; the number of Latinas in newsrooms dropped from 840 to 584; and the number of Asian American women dropped from 758 to 466" (Abbady, 2017, para. 15). In addition to the mostly White makeup of the news industry, four factors fuel the Whiteness in the news reporting: (a) overuse of White elites as sources, (b) disregard for minority organizations or groups, (c) depicting minorities as threats, and (d) dismissing stories about racism (Alemán, 2014, citing van Dijk, 2005).

The Whiteness of the news industry creates White fear when covering minority issues and groups that reflect neoliberalism's focus on individual responsibility to help justify state re-regulations at the bottom of society. For example, in covering issues related to welfare, the news reflected the political disgust toward the "welfare queen," a raced, classed, and gendered stereotype, that helped to pass the Personal Responsibility and Work Opportunity Reconciliation Act of 1996 that fulfilled President Clinton's campaign promise to "end welfare as we have come to know it" and heralded "workfare" in its place (Hancock, 2004). In addition, in covering issues related to crime, the news associate crime with Blackness that drive White fear, while invisibilizing White crimes, like White collar, rural, suburban, and hate crimes (Russell, 2009). In particular, Blacks in crime news are portrayed as more physically threatening and in political news, as more demanding than Whites (Entman, 1992). The impact on White consumers of this crime news shows an increase in White racist attitudes that sees the "black suspect in the crime story as more guilty, more deserving of punishment, more likely to commit future violence, and with more fear and loathing than a similarly portrayed white suspect" (Peffley, Shields, & Williams, 1996, p. 309). These racist news frames draw from and collaborate with the punitive paternalism and disciplinary supervision functions of Whiteness as neoliberalism.

RECOMMENDATIONS

I offer two recommendations for resisting the NRNR in the news and its impact on the nation's southern border. First, I recommend treating the militarization of the border policies as a form of racial gaslighting that obscures the supremacy of Whiteness in the nation through racial spectacles like the "war on the border" that pathologize Brown border crossers. Second, I recommend color-conscious, intersectional, advocacy journalism.

Davis and Ernst (2017) define racial gaslighting as "the political, social, economic and cultural process that perpetuates and normalizes a White supremacist reality through pathologizing those who resist" (p. 3). The process of racial gaslighting relies on racial spectacles which are "narratives that obfuscate the existence of a White supremacist state power structure" (p. 3). Psychologist use the term "gaslighting" to describe a type of abusive relationship based on distortions of reality that was popularized by the film titled *Gaslight* (1944). In the film, a murderer and burglar marries a woman under a false pretense to gain access to his prior crime scene many years later—the attic of his new wife's house—where he must continue to search for his plunder. As his searching in the attic inadvertently dims the lights in the rest of the house, the antagonist continually denies his wife's reality of dimming lights, missing items, strange noises, and occurrences in an attempt to mentally destabilize and control her.

In the case of the USA-Mexico border, the militarized border policy of United States is racial gaslighting because it is the political, economic, and social process that normalizes and defends Whiteness and its supremacy in this nation by pathologizing Brown border crossers with the worst criminal assumption for why they cross. "War on the border," "war on terror," and "war on drugs" are racial spectacles in this region based on the narrative of warfare that obscures the Whiteness of the nation at stake in this "war." Thus, the racial "war on the border" spectacle and its militarization policies are not only necropolitical and brutalizing as I describe in chapter two, but are also racial gaslighting that obscures the bi-partisan, human-made, human rights crisis in the border region that manipulates and controls border deaths as an anticipated consequence of war and not as a direct result of a premeditated policy calculation and U.S. American military interventions abroad.

Seeing the border militarization policy as racial gaslighting allows for cognitive resistance to the "war" paradigm on the border that encourage escalation over collaboration, hate over empathy. So fabled nativist claims that immigrants are criminals, invaders, rapists, commit voting fraud, steal social services, carry disease, and more can be more easily resisted as racial nightmares and fantasies if the policy discourse of "war" is treated like racial manipulations of reality rather than mere policy labels. This could allow the much-needed shift, from seeing border crossers as "illegal aliens," "illegals," and "aliens" to seeing them as economic refugees or asylum seekers, which more aptly describes the motivations to cross this border. This could also allow for the possibility of de-militarizing law enforcement efforts on the border and reducing the brutalization that occurs with the "war on the border" paradigm.

The second recommendation is a call for more color-conscious, intersectional, advocacy journalism to counter the effects of racial gaslighting at the border and beyond. Because mainstream news media is race neutral, there is no industry lens or outlook that can push back effectively against this grand scale of psychological manipulation of reality that is border militarization. Yet some journalists are challenging notions of objectivity and neutrality that dominate the corporate news reporting. For example, Pulitzer prize-winning journalist and co-founder of *The Intercept*, Glenn Greenwald states:

> Human beings are not objectivity-driven machines. We all intrinsically perceive and process the world through subjective prisms. What is the value in pretending otherwise? . . . . In essence, I see the value of journalism as resting in a twofold mission: informing the public of accurate and vital information, and its unique ability to provide a truly adversarial check on those in power. Any unwritten rules that interfere with either of those two prongs are ones I see as antithetical to real journalism and ought to be disregarded. (Keller, 2013, citing Greenwald).

Greenwald is a White, independent reporter who advocates that journalists should not deny their subjective prisms in their reporting as long as it does not interfere with providing the public with important information and checking those who wield power. Building on Greenwald's suggestion, I also add that subjectivity is intersectional. Color conscious journalism is not enough but an intersectional journalism that advocates for social justice in order to counter the racial gaslighting of border militarization policy, that hides its White supremacy not only in racial obfuscations but also hides in other categories of difference such as class, gender, sexuality, and disability as this study has demonstrated.

However, when people of color report on racial issues, they tend to be professionally attacked for their subjectivity. For example, journalist Desmond Cole who is also part of the Black Lives Matter social justice movement in Toronto, Canada and was a contributor to the newspaper *Toronto Star*. In 2015, he wrote a widely read piece for Toronto Life titled "The Skin I'm In: I've been interrogated by police more than 50 times—all because I'm black" (Cole, 2015). In April 2017, Cole protested a Toronto Police Services Board meeting to criticize the controversial police practice of carding—stopping, interrogating and collecting data on individuals without probable cause, a practice which disproportionately targets people of color in Canada.

Desmond was called into the *Toronto Star*'s office and told his protest had violated the newspaper's code of conduct. The newspaper's Policy and Journalistic Standards Manual states, quote, "It is not appropriate for Star journalists to play the roles of both actor and critic." Desmond Cole says this is not the first time he has been reprimanded by the newspaper. Last year, the chair of Torstar Corp., who was also serving as *the Star*'s acting publisher at the time, asked to meet with Desmond. The chair, John Honderich, reportedly told Desmond he was writing about race too often, and advised him to diversify his topics (Cole, 2017).

This example shows how conventional notions of journalistic objectivity helps to uphold White supremacy in mainstream news coverage. Honderich's suppression of Cole's color-conscious journalism helps to uphold the Whiteness of corporate news reporting and suppresses pushback against the racism of powerbrokers (here the practice of racial profiling by Toronto Police in their use of "carding").

These two recommendations could help turn the tide on the current, escalating rise of racist nativism on the border that treats immigrants as criminals and worse. Even though there seems to be little political will to de-militarize the border or deescalate the border discourse and little industry incentive in the mainstream news industry to promote color-conscious, intersectional, advocacy journalism, these recommendations are vital if we are to recognize that the nation's border militarization policy is a human rights crisis in defense of Whiteness.

REFERENCES

Abbady, T. (2017). The modern newsroom is stuck behind the gender and color line. *www.npr.org*, May 1, 2017. Retrieved from https://www.npr.org/sections/codeswitch/2017/05/01/492982066/the-modern-newsroom-is-stuck-behind-the-gender-and-color-line.

Alemán, S. M. (2014). Locating whiteness in journalism pedagogy. *Critical Studies in Media Communication, 31*(1), 72–88.

Alger, D. (1998). Megamedia, the state of journalism, and democracy. *Harvard International Journal of Press/Politics, 3*(1), 126–133.

ASNE. (2017). Survey: ASNE, Google News Lab release 2017 diversity website with interactive website. Retrieved from http://asne.org/diversity-survey-2017.

Axelrod, T. (2018). Trump: Border troops authorized to use lethal force "if they have to." *www.thehill.com*, November 22, 2018. Retrieved from https://thehill.com/homenews/administration/417985-trump-border-troops-authorized-to-use-force-if-they-have-to.

Bagdikian, B. H. (2014). *The New Media Monopoly: A Completely Revised and Updated Edition with Seven New Chapters*. Boston, MA: Beacon Press.

Bonilla-Silva, E. (2017). *Racism without Racists: Color-blind Racism and the Persistence of Racial Inequality in America*. New York, NY: Rowman & Littlefield.

Boykoff, M. T. (2007). Flogging a dead norm? Newspaper coverage of anthropogenic climate change in the United States and United Kingdom from 2003 to 2006. *Area, 39*(4), 470–481.

Boykoff, M. T., & Boykoff, J. M. (2004a). Balance as bias: Global warming and the U.S. prestige press. *Global Environmental Change, 14*(2), 125–136.

Boykoff, J., & Boykoff, M. (2004b). Fairness & Accuracy in Reporting. Retrieved from https://Fair.Org/Extra/Journalistic-Balance-As-Global-Warming-Bias/.

Carpenter, C. L. (2002). Of the enemy within, the Castle Doctrine, and self-defense. *Marquette Law Review, 86,* 653–700.

Chavez, L. (2008). *The Latino Threat: Constructing Immigrants, Citizens, and the Nation.* Palo Alto: Stanford University Press.

Cole, D. (2017). Journalist Desmond Cole on how the Toronto Star tried to silence his activism for black liberation. *Democracy Now!* May 25, 2017. Retrieved from https://www.democracynow.org/2017/5/25/journalist_desmond_cole_on_how_ the.

Columbia Journalism Review. (2016). 4 ways newsrooms can address a lack of diversity. *www.cjr.org,* June 15, 2016. Retrieved from https://www.cjr.org/broll/4_wa ys_newsrooms_can_address_a_lack_of_diversity.php.

Corbett, J. B., & Durfee, J. L. (2004). Testing public (un) certainty of science: Media representations of global warming. *Science Communication, 26*(2), 129–151.

Cunningham, B. (2004). Across the great divide class: Today's journalists are more isolated than ever from the lives of poor and working-class Americans. So what? *Columbia Journalism Review, 43*(1), 31–39.

Davis, J. H. (2018). Trump calls some unauthorized immigrants "animals" in rant. *The New York Times,* May 16, 2018. Retrieved from https://www.nytimes.com/2 018/05/16/us/politics/trump-undocumented-immigrants-animals.html.

Davis, A. M., & Ernst, R. (2017). Racial gaslighting. *Politics, Groups, and Identities,* DOI: 10.1080/21565503.2017.1403934.

Dolan, K. M. (2011). *Whiteness and News: The Interlocking Social Construction of "Realities"* (Unpublished doctoral dissertation). University of Illinois, Urbana-Champaign.

Domonoske, C., & Gonzales, R. (2018). Fact check: What's happening on the U.S.-Mexico border? *www.npr.org,* November 27, 2018. Retrieved from https:// www.npr.org/2018/11/27/670807343/fact-check-whats-happening-on-the-u-s-m exico-border.

Douglas, M. (1966). *Purity and Danger: An Analysis of Concepts of Pollution and Taboo.* New York, NY: Routledge.

Doyle, L., & Getler, M. (2004). Brits vs. yanks. *Columbia Journalism Review, 43*(1), 44–49.

Dunaway, J. L., Davis, N. T., Padgett, J., & Scholl, R. M. (2015). Objectivity and information bias in campaign news. *Journal of Communication, 65*(5), 770–792.

Entman, R. M. (1992). Blacks in the news: Television, modern racism and cultural change. *Journalism Quarterly, 69*(2), 341–361.

Gitlin, T. (1980). *The Whole World Is Watching: Mass Media in the Making & Unmaking of the New Left.* Berkeley: University of California Press.

Gray, H. (2000). Black representation in the post network, post-civil rights world of global media. In Cottle, Simon (Ed.), *Ethnic Minorities & the Media: Changing Cultural Boundaries* (pp. 118–129). New York, NY: McGraw-Hill Education.

Grynbaum, M. M. (2018). *The New York Times*, November 7, 2018. Retrieved from https://www.nytimes.com/2018/11/07/business/media/trump-press-conference-me dia.html.

Grynbaum, M. M., & Chokshi, N. (2018). Even Fox News stops running Trump caravan ad criticized as racist. *The New York Times*, November 5, 2018. Retrieved from https://www.nytimes.com/2018/11/05/us/politics/nbc-caravan-advertisement.html.

Herman, E. S., & Chomsky, N. (1988). *Manufacturing Consent: The Political Economy of Mass Media*. New York, NY: Pantheon.

Hickey, N. (2003). FCC: Ready, set, consolidate: The new rules are awful, but the fight is far from over. *Columbia Journalism Review, 42*(2), 5–6.

Horton, A. (2018). Why tear gas, lobbed at migrants on the Southern border, is banned warfare. *The Washington Post*, November 26, 2018. Retrieved from https ://www.washingtonpost.com/national-security/2018/11/26/why-tear-gas-lobbed-migrants-southern-border-is-banned-warfare/?utm_term=.1ce7cfd4f11d.

Jacobs, R. N. (2000). *Race, Media, and the Crisis of Civil Society: From Watts to Rodney King*. New York: Cambridge University Press.

Jordan, M. (2018). Federal judge blocks Trump's proclamation targeting some asylum seekers. *The New York Times*, November 20, 2018. Retrieved from https://ww w.nytimes.com/2018/11/20/us/judge-denies-trump-asylum-policy.html.

Keller, B. (2013). Is Glenn Greenwald the future of news. *The New York Times*, October 27, 2013. Retrieved from https://www.nytimes.com/2013/10/28/opini on/a-conversation-in-lieu-of-a-column.html.

Kil, S. H., & Menjívar, C. (2006). "The 'War on the border': The criminalization of immigrants and militarization of the USA-Mexico border." In R. Martinez, Jr. & A. Valenzuela, Jr. (Eds.), *Immigration and Crime: Race, Ethnicity, and Violence* (pp. 164–188). New York: New York University Press.

Lave, T. R. (2012). Shoot to kill: A critical look at Stand Your Ground laws. *University of Miami Law Review, 67*, 827–860.

Mbembé, J. A. (2001). *On the Postcolony*. Berkeley: University of California Press.

McChesney, R. W. (2001). Global media, neoliberalism, and imperialism. *Monthly Review, 52*(10), 1.

McLintock, C. C. (2004). The destruction of media diversity, or: How the FCC learned to stop regulating and love corporate dominated media, *John Marshall Journal of Information Technology and Privacy Law, 22*, 569.

Mindich, D. T. (2000). *Just the Facts: How "Objectivity" Came to Define American Journalism*. New York: New York University Press.

O'Rourke, C. (2018). Yes, armed U.S. civilians are heading to the border. *www. politifact.com*, November 8, 2018. Retrieved from https://www.politifact.com/ facebook-fact-checks/statements/2018/nov/08/blog-posting/yes-armed-us-civilian s-are-headed-border/.

Porwancher, A. (2011). Objectivity's prophet: Adolph S. Ochs and *The New York Times*, 1896–1935. *Journalism History, 36*(4), 186.

Rivas-Rodriguez, M., Subervi-Velez, F. A., Bramlett-Solomon, S., & Heider, D. (2004). Minority journalists' perceptions of the impact of minority executives. *Howard Journal of Communications, 15*(1), 39–55.

Russell, K. K. (1998). *The Color of Crime: Racial Hoaxes, White Fear, Black Protectionism, Police Harassment and Other Macroaggressions.* New York: New York University Press.

Samuels, B. (2018). Trump: "You know what I am? I'm a nationalist." *www.thehill. com*, October 22, 2018. Retrieved from https://thehill.com/homenews/administrat ion/412649-trump-you-know-what-i-am-im-a-nationalist.

Santa Ana, O. (2002). *Brown Tide Rising: Metaphors of Latinos in Contemporary American Public Discourse.* Austin: University of Texas Press.

Trump, D. J. [realDonaldTrump]. (2018, October 31). Our military is being mobilized at the Southern Border. Many more troops coming. We will NOT let these Caravans, which are also made up of some very bad thugs and gang members, into the U.S. [of America.] Our Border is sacred, must come in legally. TURN AROUND! Vote "R" [Twitter moment]. Retrieved from https://twitter.com/realDonaldTrump/status/1057614564639019009.

Trump, D. J. [realDonaldTrump]. (2018, October 31). It is outrageous what the Democrats are doing to our Country. Vote Republican now! http://Vote.GOP [Twitter moment]. Retrieved from https://twitter.com/realDonaldTrump/status/10 57728445386539008?ref_src=twsrc%5Etfw%7Ctwcamp%5Etweetembed%7Ctwt erm%5E1057728445386539008&ref_url=https%3A%2F%2Fwww.vox.com% 2Fpolicy-and-politics%2F2018%2F11%2F5%2F18065880%2Fnbc-racist-tru mp-ad-sunday-night-football.

Tuchman, G. (1978). *Making News: A Study in the Construction of Reality.* New York, NY: Free Press.

U.S. Census Bureau. (2018). *Older People Projected to Outnumber Children for First Time in U.S. History* [Press release]. *www.census.gov*, January 31, 2018. Retrieved from https://www.census.gov/newsroom/press-releases/2018/cb18-41-population -projections.html.

Van Dijk, T. A. (1988). *News as Discourse.* Hillsdale, NJ: Erlbaum.

Weber, J. (2016). Teaching fairness in journalism: A challenging task. *Journalism & Mass Communication Educator, 71*(2), 163–174.

Wellstone, P. (1999). Growing media consolidation must be examined to preserve our democracy. *Federal Communications Law Journal, 52*(3), 551.

West, C. (1988). Marxist theory and the specificity of Afro-American oppression. In C. Nelson & L. Grossberg (Eds.), *Marxism and the Interpretation of Culture* (pp. 17–33). Urbana: University of Illinois Press.

Index

About the Author

Sang Hea Kil is an associate professor in the Justice Studies Department at San Jose State University. She is a scholar-activist whose research focuses on the criminalization of immigrants, media analysis of the militarization of the border, and the discourse of whiteness and the nation.

CPSIA information can be obtained
at www.ICGtesting.com
Printed in the USA
LVHW030458090721
692210LV00002B/290

9 781498 561440